HANDBOOK OF
DENTAL JURISPRUDENCE AND RISK MANAGEMENT

Edited by
Burton R. Pollack, DDS, MPH, JD

Published by
YEAR BOOK MEDICAL PUBLISHERS • INC.

PSG Publishing Company, Inc.
Littleton, Massachusetts

Library of Congress Cataloging-in-Publication Data

Handbook of dental jurisprudence and risk
    management.

        Rev. ed. of: Dental jurisprudence / Oliver C.
Schroeder, Jr. c1980.
        Bibliography: p. 255
        Includes index.
        1. Dental laws and legislation — United States.
1. Pollack, Burton R., 1923–   . II. Schroeder,
Oliver. Dental jurisprudence.   [DNLM: 1. Dentistry.
2. Financial Management.   3. Jurisprudence.
4. Legislation, Dental — United States.   5. Malpractice.
6. Risk Management.   W 705 H236]
KF2910.D3H36   1987   344.73′0413   86-30419
ISBN 0-88416-550-7   347.304413

Published by:
PSG PUBLISHING COMPANY, INC.
545 Great Road
Littleton, Massachusetts 01460

Parts of this text were adapted from *Dental Jurisprudence*, edited by Oliver C. Schroeder,
Jr, © 1980 by PSG Publishing Company, Inc.

Printed in the United States of America.

International Standard Book Number: 0-88416-550-7

Library of Congress Catalog Card Number: 86-30419

Last digit is print number: 9 8 7 6 5 4 3 2 1

To Barbara (B.R.P.)

CONTRIBUTORS

Philip Glaser, DDS, CFT
President
Professional Financial Management
   Ltd.
Assistant Clinical Professor,
   Orthodontics
Department of Children's Dentistry
State University of New York at Stony
   Brook
Stony Brook, New York

Morton Glick
Consultant
Professional Liability Insurance
East Northport, New York

Bernard D. Katz, DDS, MSD, JD
Associate Professor
Department of Oral Diagnosis
College of Dentistry
University of Illinois at the Medical
   Center
Chicago
Special Assistant Attorney General
State of Illinois
Attorney at Law, State of Illinois

Alan M. Komensky, JD
Chicago
Attorney at Law, State of Illinois

Thomas H. Lawrence, CMC
Management Consultant
Chairman Emeritus
Lawrence-Leiter and Company
Kansas City, Missouri

Burton R. Pollack, DDS, MPH, JD
President, National Society of Dental
   Practitioners
Professor, Dental Health
School of Dental Medicine
State University of New York at Stony
   Brook
Stony Brook, New York
Attorney at Law, State of Maryland

Oliver C. Schroeder, Jr., JD
Director, The Law-Medicine Center
Case Western Reserve University
Cleveland
Attorney at Law, State of Ohio

Irvin M. Sopher, DDS, MD
Chief Medical Examiner
State of West Virginia
Clinical Professor of Pathology
West Virginia University School of
   Medicine
Morgantown, West Virginia

CONTENTS

FOREWORD

The first edition of this book appeared at a time when the malpractice crisis in the United States was in its infancy. Thus, while it was one of the definitive works on dental jurisprudence, it was not written with the idea of providing the dental profession with advice about how to cope with a serious problem of major proportion. The second edition has been updated to address this urgent need in the light of new legislation. To make the publication even more useful, a unique Risk Management Manual has been included as an appendix. Together, they form one of the most important dental publications to appear in recent years.

Few who read this book will find that their perceptions of dentistry as a profession remain unchanged. This is because looking at dentistry through the eyes of the law provides a perspective which is uncustomary to most readers. And because this is a new way of looking at the profession, it may at first be unsettling. Such feelings, however, should soon evaporate as readers begin to appreciate that this text is really not about how the law threatens dentistry but rather about how the law is challenging dentistry to rise to a higher level of professionalism.

The perspective of this book also provides important insights into why modern dental practice encompasses much more than the mechanics of providing diagnostic, treatment, or preventive dental services. Under the impetus of the law, the mouth has again become part of the body, and the body has been reintegrated with the mind. By detailing the importance of medical histories and informed consent, the book shows how the law has increased the relevance and importance of the basic and behavioral science foundations of dentistry. The integrative effects of the law on dentistry are also illustrated in the discussions about the interdependence of the dentist and auxiliaries in avoiding situations that give rise to legal action. No better case has been made emphasizing the need for respect and harmony among members of the dental team in a dental practice.

Most people will read this book for the sound advice that it gives about avoiding malpractice situations. But the reader will also gain an understanding of the ongoing evolution of the law related to malpractice. Armed with this understanding, the reader will be much better prepared to cope with future changes that occur, to decide what efforts to influence change in the law make sense, and to decide when opposition to change would be futile and counterproductive to the interest of the profession of dentistry.

If every dental practice were to make the study of this book and its Risk Management Manual an intra-office continuing education course, much of the fear and confusion about the crisis in malpractice would be eliminated, and most malpractice suits would be avoided. If the study of this book were to be made in the first few days of the education of every dental, dental hygiene, and dental assistant student, their perspectives and attitudes regarding the significance of all that is to follow in the curriculum and its relevance to their development into professionals would be permanently improved.

The distinguished authors of this book are to be congratulated not only for having applied their expertise to create this important book but for having expressed its concepts and advice in language we can all readily understand and apply.

John W. Hein, DMD, PhD
Director
Forsyth Dental Center
Boston, Massachusetts

INTRODUCTION

Changes that have taken place in legal issues related to the practice of dentistry since the original publication of this text in 1980 have made a second edition necessary. Unless texts on law are updated, they become outdated. Because the primary focus of the book is law and its effect on dentistry and dental practice, it was decided to publish a second edition.

A few chapters in the original text addressed generic issues and were extremely well done, and so are reproduced essentially unchanged The majority of chapters, however, have been updated to reflect the most recent changes in law. To several chapters, entirely new material has been added. The second edition contains the latest in the law and addresses the most current political, social, and legal issues facing today's practitioner and the student soon to enter the profession.

Oliver C. Schroeder, Jr, editor of the first edition and now director of The Law-Medicine Center at Case Western Reserve University School of Law, is an acknowledged expert in the subject matter contained in chapter 2. The chapter is a classic on the basic principles of law. No one could make the complexities of the legal system more understandable to nonlawyers than "Ollie."

Chapter 3 describes the legal basis of the doctor–patient relationship — contract law. Chapter 4 is designed to clarify many of the principles of contract law that apply to dental practice. Chapter 5, on the subject of patient records, is entirely new material and incorporates recent court decisions and legislative changes that affect record keeping. Chapter 6 has been updated to reflect current concern about professional liability insurance contracts and the crisis in dental malpractice.

In Chapter 7, the clarity with which Schroeder presents information on law and dental malpractice has been preserved, but updating has been done in light of current problems in the practice of dentistry. Chapter 8, on evidence as it relates to malpractice, also has been supplemented with new material.

Chapter 9 covers procedures for professional hygiene in the practice and management of dentistry. It was relevant in 1980, is relevant now, and will continue to be relevant in the future. Chapter 10 deals with the matter of consent, an important issue in light of the current malpractice crisis.

Chapter 11, on state regulation of dental practice, has been updated with specific examples, and presents trends in state legislation that affect dental practice. Chapter 12 has undergone a major revision because of the changing tax laws affecting corporate and nonincorporated practice. Chapter 13 has remained unchanged, but because forensic dentistry is increasing in importance as a community service, the chapter is included in this new text.

Chapters 14 and 15 bring to the surface current concerns of the dental profession, including legal, social, and political threats to the system and practice.

Chapter 16 presents, in capsule form, the "do's, don'ts, and maybes" of law in everyday dental practice. Many questions have been added to the original chapter , and many answers to old questions have been changed because court decisions have changed the law and new legislation has been enacted.

Appendix I, on risk management, represents the practical application of all that is presently known about the laws regulating dental practice. The material that it is based on is specially adapted to dentistry and has its foundation in litigation involving health practices. It is "must reading" for those practitioners who wish to practice in a claims- and worry-free environment.

A careful reading of this text will enable the dentist, student, and educator to understand and prepare to deal with current issues of dental jurisprudence.

Burton R. Pollack, DDS, MPH, JD

1 Why This Handbook?

Oliver C. Schroeder, Jr.

Jurisprudence is more than the rules of conduct generally associated with the word "law": it is the philosophy or science of law. Thus, dental jurisprudence is the philosophy or science of law concerned with dentistry — its education, its research, and its practice.

Several conditions in modern dentistry are having profound impacts on dental practice: the explosive growth of the biologic and dental sciences, the rapid change of basic experimental methods, and the introduction of modern electronics and computers. To this list the author would add three other important indicators of the changing practice of dentistry: the presence of third party payers who are changing the dentist–patient relationship; the unionization of dentists into trade groups to protect their economic interests and rights to practice; and the participation of dentists as coequal members of the health delivery team. These profound changes now being experienced in the dental sciences and practice indicate the need for a new look at an old problem. We need to look at how dental practices relate to the legal demands of American society as we enter our third century.

This volume does not necessarily supersede such excellent publications as those of Sarner,[1] Willig,[2] and Howard and Parks.[3] Each of these works presents an intelligent and helpful analysis of the legal rights and duties of dentists that concerned dental practitioners and students will find useful. However, this present text examines additional aspects of dentistry as it relates not just to law, but more importantly, to justice: justice for the dentist, justice for the dental patient, and justice for the community. This approach includes substantial segments concerning the legal rights and duties of dentists.

The volume also seeks to meet the desires of practicing dentists by responding to their specific legal concerns as elicited in response to our questionnaire (Appendix II). One thousand practicing dentists randomly selected from all those associated with American schools of dentistry received the questionnaire; 27% of those contacted responded. The breadth of concerns and the degree of interest in the various legal matters presented were measured by an analysis of each item on the questionnaire. We have sought to respond to these interests throughout this book not only by setting down the rules of law, but also by indicating their practical significance.

Our analysis of the returns revealed the wide interest of dental practitioners in all phases of the law. Of special significance to us, however, were those categories that were of interest to more than 40% of the respondents. Negligent care of the patient was of concern to 60%. Informed consent matters and licensure were the selections of over 50% of those responding, and matters involving insurance companies as third party payers generated interest in half of the responders. Contractual matters concerning fees and the dentist's participation in the administration of justice by preparation and submission of records and reports were also areas in which more than 40% of the respondents indicated interest.

Even more important were the 56 respondents who wrote additional comments of concern under the several general subject areas. Some of these comments are reproduced here verbatim to provide a feel for the general attitudes of some dental practitioners toward specific legal problems:

1. "Emergency treatment (oral and maxillofacial) in hospital — liability for alleged deformity." "Doctors who carelessly criticize dental treatment previously rendered."
2. "Negligence in informing patients fully of their diseases and need for treatment — periodontal needs a major problem — also dentists who prefer not to provide certain kinds of treatment, ie, pedodontics, who tell parents that minimal or no care is needed. 'Negligent care of patients' covers a

very wide variety of problems, for it can be outright fraud, exceedingly poor dental care, lack of proper treatment, more treatment than needed, and so forth."

3. "Lack of national licensure (lack of reciprocity), state lines, restriction of trade."

4. "Regulations involving dental education specifically tying federal support to requirement of expanded auxiliary utilization training."

5. "Government support of and/or training of health care personnel and associated programs which duplicate (and therefore compete with) existing methods of providing health care by the private sector."

6. "Though it may not be strictly a legal matter, I am concerned about positive aspects of discipline such as peer review of treatment (similar to hospital rounds and tissue committees for physicians)."

7. "Attorneys and third parties freely impose on the time of a dentist, expecting it to be free. When an hourly rate is quoted for the time to be expended, all of a sudden the need for the reports no longer exists." "Responsibility in uncovering real or assumed evidence of nondental significance by direct observation of patient and/or his or her x-rays in child abuse, drug abuse, or neglect."

8. "Accidents on premises."

9. "Excessive involvement of lawyers in unreasonable malpractice suits."

10. "Failure to report suspected child abuse as required by state child protective laws."

11. "Negligence in continuing education; insufficient physical examination by dentist; insufficient diagnostic acuity."

12. "Limit of dentist's liability once a treatment has begun."

13. "Should have national licensure from any approved college of dentistry with office quality check at least every 5 years in your own office. Look at patients and patients' records as a bank examiner would a bank."

14. "General anesthesia."

15. "The profession must give up its monopolistic attitude toward the public."

16. "The biggest concern is with the ignorant patient who cannot understand the dentist is not God and therefore becomes dissatisfied."

17. "Negligence in allowing improperly trained auxiliaries to perform duties they are not allowed to do by State Dental Practice Acts."

18. "Common negligence: failure to perform thorough examination; failure to inform patients when they have periodontal disease."
19. "Standards for radiation and diagnostic treatment; pacemaker interference; successful treatment standards."

In addition to the individual dentist's responses, information from the American Dental Association is helpful in understanding how the dental profession interacts with the law. The Council on Legislation of the American Dental Association periodically makes available abstracts of legal decisions, either decisions rendered by courts or administrative decisions handed down by governmental agencies, involving dentists. The overwhelming number of these decisions cluster about several general areas of law. The subjects of these abstracts are presented below as a list of general topics and specific subissues found in each area:

Malpractice cases
    Failure to diagnose
    Anesthetics
    Paresthesia
    Bridge and crown, dentures
    Informed consent
    Surgical injury
    Extraction
    Nerve damage
    Referrals
    Drugs
    Malpractice insurance
Licensure and practice cases
    Membership in a dental organization
    Liability to employees
    Laboratory employees
    Criminal convictions
    Requirements for licensing
    Discipline by dental society
    Dental group practice
    Technicians
    Right to review when license suspended
Practice management and business cases
    Advertising
    Sale of practice
    Professional corporations
    Taxes

Collection of fees
Dental insurance
Crimes
Government regulations
Employer-employee relations
Zoning
Investments
Fee collections
Social concern cases
Fluoridation
Legal procedure cases
Statute of Limitations
Court appearances
Evidence

This volume also offers material essential to comprehend the proper relationships among three concepts that primarily affect modern dentistry: health, justice, and ethics. The practice of today's dentist, while traditionally involving the specialized health knowledge and technological skill developed in both predental education and schools of dentistry, has now become an integral part of the whole life experience, as have the practices of other health professionals, such as physicians, surgeons, and nurses. Dentistry is no longer practiced solely by the dentist. Patients, lawyers, government bureaucrats, insurance company representatives, labor union officials, and lay citizens all have a stake in the outcome of dental care. They are demanding a voice in the important decisions being made in dental health. While it is enjoyable to be so popular, it is also exasperating to have one's daily practice profoundly influenced by others who have neither a professional dental education nor health care experience.

With this volume we hope to relieve much of this exasperation and to generate considerable understanding of the legal aspects of the practice of dentistry. We hope to encourage the dental practitioner to make his or her concern felt in the legal practices and procedures. Better dental jurisprudence will not only elevate the dental profession, but it will also better serve the human society of which it is a most important component.

Ed. — Although this chapter was completed in 1979, it is interesting to note that the concerns of the dentists 7 years later have not changed to any appreciable extent, nor have the issues. The only change has been in the intensity with which some of the issues have impacted dental practice, eg, those that relate to malpractice.

6

REFERENCES

1. Sarner, H. *Dental Jurisprudence*. Tampa: W. F. Poe Associates, Inc., 1963.
2. Willig, S.H. *Legal Considerations in Dentistry*. Baltimore: Williams and Wilkins Co., 1971.
3. Howard, W.W. and Parks, A.L. *The Dentist and the Law*. 3rd Ed. St. Louis: C. V. Mosby Co., 1973.

2 Basic Principles of Law

Oliver C. Schroeder, Jr.

The four broad areas of law — contracts, crimes, property, and torts — have set down the fundamental rules of conduct for the Anglo-American common law system, now nearly 1000 years old. The basic first-year curricula in practically all American schools of law concentrate on these four basic areas.

The rules of conduct promulgated as laws in these ancient fields of knowledge are not so much the result of intellectual deliberation in the chambers of legal scholars as of practical experiences on the highways, in the marketplaces, and in the homes of citizens. Some human event occurred. Persons involved felt or believed injuries had been imposed upon them for which they were entitled to legal redress. The event and its results were taken to a court, where the judge listened to the facts presented by both parties in the dispute. After the presentation of evidence, in what has been defined as the adversary process, the judge applied the law. The law came from precedents; what other courts had decided in prior cases were the rules of conduct. If no precedents existed, the law was derived from what the judge considered, through rational reasoning and human morality, would provide a peaceful, orderly, and just community.

This common law process of the development of legal principles is the heart of the American legal system today. Several helpful quotations from persons of great stature in the law will provide a better understanding of this profoundly significant process.

In 1954, Chief Justice Shaw of the Massachusetts Supreme Judicial Court wrote:

> It is one of the great merits and advantages of the common law, that, instead of a series of detailed practical rules, established by positive provisions, and adapted to the precise circumstances of particular cases, which would become obsolete and fail, when the practice and course of business, to which they apply, should cease or change, the common law consists of a few broad and comprehensive principles, founded on reason, natural justice, and enlightened public policy, modified and adapted to the circumstances of all the particular cases which fall within it.[1]

The late Roscoe Pound of Harvard Law School, considered by many to have been America's most distinguished legal scholar, explained this ancient common law process in these words:

> What it all comes to is that we make the best practical adjustment we can by experience developed by reason and reason tested by experience in order to solve problems of human relations in a complex social and economic order which do not admit of satisfactory solution by simple moral maxims as universally valid. But this does not necessarily drive us to the extreme of the believers in government as a regime of force. We still believe in justice as the ideal relation among men and seek to understand our idea of that relation and conform to it as best we can. What we have never been able to do is to reduce the ideal to details for everyday application. It has always proved unreasonable to reduce the reasonable to chapter and verse of rules. But rules we must have if our adjustment of relations and ordering of conduct are to be tolerable. Men will not long submit to arbitrary subjection of their wills to the wills of others.[2]

An inevitable part of the law-making process is the constant conflict between man's natural right to complete freedom and his community's need for controlling that freedom to protect and secure other human beings. Sir William Blackstone, England's preeminent legal scholar, wrote these words to explain his perception of this law-making procedure:

> Every man, when he enters into society, gives up a part of his natural liberty, as the price of so valuable a purchase; and, in consideration of receiving these advantages of mutual commerce, obliges himself to conform to those laws which the community has thought proper to establish. And this species of legal obedience and conformity is infinitely more desirable than that wild and savage

liberty which is sacrificed to obtain it. For no man, that considers a moment, would wish to retain the absolute uncontrolled power of doing whatever he pleases; the consequence of which is, that every other man would also have the same power, and then there would be no security to individuals in any of the enjoyments of life. Political, therefore, or civil liberty, which is that of a member of society, is no other than natural liberty, so far restrained by human laws (and no farther) as is necessary and expedient for the general advantage of the public. Hence, we may collect that the law, which restrains a man from doing mischief to his fellow citizens, though it diminishes the natural, increases the civil liberty of mankind. And Locke has well observed "where there is no law there is no freedom."[3]

Much of Blackstone's basic philosophy as expounded in his *Commentaries on the Law of England* (1765) emerged from such court decisions as those of Sir Edward Coke, when he stated:

The law of nature is that which God at the time of creation of the nature of man infused into his heart, for his preservation and direction; and this is *lex aeterna*, the moral law, called also the law of nature. And by this law, written with the finger of God in the heart of man, were the people of God a long time governed, before the law was written by Moses, who was the first reporter or writer of law in the world.[4]

With the twentieth century and the rapidly changing conditions in human society brought on by such dynamic forces as industrialization, urbanization, and, later, science and technology, new processes were demanded if peace, order, and justice were to be society's lot. The law process must not only resolve conflicts which arise between and among people; it must also plan and program human society to assure the prevention of the conflicts disruptive of both individual and community well-being.

Dean Pound termed this newer process in legal decision-making "social engineering":

There are very many of us but there is only one earth. The desires of each continually conflict with or overlap those of his neighbors. So there is, as one might say, a great task of social engineering. There is a task of making the goods of existence, the means of satisfying the demands and desires of men living together in a politically organized society, if they cannot satisfy all the claims that men make upon them, at least go round as far as possible. This is what we mean when we say that the end of law is justice.[5]

Whether it is the ancient decision-making process of the court case rendering a decision to resolve a human conflict, or whether it is the modern decision-making process of legislation and administration to plan and program law for the community welfare, what is really at work has best been described by Edmund Burke:

All government — indeed, every human benefit and enjoyment, every virtue and every prudent act — is founded on compromise and barter.

Once this legal process of lawmaking through judicial decision or legislative enactment is understood, the role of the law professional, the lawyer, can be analyzed. It is his or her professional duty to participate in the process by representing one party or one legal theory, then to "lock" intellectual horns and moral convictions with his or her counterpart representing the other party or another theory. In the rational give-and-take there emerges a settlement, adjustment, accommodation, resolution, and harmonization of the opposing forces. The individuals and the community move on to the next challenge which the law process must digest. It is the system that works and to which judges and lawyers owe obedience and loyalty.

REFERENCES

1. *Norway Plains Co. v. Boston and Marine Railroad*, 1 Gray 263.
2. Pound, R. Natural natural law and positive natural law. 68 *Law Quarterly Review*. 330, 335–336, 1952.
3. Hickey, W. *The Constitution*. Philadelphia: 1854, p. XXVI.
4. *Calvin's Case* 77 English Reports 377 (1608).
5. Pound, R. *Social Control Through Law*. New Haven: Yale University Press, 1942, p. 64.

3 Contracts: The Creation of Legal Rights and Duties

Alan M. Komensky
Burton R. Pollack

The purpose of this chapter is to acquaint dentists with the complexities of the law of contracts. The more knowledge dentists have of contract law, the better they can conduct their daily business affairs. Because of the complexity of contract law, however, the dentist should consult an attorney prior to entering into any contract. It is much simpler to solve problems during the formation of a contract than after a breach occurs.

DEFINITION OF A CONTRACT

Contract principles rest upon the individual's desire to make a portion of his future life certain. A dental student pays the school of dentistry tuition, exchanging money for schooling. The student now has made firm plans for the academic year that follows. Contract principles also permit improvements in life (at least, the individual perceives it as an improvement) by exchanging what a person has at present for something in the possession of another person. Thus, contract principles rest on both the present and future desires of individuals.

The *Restatement of Contracts*, the standard legal text, defines a contract as "a promise or set of promises, for breach of which the law gives a remedy or the performance of which the law in some way recognizes a duty." Every contract consists of four main requirements. First, the subject matter of the contract must be legal. Second, the contracting parties must reach an agreement. One party, the offeror, must make a definite offer; the second party, the offeree, must accept the terms of the offer. Third, there must be consideration, that is, something must be given by the offeree to the offeror in exchange for the bargain. Finally, the parties must have contractual capacity, which means they must understand the significance of what they are doing and usually must be over the age of minority (in most jurisdictions, age 18).

A contract can be formed in one of three ways: it can be expressed by agreement; it can be implied through conduct; or it can be a quasicontract, which is a kind of relief given by the court to prevent unjust enrichment.

Mutual Assent

Contracts are formed by mutual assent, which is a meeting of the minds to agree to the same bargain at the same time. Mutual assent is measured by an objective standard by which each party is bound to the apparent intention which that party manifests to the other. All parties must intend to enter the agreement, understand the terms of the agreement, resolve to be bound by the agreement, and provide something of value to the agreement. In legal terms, there must be an offer, an acceptance, and consideration (the thing of value). Comprehension of this crucial formation procedure in contract law is required if a dentist is to become a party to a legal contract, such as to provide dental services to a patient, to purchase supplies from a supplier, or to buy land on which to construct an office.

Offer

The offer is a proposal by one party to provide some goods or some service in exchange for something of value, usually money. It requires of the offeror (the person making the offer) a display of a present intent to enter into a contract. When the offer is in writing, this intent becomes obvious; hence, written offers are to be encouraged. A communication will be considered an offer only if it demonstrates a reasonable expectation that the offeror is willing to enter into a contract according to what he or she has stated. An orthodontist who offers to provide dental care to a patient can assure a better contract by putting in writing, as precisely as possible, the nature and the cost of the services he or she will provide to the patient. When an offer is given orally, the legal effect is the same; however, what the offeror says and what the offeree hears may not be the same, because oral statements tend to be more easily misunderstood than written statements. Arguments are generated because the dentist will say one thing and the patient will hear another. Thus, no mutual assent exists and no contract in law has been established.

Surrounding circumstances as well as words can manifest the intent of both parties to enter into an agreement. A patient makes an appointment with the dentist every 6 months for a prophylaxis. The course of the past relationship between the dentist and this patient, and the customary practice with other patients, will indicate that when the dentist accepts the appointment; both parties to the contract mutually intend a contract for dental service.

The law insists that the terms of the offer be definite and certain. Five essential ingredients are required to provide this certainty and definiteness: (1) a specific party to whom the offer is made, (2) a specific subject matter of the offer, (3) a specific time for performance of the contract or a reasonable time period that can be ascertained from the circumstances, (4) a specific price for the goods or services, or one that is capable of being determined by some definite process, and (5) communication of the offer from the offeror to the offeree.

The Specific Party The determination of whether an offer has been made is an essential factor in determining whether any contractual rights exist. The subject matter of the offer must be definite, and the **offeree must be identified. If a dentist places an advertisement in a** newspaper that is consistent with the specifications of *Bates and O'Steen v. State Bar of Arizona*, 433 U.S. 350 (1977), stating that he will provide a full denture for $350, no offer has been made because no specific offeree can be identified. Any person reading the advertisement could come in and ask for a denture at $350. The dentist would be under no contractual obligation to make such a denture for any specific person answering the advertisement. Note, however, that the dentist could be found liable for unfair advertising practices.

If the same dentist advertised a full denture for $100, but qualified the advertisement by adding, "To the first patient the day after the date the advertisement appears," then the dentist has made a definite offer to a specific person. Only one person could be the first patient on the given day; that person could bring suit for breach of contract if the dentist refused to comply with the terms set out in the advertisement. Thus, the offeree is clearly identified, the offeror is the dentist, the goods are a full denture, and the consideration is $100.

The Specific Subject Matter   The subject matter of the offer must be definite. If the law considers that the intent of the parties is to make a contract, the law will often recognize a contract relationship by implying certain elements omitted or left in doubt. Missing terms of a contract, even though deemed material, can be supplied by the court as long as some objective standard exists to determine the missing terms. In real estate transactions, an offer must identify the land and the price. In contracts for the sale of goods, the goods must be specifically described in the contract so as to be capable of being readily identified. A contract to buy all of one's requirements from a certain party is capable of being made certain by examining objective extrinsic facts, since good faith is assumed on the part of all parties. If a dentist contracts to purchase all the amalgam he will need for 1 year from a specific supplier, that contract is enforceable since the amount of amalgam a dentist uses in 1 year is easily determined by examining his records.

Indefinite price and indefinite time of performance are terms capable of being set within reasonable bounds by the court through an examination of the mutual intent of the parties. Obviously, however, this process generates conflicting arguments. The fundamental purpose of a contract, to make a definite and certain agreement on a present exchange or on a future action, becomes more difficult.

Certain offers that contain alternatives or options are recognized as legally enforceable, especially in the commercial area of contract where practices and experiences of the marketplace are well established from several centuries of development of the law merchant. Dentists are wise to avoid such indecisive features as options or alternatives, however, for marketplace customs may not be geared to dental office needs. Better to be certain and know your rights, than to be uncertain and surprised by your duties.

Indefiniteness in a contract term can be cured by part performance of the contract. Part performance is splendid proof of mutual assent to the agreement; any indefinite term of the contract, which might otherwise negate a mutual agreement, can be washed away where one party partially performs and the other party accepts that performance. Thus, a contract exists despite the original indefiniteness of the agreement.

Employment contracts are generally one exception to the time of performance rule; such agreements do require a definite time period for performance. Thus, a dentist should hire a hygienist for 30 days, 6 months, or 1 year. In addition to being specific about the duration of employment, all other terms of an employment contract should be specific in order to prevent misunderstandings from arising in the working relationship. Salary, vacation, sick leave, medical insurance, pension plan, and any other benefits should be stated in the contract and drafted in terms the employee understands.

When a dentist hires a dentist as an associate, the contractual arrangement becomes very complex. Both parties will want to protect their rights as best they can; both should have professional representation in negotiating an employment contract. The employer dentist should insist that all duties and responsibilities of the employee be stated in the contract. The salary arrangement, working hours, record keeping, payment of taxes, social security, insurance, and patient allocation should also be written in the contract. The more comprehensive the contract, the more certain both parties are of their rights and the less chance of a dispute arising later (see chapter 4).

Communication of the Offer Another vital element of the offer to contract is communication of the offer to the offeree. This can be done in several ways. The language used may show that an offer was made. For example, the statements, "I offer," "I quote," "I am asking," or "I will sell for" are clearly offers. Language which is not specific may be construed as an invitation to bargain. An offer can also be established by the circumstances surrounding a transaction or by the prior practice and relationship of the parties.

Ambiguities are always potential disrupters of contracts. When a word or an idea is capable of two meanings, the law cannot easily determine which meaning the parties intended. Thus, latent or patent ambiguities generally cannot be corrected by legal action, and no contract can exist.

Mistakes also present a mutual assent problem. If the offeror makes an innocent mistake and the offeree accepts the offer not knowing of the mistake, a contract exists. But if the offeree knew of the offeror's innocent mistake or was chargeable with such knowledge of the error, no contract exists. Where the mistake relates to a material part of the contract and the mistake is mutual, there will be no binding contract; the contract is voidable at the request of either party. Usually, if a mistake is unilateral, the contract cannot be avoided.

Rules for Contract Construction Over the years, the law has formulated rules for construction of contract documents, or proceedings, which may be helpful to a dentist. If the communications are numerous, or stretch over a long period of time, they are construed as a whole, with particular provisions subordinate to the general intent. Business custom and usage in the place where the contract is made, or is to be performed, will be used to interpret the contract. Words are construed according to their ordinary meanings, unless they are used in a technical sense (which dentists may do in providing their special dental care). If inconsistencies exist between written and spoken words, the written words prevail. The law will attempt to interpret documents or conversations in order to give effect to the contract, because the law has a general purpose to uphold private arrangements embodied in contracts.

Of utmost importance to dental contracts of all types is the "parol evidence rule." This rule simply means that when an understanding has been reduced to writing, and both parties have agreed that the writing embodies all parts of the understanding, the writing becomes the full and final agreement. Matters discussed but left out of the written agreement cannot be brought up later to add or change the written promises. The only exceptions to this important contract rule are: that the writing is a forgery, or sham; that fraud, duress, or mistake exist in the writing; that the extrinsic parol evidence is needed to explain ambiguous terms in the writing.

Acceptance   The offeree's act of acceptance locks the offeror into the mutual assent needed for the legal contract. Obviously, only the person to whom the offer is made can accept. A valid method of acceptance must be used. The acceptance must be absolute and unqualified. Beware of a condition placed on the offer by the offeree in his or her alleged acceptance. The presence of such conditions may render the communication a counteroffer rather than an acceptance. In matters covered by the Uniform Commercial Code, such as a contract for the sale of dental supplies, the insertion of different terms in the acceptance is not a rejection of the offer unless the offer itself expressly limits acceptance to the offeror's terms. The additional terms of the offeree are proposals for additions to the contract. This rule is applicable only between merchants.

Courts have uniformly ruled that the construction of an appliance by a dentist for a patient constitutes the sale of services, and not the sale of goods. Therefore, dental appliances are not governed by the Uniform Commercial Code.

Another areas of concern is the offer which states or implies that silence of the offeree will be deemed acceptance of the offer. A prime example is a book club solicitation requiring return of a postcard to decline membership. Many jurisdictions have enacted statutes to protect consumers from such unsolicited goods. However, if the offeree uses the goods, his or her acceptance is implied by law and a contractual obligation to pay exists.

Acceptance of an offer can be inferred from conduct. Silence, while generally not an acceptable mode of acceptance, can constitute acceptance if there is a mutual agreement that silence will serve as a valid acceptance. An acceptance transmitted by unauthorized means may still be effective if actually received by the offeror while the offer is still in existence.

A dentist receives an offer to purchase a new handpiece from a person selling dental supplies, who tells the dentist that the handpiece can be ordered by mail during the next month. That afternoon, the dentist orders one handpiece by mailing an order. The next day, the supplier calls the dentist and revokes the contract. The revocation is ineffective; the dentist validly accepted the offer at the moment of posting the order.

Termination of Offer   Offers must end. The law will terminate offers when a reasonable period of time in which the offeree should have accepted lapses. The offer also ends by operation of law if the subject matter of the offer is destroyed. Death or insanity of either party obviously ends an offer because a mutual meeting of the minds is not possible since no mutual assent can be provided. If the contract has become illegal because of an intervening development after the offer was tended, the law also terminates the offer.

Offers can also be terminated by the acts of the parties. The offeror may revoke the offer at any time before its acceptance. The revocation must be communicated to the offeree by the offeror or by indirect communication from a reliable third party. Offers also are ended by the offeree's rejection of the offer. If an offeree makes a counteroffer, that counteroffer serves as a rejection of the original offer.

An option is an offer in which the offeror's power to terminate the offer is limited. The option guarantees that the offer will remain open for the period of time stated in the contract if the offeree has furnished consideration in return for the promise to keep the offer open. If a dentist wants to sell a dental chair for $500 to another dentist and the prospective buyer is not certain he wants the chair, the prospective buyer can offer the seller a sum of money to keep the offer open for 1 week. The prospective buyer can then accept the offer to buy the chair for $500 any time during that week. If the seller is a merchant and gives assurances in a signed writing that an offer will be held open despite a lack of consideration, with no period of time specified, the offer will remain open for a reasonable time, but no longer than 3 months.

Consideration

Consideration and mutual consent as set forth in the offer-acceptance rules are the two basic elements of contract. Consideration requires that something be bargained for by the parties. Furthermore, what is bargained for must have some value or must be legally sufficient to serve as consideration for the contract.

A threshold problem is whether a bargain, or a gift, was mutually intended. Some promises may be only conditional gifts instead of bargaining contracts. The law generally provides that if the act by the promisee would be a "benefit" to the promisor, a bargain rather than a gift situation exists. Thus, promises by wealthy individuals to give $500 if a particular relative does not smoke or drink until age 21 have been upheld as contracts, and not gifts, because by refraining from these acts, the relative is conferring a benefit on the family name. In doubtful cases, the law tends to hold that a bargain, and not a gift, was intended because we presume that a natural human trait is not to give wealth away, but to exchange wealth in a bargain. Where an act has been done before the promise has been made to perform it, no bargain exists; such consideration is insufficient to establish a contract.

Moral consideration, as distinguished from economic consideration, will not support an enforceable contract in most states.

If a gratuitous promise, moral consideration, or past consideration is present, an enforceable contractual promise may be found if the promisee has materially changed his or her position in relying on the promise and suffered detrimental effects. This principle of "promissory estoppel" has important ramifications for individuals and is the source of considerable litigation. The promisor is estopped from denying that the contract is enforceable in the following circumstances: (1) the promisor made a gratuitous promise upon which the promisee might reasonably be induced to reply; (2) the promisee actually did rely; (3) the reliance was reasonable under the circumstances; (4) as the result of such reliance, the promisee has suffered substantial economic detriment; and (5) injustice can be avoided only by holding the promise enforceable. The doctrine of promissory estoppel is accepted in most states today and represents a major change from the old contract principle requiring consideration.

For example, suppose that a dentist desires to rehabilitate the dental office building. The mortgage holder says to the dentist, "Go ahead, I won't foreclose on you if you miss some mortgage payments." The dentist, relying on this statement, rehabilitates his building but misses some mortgage payments because of a cash flow problem. The law in fairness will "estop" the mortgage holder from asserting the legal right to foreclose because the mortgage holder's statement induced the dentist to rehabilitate, and the dentist relied on the statement and did so.

The definition of "legally sufficient consideration" has puzzled the law for a long time. Most courts will say the act or promise to perform must impose a legal detriment, rather than a legal benefit, on the party who acts or promises. Some courts will hold that either of these conditions is sufficient to meet the consideration requirement. What are the legal detriments? Economic values, such as the payment of money, the conveyance of chattels (personal property), and the performance of services are obviously legal detriments. Noneconomic detriments, such as going to the dentist at the request of the offeror, can be legal detriments. Forbearance to sue on a claim is also sufficient consideration. Extending the date to pay a debt can also be a noneconomic legal consideration.

At common law, if a person has a preexisting legal duty to perform an act, it cannot constitute legal consideration. For example, police officers have a legal duty to apprehend criminals; thus, they cannot provide the legal consideration necessary for a reward contract by arresting the suspect.

Fairness of the value of the consideration is irrelevant in the law of contracts. The law does not consider whether the price enacted for the act or promise is equivalent to the value of the act or promise. Even though fairness of the bargain is not an issue in law, both parties are required to have given legally sufficient consideration. A promise to pay a debt banned by the expiration of the legal time to file a lawsuit to collect the debt (Statute of Limitations) or to pay a debt discharged by bankruptcy are both enforceable without consideration. A promise to pay a contract previously voidable due to infancy, duress, or insanity is also enforceable without legally sufficient consideration. Even guarantees in writing to pay the debt of another, with only the recitation of a purported consideration, are now becoming enforceable.

BARRIERS TO CONTRACTING

Statute of Frauds

Probably the most important contract legislation ever enacted in the Anglo-American legal system was the Statute of Frauds. Enacted by the English Parliament in 1677 primarily to prevent fraud and perjury in contract situations, the statute required that the actual terms of an agreement be in writing and signed by the person charged with the obligation to perform. This legislation, therefore, became a source of evidence in contract relationships. Each jurisdiction within the United States has enacted a Statute of Frauds. Although the specific provisions vary from state to state, the general principles are similar.

If one who is not liable for a debt makes a promise to a creditor to discharge the present or future debt of a third person debtor, such a contract must be in writing. Dental care contracts may well involve such matters when the person promising to pay has no legal duty to support the third person who receives the dental care. In order to hold the guarantor, the practitioner must have a writing signed by the promisor to prove the dental service claim. If no such writing can be presented, the contract is unenforceable and the promisor has a solid defense against the dentist's claim. A typical situation arises when employers refer employees to their dentists. If in the referral the employer states, "Provide the care, and if the employee does not pay you, I will," the agreement must be in writing and signed to be enforceable, because it is a promise to pay the debt of another and comes within the Statute of Frauds. However, if the employer states, "Provide the care, and I will pay for it," such a statement creates an "original" debt and does not require writing to be enforceable.

Contracts for the sale of land or any interest in land also fall within the provisions of the Statute of Frauds. This includes not only land, but also fixtures, easements, mortgages, liens, and growing timber on such property. Dentists seeking to purchase land for dental practice and investment have no enforceable contract if only an oral agreement has been reached. Leases for over 1 year in length must be in writing. Thus, an oral 2-year lease agreement for dental office space has no legal significance until it is reduced to writing and signed by the parties who are obligated to perform.

Contracts for the sale of goods generally exceeding $2500 ($500 in a few states) in price are required to be in writing. Contracts for services such as dental care are not included within this rule, even if goods are supplied as a part of the contract obligation. Goods are defined as tangible, movable property, and would include dental supplies procured by a dentist where the price exceeds $2500. Exceptions to this provision of the Statute of Frauds exist where the buyer-dentist accepts and receives all or part of the goods, or where the contract is for the production of special goods for the buyer that are not suitable for another, and a substantial start on their production has been made or partial payment has been given by the buyer. Full performance on one side takes the contract out of the Statute of Frauds.

Contracts that cannot be performed within a year are also within the Statute of Frauds. The 1-year period begins on the date the contract is executed. Contracts for the employment of dental personnel whose term of employment is to exceed 1 year fall within the Statute of Frauds and should be reduced to writing. If the terms of the contract indicate it is impossible to perform within 1 year, such as contracts for orthodontic care, then a writing is required. However, where the contract is impossible to perform within a year but one party has fully performed his or her obligation, most courts take the entire contract out from the Statute of Frauds and will enforce the oral promise. In some jurisdictions, courts have ruled that even though orthodontic services often require more than a year to complete, they are not within the Statute of Frauds because they may be considered on a visit basis rather than considering the contract to be on a total treatment basis.

A contract made by an agent for a principal falls within the Statute of Frauds and is required to be in writing. The agent's authority to contract such an agreement must also be in writing.

What must the writing contain? The identities of the contracting parties, a description of the subject matter of the contract, a statement of its terms, conditions and the consideration given, and the signature of the person sought to be legally charged to fulfill the agreement are all required. A written signature is not always necessary; a letterhead has been held to satisfy the signature requirement of the Statute of Frauds.

Most states will permit restitution from the party receiving the benefits of an oral contract that is deemed unenforceable because of a failure to comply with the Statute of Frauds. The amount of restitution in this quasicontract action is the fair value of the benefits conveyed (*quantum meruit*), not the orally agreed contract price.

If a party, by word or deed, represents that he or she has or will put the agreement in writing, or will waive the Statute of Frauds as a defense, and the other party relies on this representation to substantial detriment, the courts will apply the estoppel doctrine and prohibit the use of the Statute's defense.

Contractual Capacity

Minors have no legal capacity to contract, except for the reasonable value of necessaries. Dental care is such a necessary, but the value of the services is not the contract price. It is the reasonable value of such services in that locale (*quantum meruit*). The age of 18 is now generally the age of majority in the United States when full rights to contract are given to a person. What is a necessary depends on the minor's station in life. Although minors generally lack the capacity to enter into a contract binding on themselves, the promises of an adult, if found contractual, are binding on the adult if made to a minor.

Mental incapacity, at any age, precludes capacity to contract. If a person lacks understanding of the purpose, the effect, or the nature of the agreement, then incapacity exists. Poor judgment due to emotional problems is not such a condition. Drunken or drugged persons present problems of only temporary incapacity.

A dentist should discuss the course of treatment, fees, home care, follow-up visits, and informed consent prior to giving the patient any medication or anesthetic (see chapter 10). Each situation is resolved on its own facts, with the basic test being whether the party understood what he or she was doing.

Illegal Contracts

If a dentist does not have a license as required by stated law, any contract made for services controlled by the licensing is illegal. No recovery is allowed either on the basis of the contract or quasicontract restitution. If the state law requires that a dentist reregister the license at regular yearly intervals, and the dentist fails to comply, any of the fees charged during the period of failure to register are not recoverable by the dentist. If the seller of goods or services does not know they will be used for an illegal purpose, a valid contract exists. Obviously, the seller must do nothing in furtherance of the illegal action or he or she will be barred from recovery by the illegality. The effect of illegality is to make the contract void and unenforceable.

Exculpatory agreements by which a person relieves himself of liability for his own wrongful acts are illegal. Dentists cannot provide in a dental care agreement that they will not be held liable for negligent dental care.[1] However, informed consent forms are valid and will serve as a defense if one is sued for the collateral effects of a dental procedure. The patient must be told of the collateral effects of the procedure in understandable terms before consenting to those risks. Informed consent is no defense if negligence on the part of the dentist is the cause of the collateral risk (see chapter 10 for an in-depth discussion of informed consent).

Contracts made by fraud, duress, or mistake may be rescinded or enforced by the innocent party. Thus, the innocent person is given a defense which may or may not be used to make the contract unenforceable.

In recent years, a strong movement for fairness has entered the contract field of law. A court will look to many factors in determining whether a contract is "unconscionable," that is, whether it is so harsh and oppressive to one side that the court will not enforce it. Price is one factor. Other factors include time for performance and allowance for the maker of the contract to breach while firmly binding the other party. When parties to a contract are in substantially unequal bargaining positions, the contract produced is termed an "adhesion" contract. If one party is forced to adhere to contract terms that are unconscionable, oppressive, or grossly unfair because of weakness in bargaining capacity, courts apply a general public policy to deny enforcement of such provisions. The principle of unconscionability is applicable to contracts for the sale of goods as well as those for personal services such as in medicine and dentistry.

A case decided in New York is an exellent example of an adhesion contract in the health care field. A patient with only a high-school education entered into a contract with a plastic surgeon, who had both a dental and medical degree, agreeing to forego her right to court action in favor of binding arbitration in the event of a claim of negligence against the plastic surgeon. The court declared the agreement unen- forceable as an adhesion contract, stating that the parties were not in an equal bargaining position because of the disparity in the education of the parties, and because the only way for the patient to receive the services of the doctor was to enter into an agreement that placed the patient at a considerable legal disadvantage.[2]

THIRD PARTY CONTRACTS

Dental practice often involves third party contracts. All third party payer contracts, such as private health insurance policies for dental patients or labor union contracts with dental care provisions, are representative of such contracts.

The primary concern is whether a third party can enforce a contract made by two other parties for the benefit of the third party. If the contract is primarily for the benefit of this third party, the third party can enforce such a contract. Extrinsic evidence outside the contract agreement may be used to prove such a benefit. If the third party is named in the contract, either individually or as a group, this constitutes strong support of the interest to benefit the third party. Once the third party's rights become vested or fixed, no rescission by the contracting parties can deny the third party's contract rights.

ASSIGNMENT OF CONTRACTS

Contractual benefits or rights can be assigned by one party to an independent third person, thereby replacing one party to the contract with a wholly new party. If the contract is one involving personal services, such as dental care, it cannot be assigned. Thus, if a dentist contracts with a person to perform a full mouth examination, panorex radiograph, and prophylaxis for $50, and the patient does not want to fulfill the contract but has a friend go in for the examination, the dentist does not have to treat the substitute patient under the original contract. A contract provision specifically stating that no assignment can be made will also bar an assignment. Insurance contracts are generally not assignable because different people pose wholly different risks for the insurer. Personal credit contracts where a substitution of debtors is contemplated are also nonassignable. If the assignment of rights would substantially change the obligor's duty, assignment cannot be made.

No formality is needed to assign a contract, the only requirement is the presence of the intent to transfer present contractual rights to the assignee by the assignor. Any assignment given for consideration is irrevocable. A gratuitous assignment is removable at any time by the assignor. If the gratuitous assignment is accompanied by the delivery of a token consideration, such as a stock certificate or a savings passbook, then it be comes irrevocable. An assignment in writing without consideration is also irrevocable. If the assignee of the gratuitous assignment relies to his detriment on the assignment, then it cannot be revoked.

Once the assignment is made, the assignee can hold the promisor directly. Once the promisor knows of the assignment, he or she must render performance to the assignee. All rights that the promisor had against the assignor still prevail against the assignee.

DELEGATION OF CONTRACT DUTIES

In general, any duty in the contract may be delegated to another to perform. However, personal service contracts requiring judgment and skill, such as dental care agreements, cannot be delegated where the performance of the professional is required, no matter how competent the person to whom the duty is delegated. When professional practices change with the development of new health skills and knowledge, and the changes are recognized in practice and by licensing laws, duties once nondelegable can become delegable. The dental hygienist's role in contemporary dental health practice is the prime example.

Legal matters involving both assignments of contracts and delegation of contract duties generally become complex. Legal counsel is mandatory for any person desiring to assign contracts or to delegate duties.

PERFORMANCE OF A CONTRACT

Performance issues are concerned with which party has breached the contract. Provisions of the contract may include either covenants or conditions. A covenant is an absolute promise to perform or refrain from doing something, and can be unconditional or conditional upon the existence of some set of circumstances. Failure to perform such provision breaches the contract. A condition, on the other hand, is an event or a nonevent which establishes or eliminates the absolute duty to perform. Failure of a condition does not breach the contract.

Generally, the contract words will distinguish whether a covenant or a condition was intended by the parties. The parties' intentions prevail. Business and professional customs also help to make this distinction. Ordinarily, doubtful provisions will be interpreted to be covenants instead of conditions.

Conditions are of three kinds: precedent, concurrent, and subsequent. If the condition is construed as precedent, no absolute duty to perform is present until the condition happens. Dentists can become involved in such a situation where the patient's satisfaction with the dental care is required before the absolute duty to pay the dentist's professional fee arises. The wise dentist will generally avoid such a situation. Concurrent conditions are mutually dependent acts capable of being executed almost simultaneously. If a dentist established a clinic where cash payment for dental services is required, the condition — the performance of dental services and the payment — would be concurrent. Conditions subsequent will extinguish the absolute duty to perform. If a dentist gives a patient the right to return a denture after using it for a period of time, the return of that denture extinguishes the patient's absolute duty to pay for the denture. Courts do not favor conditions subsequent. The defendant-promisor in contract breach litigation must prove the condition subsequent, while the plaintiff-promisee has the burden of proving a condition precedent.

Express conditions are specified in the contract. Implied conditions are inserted in the agreement by the law because they represent conditions necessary to fulfill the broad contractual purpose or conditions of good faith which the parties would probably have agreed to if they had thought about them. Implied conditions in all contracts will include an obligation of good faith to perform or enforce the contract.

Conditions precedent or concurrent may be excused by the law, thereby creating the absolute duty to perform. If either party wrongfully prevents or hinders the occurrence of the condition, it is legally excused as a requirement. Wrongful means not only bad faith, but includes the situation where the other party would not have reasonably thought of, or assumed, the risk of such a happening.

Even if the time of performance has not arrived, if from all the facts and circumstances it is clear that one party will not perform when performance comes due, this party's prospective failure to perform excuses the other party's duty to perform. This is the theory of anticipatory breach of contract. If a patient contracts with a dentist to have all of his teeth extracted on December 10, and then tells the dentist on November 10 that he does not want the extractions, the dentist can bring an action on November 10 for breach of contract. Needless to say, if matters have progressed to such a state, legal counsel is mandatory, for the rules, though definite, are complex.

DISCHARGE OF A CONTRACT

A contract may be discharged in one of several ways. Contracts may be discharged if the condition subsequent occurs. When the contract is still not executed by either party, an express agreement to end the contract, termed mutual rescission, is accepted as a discharge. Modification of the contract by mutual assent does not destroy the original agreement as does rescission, but it does amend the original contract to produce a new understanding. Discharge of a contract is also produced by creating a subsituted contract. A written release will also discharge a contract. In some jurisdictions, new consideration to support the release is required, but in other sates no such new consideration is needed.

Accord and satisfaction is another way to discharge a contract. If a patient owes a dentist $2000 and agrees to give the dentist an automobile in payment, the promise to give the auto is an accord. The acceptance of the auto by the dentist is satisfaction. The delivery discharges both the accord agreement and the prior contract. Discharge by account stated occurs when a dentist has a patient who also supplies the dentist with goods for his or her services. When several transactions have occurred, both parties may fix a final balance due. This agreement is a new contract called the "account stated," which becomes the only enforceable contract, merging all the previous contracts into one and discharging the previous contracts.

A major area of legal difficulty in the law of contract discharge is impossibility of performance. If without the fault of the promisor, it becomes objectively impossible to fulfill the contract duty, and this duty is the major element of the contract, both parties are discharged from the contract performance. When a patient contracts with an orthodontist to have all his teeth straightened, and, before treatment commences, all of the patient's teeth fall out due to periodontal disease, both parties are discharged from performance. Objective impossibility means that no person could perform. Subjective impossibility means that, although the promisor cannot perform, someone else could perform. The promisor must assume the risk of his own inability to fulfill the contract duty when he agreed to the contract. The promisor is not to be discharged from his contractual promise.

The impossibility must arise after the contract is made. If the promisor agrees to do an impossible thing at the outset, no contract ever came into existence and no discharge is needed.

Objective impossibilities will be found when performance becomes illegal due to a law change, performance becomes impossible due to an act of government, or the subject matter of the contract is destroyed. In a personal service contract, such as a dental care contract, if the dentist dies or is struck with an incapacitating illness, contractual impossibility exists.

Temporary impossibility, such as illness of the dentist, merely suspends performance; it does not discharge performance. Partial impossibility, such as inability of the dentist to get gold for restorations because of a new law, discharges only that portion of the contract now impossible to perform. If performance is still possible but the purpose of the contract has been eliminated by an intervening event, courts will hold the contract discharged on the grounds of frustration of contract purpose.

STATUTE OF LIMITATIONS

Legal actions must be brought within a certain time period, depending on the nature of the action and the state where the action is to be brought. Depending on the jurisdiction, lawsuits for breach of oral contracts generally must be brought within 4 or 6 years of the breach, or when the breach reasonably should have been discovered. Breaches of written contracts may have a time period up to 15 years or longer, depending on the law of the local jurisdiction. The Statute of Limitations does not discharge the contract, but it does give the defendant an impregnable defense which the defendant can raise affirmatively to bar liability for the breach. Technically, the breach remains, but the remedy is ended.

BREACH OF CONTRACT

Failure to perform, where there is an absolute duty to do so and no discharge has been effected, gives rise to a legal breach of contract. The legal effect of the breach depends on whether it is material or minor. This decision requires legal counsel.

A minor breach will not give rise to damages for breach of the entire contract. It will temporarily suspend any duty of counter-performance and will give rise to a suit for any damages caused by the breach. Where a material breach occurs, the nonbreaching party can treat the contract at an end, and sue for all remedies for breach of the entire contract.

The law provides various remedies for the breach. Damages are most frequently awarded. Specific performance is available when damages would be an inadequate remedy, such as when the subject matter of the contract is unique and cannot be purchased elsewhere. All parcels of land are considered unique, as are works of art and antiques. Rescission of the contract and restitution of the benefits conferred are also available in certain situations. Quasicontractual actions are allowed where there is a failure to pay money for performance already given by the innocent party. The measure of payment is the reasonable value of the benefit rendered (*quantum meruit*), not the contract price. A new remedy now emerging, particularly in products liability cases, is a tort action in favor of the injured party.

In dentistry, a suit for breach of contract due to substandard care could be brought. However, it is more likely that an injured patient would bring a suit for malpractice under tort law, because that theory allows recovery for pain and suffering. Breach of contract suits against dentists are usually brought when the dentist guarantees the results of treatment. If the dentist states to a denture patient, "You will eating steak in two months," and at the end of 2 months the patient cannot eat steak, the dentist has given an express warranty and successfully could be sued on that basis. A suit for breach of warranty is a contract action. A contract action usually has a longer Statute of Limitations than does a tort action, although the recovery by the injured party may be less because recovery for pain and suffering is not usually awarded in contract actions.

DAMAGES

Damages for breach of contract is a remedy of broad scope. The injured party is entitled to compensatory damages, which include the value of the benefit of the contract bargain as far as it is feasible to determine. There is a standard legal formula to determine this value depending on the type of contract involved — sale of goods, sale of land, employment contract, construction contract. Compensatory damages also include direct and consequential losses. Faulty dental treatment is measured by the cost to get the treatment completed (direct damages) and the amount of wages lost for being off work because of the resultant dental complications (consequential damages). Compensation for pain and suffering is called special damages. Direct and consequential damages are known as general damages.

The measure of damages in the case of employment contracts depends upon whether the breach was by the employer or employee. Where the breaching party was the employer, the standard measure of the employee's damages is the full contract price. When the breaching party is the employee, the employer will be entitled to the costs of replacing the employee.

Punitive damages are not available as damages in contract situations unless specified in a particular statute. Breach of a promise to marry is one exception, yet in some states such actions are forbidden.

Nominal damages are recognized in law where a breach is proven but there is no actual loss. Such damages permit a party to establish its legal contract right by getting a verdict for $1 and charging the cost of the litigation to the defendant.

In breach of contract cases, the nonbreaching party has a legal duty to mitigate damages. In sales contracts, this would require the sale to another purchaser, thereby offsetting the contract price due from the breaching purchaser. In employment contracts, mitigation requires that other employment be located to keep the damages from reaching the standard measure. In manufacturing and construction contracts, no duty exists to find another purchaser, but there is a duty not to add to the costs of production after being notified of the breach.

Contracts may include provisions for specified predetermined damages in event of a breach. If the damages would be difficult to determine at the time the contract is made but a reasonable estimate is possible, courts will uphold such prior determined liquidated damage clauses.

CONCLUSION

The dentist, both professionally and privately, enters into many contracts and should ask several questions in the process of making and fulfilling contracts. Was a contract offer made? Has an effective acceptance been rendered? Is there adequate consideration for a contract? Are there third party beneficiary rights or duties in the contract? Can assignments or delegations be made under the contract? Has the contract been performed? Lawyers can advise on these matters where doubt may arise in the dentist's mind.

While general rules of contract set forth in this chapter should serve to alert the practitioner to the broad and sweeping aspects of contract law, at least three specific contract matters are currently of prime importance to dentists: (1) the dentist-patient contract relationship; (2) the insurance contracts that protect a dentist in his legal duties and secure to a dentist his regal rights; and (3) the professional dentist corporation as an example of contract planning for tax and pension benefits. Each of these specific matters requires separate discussion in the following three chapters.

REFERENCES

1. *Proubiansky v. Emory University et al.,* 275 S.E. 163, aff'd 282 S.E. 902 (1981).
2. *Minor v. Walden,* 422 N.Y.S.2d 335, (1979).

4 Contract Law and the Dentist-Patient Relationship: Legal Forms of Practice, Patients of Record, and the Right to Advertise*

Alan M. Komensky
Burton R. Pollack

CONTRACT LAW AND THE DENTIST-PATIENT RELATIONSHIP

Contract law governs the relationship of the dentist and the patient. Except in special situations under the Statute of Frauds, described in chapter 3, the terms of the contract between the dentist and the patient do not need to be in writing to be enforceable. The written contract serves as evidence that an agreement between the parties was reached. The terms may be expressed or implied. Those that are usually expressed include the fee, the nature of the treatment to be performed, the time in which the treatment is to be completed, payment arrangements, etc.

---

* Sections written by Mr Komensky have been copyrighted by the American Dental Association. Reprinted by permission.

Implied Duties of the Dentist

In the absence of express terms stated in a contract, the courts, in a series of cases decided throughout the country, have identified duties owed to the patient simply as a result of the doctor-patient relationship. Although most of the cases refer to physicians, they would apply to dentists as well. In accepting a patient for care, the doctor (physician or dentist) warrants that he or she will:

1. Use knowledge and skill with reasonable care in the provision of services in keeping with the standard of other practitioners of the same school of practice in the same or a similar community;
2. be properly licensed, registered, and meet all other legal requirements to engage in practice;
3. maintain a level of knowledge of current advances in the profession;
4. use methods that are employed by at least a respectable minority of the practitioners in the community, or in a similar community;
5. employ competent personnel and provide for their proper supervision;
6. not use experimental procedures;
7. obtain the informed consent of the patient before instituting an examination or treatment;
8. not abandon the patient;
9. charge a reasonable fee for services based on community standards;
10. ensure that care is available in emergency situations, or in the absence of the practitioner;
11. not permit or direct any person acting under his or her direction to engage in any unlawful act in the provision of care;
12. keep the patient informed about his or her progress;
13. not undertake any procedure for which the practitioner is not qualified, either by law, training, or experience;
14. complete the care in a timely manner;
15. keep accurate records of the diagnosis and treatment of the patient;
16. maintain confidentiality of information gained from the patient or as a result of treatment;
17. inform the patient of any untoward occurrences in the course of treatment;
18. make timely referrals and request necessary consultations;

19. comply with all laws regulating the practice of the profession;
20. take all necessary precautions, consistent with the patient's medical history, in the treatment of the patient;
21. practice in a manner consistent with the code of ethics of the profession.

Guarantees

Guarantees made by the dentist would constitute express terms in the contract. To make claims about the outcome of care that could be interpreted as guarantees is unethical, in some jurisdictions illegal, and from the viewpoint of the law, extremely foolish! It may result in the loss of a suit based upon breach of contract rather than on malpractice. In breach of contract suits, negligence need not be shown, and expert witnesses are not required. In many jurisdictions, unless an express guarantee is made by the provider of care, breach of contract suits brought against health providers are held to the same rules of law as suits in negligence. In a few jurisdictions, for a guarantee to be enforceable in the delivery of health care, it must be in writing and supported by consideration specifically attached to the guarantee.

Implied Duties of the Patient

The patient, in accepting the contract for care, warrants that he or she will:

1. keep appointments;
2. cooperate in care;
3. pay a reasonable fee;
4. make timely payments;
5. notify the practitioner of a change in health status.

Termination of the Doctor-Patient Relationship

The contract to provide care terminates when:

1. either party dies;
2. the patient is cured of the specific disease for which the patient sought treatment;
3. the doctor and patient mutually agree to terminate the relationship;
4. the patient terminates the relationship;
5. the doctor terminates the relationship.

The risk to the dentist in unilaterally terminating the relationship is the possibility of being charged with abandonment.

Abandonment

To terminate care before it is complete, or to refuse to treat a patient of record, may bring allegations of abandonment. In cases where patients are hospitalized, failure to visit the patient at regular intervals may also constitute abandonment. To avoid such claims, the courts have provided some helpful guidelines:

1. The patient must be given adequate time to obtain substitute care.
2. The withdrawing dentist should agree to cooperate in the future care of the patient by making all the patient's records, reports, and radiographs available to the new dentist.
3. Care must not be discontinued at a time when the health of the patient may be compromised.

It is wise always to have the patient select the new dentist.

Specific Performance in Health Care

In some situations, described in the preceding chapter, when a contract is breached, money damages will not adequately compensate the injured party for the breach. Thus in a contract for the sale of real estate, antiques, or art, the court will order the seller to deliver the article of sale. It is termed "specific performance." In contracts to provide health services, courts do not apply specific performance. Doctors are not required to perform services they do not wish to perform, even if they agreed to do so at some prior time. However, money damages may be awarded to patients for the breach. How foolish it would be for a court to order a cardiologist to perform open heart surgery that he or she did not want to perform. The same reasoning is applied to dental care.

FORMS OF DENTAL PRACTICE

The legal form of dental practice often determines the rights of the dentists and affects the contractual relationship with patients. When two or more dentists practice together, the contractual relationship between the patient and the provider takes on many complexities. These relate to ownership of the patients' records and control of the practice. Ultimately, many of the duties that flow from the relationship between the practicing dentists and their individual responsibilities to the patient must be decided by the courts. The form of the practice relationship may be the critical issue in making the determination of responsibility.

Dentists may limit their relationship to sharing facilities, while maintaining completely independent practices. The extent of their patient interchange may only be to provide emergency care in the absence of the treating dentist. Such an arrangement carries with it few, if any, complications about the right to the patients' treatment records and other matters related to dental practice. Technically, it is not a form of an associateship. However, if the practice appears to patients to be a partnership, the courts may treat it as one. This may be important in the consideration of liability in malpractice claims. If both names are on the stationery and the bill heads, and if patients are shared, even though the dentists are not partners, they may be treated as partners.

Other forms of practice relationships between dentists may bring with them many complications, including, but not limited to: who controls the practice; the right to patient records when the arrangement is terminated; the right to patient lists; announcements to patients; and where and when a new office is opened by the departing dentist. The following sections will examine the problems and suggest ways to avoid difficulties.

ASSOCIATESHIPS

An associateship is any form of arrangement in which two or more dentists have a common interest in the practice of the profession. An associateship in dental practice may take many forms: owner-independent contractor; employer-employee; partnership; or shareholders in a professional corporation. Each has its risks and benefits. Each has its advantages and disadvantages. Each has its pitfalls and ways to avoid them. Unfortunately, many of the problems may find their way into the courts for resolution. The way to completely avoid the complications of associate practice is to practice alone. But in spite of the complications, the disadvantages of solo practice have led to the trend to associate practice.

Most difficulties in any form of associateship arise when the relationship is dissolved. In each form of associateship, the difficulties are somewhat different, as are their resolutions. Avoiding the problems also varies depending on the form of the relationship.

Independent Contractor

An owner-independent contractor is a form of associateship in which one individual or a group of individuals owns the practice and employs another dentist as an independent contractor. The owner shares in the fees generated by the independent contractor-associate, who does not share in the fees generated by the owner-associate. In theory, the independent contractor maintains his or her practice within the overall practice of the associates. Theoretically, independent contractors control their practices, provide for their own supplies, maintain their own patient records, send out bills on their own bill heads, etc.

The critical factor looked at by the courts seems to be whether the share of earning is paid in gross, or whether the owner takes out social security, withholding taxes, and workmen's compensation. In the absence of a contract, these issues may become important.

A major problem may arise if a suit is entered by a patient of the independent contractor for malpractice. Access to the records may present some difficulty to the independent contractor in the defense of the suit. Also, the owner may attempt to escape liability for the acts of the independent contractor.

If the relationship ends in the absence of a contract, disputes may arise as to access to patients of record of the independent contractor by the independent contractor, and access to the records themselves. Announcements to patients about the dissolution of the associateship that include the location of the new office of the independent contractor may bring up serious problems and may require court resolution.

The only way to avoid such disasters in relationships is to enter into a written contract that addresses many of the issues in advance of entering into practice.

Employee

From a professional standpoint, the relationship that distinguishes an independent contractor from an employee is the degree of control the employer-associate has over the practice. Theoretically, the employer has complete control over all aspects of the employee's practice, while the independent contractor exercises total control over his or her practice. All patients of the employee may be assigned. Treatment planning may be under the exclusive control of the employee. All patients, even those brought into the practice by the employee, may be considered patients of the practice. On dissolution, the employee may be left with no tangible benefits of the time spent in the practice.

No matter what the other arrangements, the courts usually consider control over the practice and the payment of taxes and other financial responsibilities when distinguishing between an employment relationship and a principal independent contractor relationship. This may become important in fixing liability in malpractice litigation, and in the rights of the individuals on dissolution of the associateship where no contract was entered into by the parties. The rights may affect access to patients' records, announcements to patients of record, and the time and place of relocation of a practice.

Partnership

Partners have a common interest in the practice. Each shares in the profits generated by each of the partners. The share is determined by the agreement. Partners may share the treatment of patients or may maintain their own practice. Partners generally share space, equipment, personnel, expenses, etc. Their names usually appear together on stationery and business cards. It is rare for partners not to have a written agreement that spells out all the terms and rights of each partner should the partnership dissolve. Each partner may be independently liable for the negligent acts of other partners under the legal doctrine of vicarious liability. Patients of records are usually patients of the partnership, even if treated by one of the partners.

Professional Corporations

Professional corporations became popular when federal legislation made them financially attractive. However, The Tax Equity and Financial Responsibility Act of 1982 virtually eliminated all of the benefits. One of the benefits that remains relates to liability of shareholders for the negligent acts of other shareholders. Only the negligent shareholder, along with the corporation, is liable. Innocent shareholders generally escape liability. For additional information on professional corporations, see chapter 12.

THE ASSOCIATE CONTRACT OF AGREEMENT

It is advisable, before entering any form of relationship with another dentist, to seek the advice of an attorney. To enter a relationship without a written agreement, or with a written agreement but without the advice of an attorney, can lead to many legal difficulties when the relationship terminates. "Trying it out" before the contract stage is a mistake many young practitioners make in order to seek employment. Under these circumstances, the employer has all the advantages, while the employee-associate gains only bitter experiences and wasted time.

Terms of the Agreement

1. Controls of the practice: scheduling appointments, treatment planning, decisions on who to treat, working hours, who sets the fees, who does the billing, name on door and stationery, who signs insurance forms, hiring and supervision of auxiliaries, assignment of office space.
2. Patient and office records: Maintenance of, storage of, access to, who makes entries to.
3. Finances: percentage to each, money due on billing or collection, guarantee minimum, cost of overhead, maintenance of equipment, cost of remodeling, who pays laboratory bills, supplies, utilities, taxes.
4. Benefits: Payment of health insurance, loss of earnings insurance, vacations, continuing education, cost of professional liability insurance.
5. Options for future relationships: partner, etc.
6. On dissolution: notice required, right to contact patients, right to patient records, restrictive covenants (where to relocate and when to relocate).
7. Illness, disability, and death provisions.

Professional Liability Insurance

Each associate should have his or her own professional liability insurance. It is essential that all associates be insured by the same carrier. Serious problems may arise if more than one associate is sued because of a single act and each has a different insurance carrier. It results in each being represented by different attorneys having different proprietary interests. The insurance company should be made aware of the associateship and its legal nature. For additional information, see chapter 6.

PATIENTS OF RECORD

Determining who is a patient of record is an important ethical and legal consideration in a multipractitioner office, especially when the agreement of practice does not state which patients are the patients of record for each dentist. The problem becomes even more complicated when two dentists practice together with no written agreement. The question of who is a patient of record when an agreement is unclear or when none exists has been considered by a California court.

Following is a discussion of Dr Owner v. Dr Employee (names are fictitious) involved in the California court. The parties were two dentists who practiced together until one decided to open his own office. This decision does not settle the question in every situation, but it does show how one case was handled by the courts.

Owner v. Employee, 254 C.A.2nd 919 (1967)

The facts in this case are familiar to any dentist who has practiced with an associate. Dr Owner, an established dentist in need of assistance, entered into an agreement with Dr Employee, whereby Dr Employee would be Dr Owner's associate, to be appointed patients solely on the basis of available time. Dr Employee was to receive half the fees from patients he treated, less laboratory fees. The patients' records for both dentists were kept in the same file; however, each patient's record bore the name of the treating dentist.

After 18 months, Dr Employee decided to establish his own practice. He rented an office about half a mile from Dr Owner's office and duplicated the records of the approximately 900 patients he had been treating. Employee then gave Owner notice of termination of the agreement of association and sent announcements of his new location to the patients whose records he copied. In addition, Employee sought to collect for services rendered during his association with Owner, while Owner sought to collect for treatment completed by Employee before termination of the agreement. Most of the 900 patients contacted by Employee decided to continue with him at his new location.

Because the agreement of association did not state the rights each dentist would have to patients' records upon dissolution, Owner sued Employee for the wrongful taking of patients' records; Employee countersued for damages resulting from restraints of trade. The trial court decided in favor of defendant Employee; the verdict of the trial court was upheld by the California Court of Appeals.

Who are Patients of Record?

The California Appellate Court first concluded that because both dentists agreed to abide by the rules and regulations of the American Dental Association (in force at that time, but no longer applicable), Dr Employee had the right to send announcement cards to "other dentists, other health professionals, and to patients of record." The court then considered who was a patient of record.

The court found that Dr Employee was not an employee of Dr Owner because Owner did not withhold Social Security or other employment taxes from Employee's pay; Employee paid self-employment taxes. Records were kept according to the name of the treating dentist. Patients were treated by only one dentist, and the majority of Dr Employee's patients considered him their dentist because they continued to see him at his new location. The court concluded that Dr Employee did not act in bad faith because the ADA Principles of Ethics had not been violated.

The case of Owner v. Employee did not completely solve the problem of defining a patient of record, because the court was only faced with a partnership situation where each patient was always treated by the same dentist.

The Court did state in 254 C.A.2nd 924:

> Obviously, if respondent [Dr. Employee] was a mere employee of appellant [Dr. Owner] he could not take with him such things as patient lists and records upon termination of his employment, nor could he solicit the patients of his former employee...

However, this strong statement is not binding upon later courts because the Owner v. Employee court was not presented with that problem. Furthermore, a court in another jurisdiction may rule differently.

Although the question of patients of record in an employer-employee situation is not settled, certain criteria would be scrutinized by the court in deciding whether the patient was a patient of record of the employee dentist. These would include: Is the patient treated by both employer and employee? Is the patient treated only by the employee? Whom does the patient consider his dentist?

In the absence of an employment contract, the determination of whether a dentist is an employee hinges on the facts of each legal situation. The California decision indicates that the court would apply a liberal test in determining who are patients of record, and would be less willing to find an associate dentist an employee. In any event, if the associate dentist is determined to be an employee, a court would be less likely to rule in the associate dentist's favor concerning which patients' records he is entitled to upon dissolution.

AN OUNCE OF PREVENTION

The problem of determining the patients of record for each dentist can be eliminated by the execution of a written agreement addressing the issue when two dentists agree to practice together. In the case where the owner of an office hires an employee, the owner will probably want a clause in the assistant's employment contract stating that any patient the employee treats is the patient of record of the employer, and the employed dentist is not entitled to any patient records upon termination of employment. In cases involving joint ownership of the office, such as in a partnership or a professional corporation, an agreement as stringent as that used in the employer-employee office would probably not be feasible.

There are three basic types of agreement that could be used to allocate patients in a dental partnership or professional corporation. The first would require that all dentists keep separate records of the patients they treat; upon dissolution, those patients become patients of record of the treating dentist, and the treating dentist is entitled to their records. The second agreement would allow each partner to send announcement cards to any patients of the dissolving partnership or corporation. The third type of agreement provides for the patients to determine which dentists they wants to treat them in the future. This is accomplished by the dentists' agreeing to send out letters following dissolution, the text of which informs the patients of the dissolution and asks patients to specify on a postal response card which dentist they want in the future. If the response card is not returned, the file could be allocated on the basis of the last dentist to treat that patient.

These are just a few examples. The best arrangement depends on many factors, including type of ownership of the office and whether each patient is always treated by the same dentist. Before entering into any agreement to allocate patients, all aspects of the practice should be discussed with competent legal counsel.

THE RIGHT TO ADVERTISE

The California case was heard before a major change took place in this country that permitted attorneys, physicians, dentists, and a host of other professionals to advertise. The celebrated case of *Bates and O'Steen v. The State Bar of Arizona*, 53 L.Ed. 2nd 810 (1977), decided by the United States Supreme Court, broke the barrier to the prohibition of advertising by professionals. The states were first to change their laws that prohibited advertising by professionals. Prohibitions against advertising stated in codes of professional ethics, particularly those of medical and dental organizations, were resistant to change. But after a series of cases instituted by the Federal Trade Commission, through a series of consent orders and court decisions, they complied. It took several years, but now there are no prohibitions against advertising, either by the states or by the professional organizations.

The situation in New York is an excellent example of the change in state laws that regulate advertising by professionals. Prior to 1977, the only announcements permitted by dentists in practice were to their patients of record. This attitude was reflected in the ADA Code of Ethics, and was relied on by the California court in the Owner v. Employee case described above.

Within several months after the Bates decision, The Board of Regents of the State of New York declared only the following to be unprofessional conduct (Section 29.1, *General Provisions for all Professions* of the *Rules of the Board of Unprofessional Conduct*):

(12) advertising or soliciting for patronage that is not in the public interest:

(i) Advertising or soliciting that is not in the public interest shall include but not be limited to advertising or soliciting that:

(a) is false, fraudulent, deceptive, misleading, sensational or flamboyant;
(b) represents intimidation or undue pressure;
(c) uses testimonials;
(d) guarantees any service;
(e) makes any claim relating to professional services or products or the cost or price thereof which cannot be substantiated by the licensee, who shall have the burden of proof;
(f) makes any claim of professional superiority which cannot be substantiated by the licensee, who shall have the burden of proof;
(g) offers bonuses or inducements in any form other than a discount or reduction in an established fee or price for a professional service or product.

(ii) The following shall be deemed appropriate means of informing the public of the availability of professional services:

(a) informational advertising not contrary to the foregoing prohibitions; and
(b) advertising in a newspaper, periodical or professional directory or on radio or television of fixed prices, or a stated range of prices, for specified routine professional services, provided that there is an additional charge for related services which are an integral part of the overall service being provided by the licensee and the advertisement shall so state, and provided further that the advertisement indicates the period of time for which the advertised prices shall be in effect;

(iii) (a) all licensees placing advertistments shall maintain or cause to be maintained, an exact copy of each advertisement, transcript or videotape thereof as appropriate for the medium used, for a period of one year after its last appearance. This copy shall be made available for inspection upon demand of the Education Department . . .

(b) a licensee shall not compensate or give anything of value to representatives of the press, radio, television or other communications media in anticipation of or in return for professional publicity in a news item;

(iv) No demonstrations, dramatizations or other portrayals of professional practice shall be permitted in advertising on radio or television.

Section 29.5 of the Rules is specific for dentists:

(a) claiming professional superiority or special professional abilities, attainments, methods or resources, except that a practitioner who has completed a program of specialty training approved by the Board of Regents in a specialty recognized as such by the Board of Regents, or who can demonstrate to the satisfaction of the department the completion of the substantial equivalent of such a program, may advertise or otherwise indicate the specialty. A practitioner who has completed all of the requirements for specialty qualification except an examination may advertise or otherwise indicate the additional training which has been acquired. The phrase "practice limited to" shall be deemed a claim of special professional abilities, and may be used only by dentists who have completed specialty training satisfactory to the department or dentists who have restricted their practice to a dental specialty prior to January 1, 1979.

Similar changes were made in the ADA code of ethics. The current *ADA Principles of Ethics and Code of Professional Conduct*, revised in January 1983, states:

Section 5-A, Advertising
Although any dentist may advertise, no dentist shall advertise or solicit patients in any form of communication in a manner that is false or misleading in any material respect.

As a further condition of the consent order entered into by the ADA, the association agreed that all codes of ethics adopted by constituent and component societies of the ADA must conform to those of the ADA.

It is interesting to compare the above statement relating to advertising in the latest *ADA Principles of Ethics* with the statement made in 1977, before the consent order of September 1979 was entered into:

Section 12 — Advertising
Advertising reflects adversely on the dentist who employs it and lowers the public esteem of the dental profession. The dentist has the obligation of advancing his reputation for fidelity, judgment, and skill solely through his professional services to his patients and to society. The use of advertising in any form to solicit patients is inconsistent with this obligation.

Thus, all prohibitions against advertising were eliminated from state laws and the code of ethics of the profession. Announcements to patients of record no longer have any significance, and, barring an express condition in a contract, restrictions on announcements to patients will not be supported by the courts.

Other Constraints (Restrictive Covenants)

When associated dentists enter practice under a formal arrangement, there usually are conditions in the contract relating to the rights of each dentist on the dissolution of the association. Some of the conditions state what the departing associate may or may not do. The restraints are termed restrictive covenants. Generally, if the covenants are reasonable, legal, and not against public policy or interest, they will be upheld by the courts. Under contract law, there usually is sufficient consideration to legally support a restrictive covenant.

It is reasonable to expect that a dentist-employer, or the senior partner working with an independent contractor dentist, or a junior partner, would have great concern about the practice based on the actions of a departing junior dentist. Often the senior, remaining dentist will not want the departing dentist to have access to patient lists, to be able to remove patient records, to be permitted to contact former patients about the move of the departing dentist to a new location, etc. All are reasonable concerns of the remaining practitioner, and, if properly presented in a contract, will probably be upheld by the courts.

However, difficulties have arisen when restrictive covenants relate to the number of years a departing dentist is to refrain from entering practice within a prescribed geographic area. The remaining dentist does not wish to have the departing dentist within easy reach of patients that the remaining dentist may consider patients of the practice rather than patients of the junior dentist. Avoiding competition with a former associate is a legitimate concern of the senior, remaining associate.

The question that should be addressed in designing restrictive covenants that relate to relocation is whether the restrictions are reasonable for all parties. Barring relocation within a 50-mile radius for a period of 20 years is clearly unreasonable. A more reasonable restriction would be to bar relocation for 3 to 5 years within a radius of 5 to 10 miles of the location of the remaining dentist. However, it is impossible to predict the action of a court in deciding location and time restrictions when health care providers are involved. Access to health providers by the community weighs heavily in the determination of whether limiting health facilities is in the public interest. It is wise not to count too heavily on court support of restrictive covenants. However, it is best to make certain they are not unreasonable.

Another potentially problem-causing issue in the separation of associates relates to forms of practice that require continuing care, such as the practice of orthodontics and periodontics, as compared with episodic practices such as oral surgery. Even if the agreement of an orthodontic practice restricts a departing dentist from contacting his or her patients and does not permit the removal of patient records, the courts are likely to find that such an agreement is against the best interest of the patient. Unless the patient was informed of the private agreement between the dentists, which was clearly to their disadvantage, the agreement may not be supported by the court.

Summary

Associateships take many legal forms, and the one selected should reflect the style in which each associate wishes to practice. Before entering into any associateship, each dentist should carefully examine his or her individual goals in practice. Written contracts of agreement are essential in defining rights and responsibilities. Unless the contract is specific in its terms, difficulties will surface on the dissolution of the associateship. Although the California case helped settle some of the problems in defining patients of record, it did not address itself to all the situations in which a definition of patients of record would be needed. The issue of the possession of patients' records will present a difficulty as long as two or more dentists continue to practice without a formal agreement that addresses this question.

The rights of partners, associates, or employees should be determined in writing in the partnership agreement, employment contract, or bylaws of corporate practice before the association is established.

5 The Management of Patient Records

Burton R. Pollack

INTRODUCTION

"Dentists seem to be among the worst record-keepers. It is not unusual for the complete dental records to consist mainly or solely of a billing chart. Such scant records should be considered malpractice in and of themselves."[1]

An accurate record of the diagnosis and treatment of the patient is as important a part of care as the treatment itself. Failure to maintain an accurate record may result in injury to the patient at a subsequent treatment episode. Originally, the purpose of recording a patient's treatment was for the doctor to recall what had been done, and, in some cases, to arrive at and justify to the patient the charge for the service.

Traditionally, there was no requirement to maintain a record of the patient's treatment. Over the years, however, the patient's record has become very important — to the patient, the treating doctor, society, the system of justice, and the payer of services. Statutory law, case law, and professional ethics have had major effects on record-keeping. Issues of ownership, confidentiality, access, accuracy, content, and maintenance have been addressed by the courts, legislatures, and professional organizations. The law and society, over the years, have converted the informal notes made by the doctors about patients' care into legal documents that have achieved a level of importance far exceeding their original intent. This chapter will trace the evolution of the patient's record as a legal document and will address many of the more important aspects of record-keeping by the dentist.

PURPOSE OF THE PATIENT'S RECORD

In addition to playing an important role in the outcome of malpractice suits, the patient's record also serves as:

1. a permanent and accurate record of the medical and dental histories and all dental services rendered to the patient, including diagnostic, treatment, consultative, etc; as well as a record of treatment reactions and outcomes;
2. documentation, should information about the condition or treatment of the patient become necessary in legal proceedings;
3. an assessment of the quality of care rendered to the patient;
4. a source of data for research purposes, either formal or to contribute to the professional experience of the provider;
5. a document in the provision of care as required by third party payers;
6. a means of communication among health care providers involved in the care of the patient.

OWNERSHIP: CASE LAW

During the past 50 years, the question of ownership of patients' records has taken a dramatic turn, the extent of which has not been fully realized by the average practicing dentist. Many dentists maintain the records of their patients in a manner consistent with the standards of the turn of the century. They treat the record as if it were their exclusive property, and, when requested to do so, will turn the record over to a succeeding practitioner solely as a courtesy rather than as a requirement. At one time, this practice was supported by the courts.

The first case of major importance was *McGarry v. J. A. Mercier Co.*, decided by the Supreme Court of Michigan in 1935. The plaintiff was a physician, the defendant a highway construction corporation doing business in Michigan. The company engaged the plaintiff to provide medical care for an injured employee. The service was provided in accord with the agreement, but upon the submission of the bill by the physician for the services to the company, he was refused payment. The company demanded that the radiographs taken by the physician of the injured employee be examined by other physicians. Until the request was satisfied by the physician, the company refused to pay for the services. The physician entered suit to collect the fee. The company's defense for nonpayment was that the radiographs were not made available to other physicians. The issue to be decided by the court was the right of the payer to the radiographs of the physician. The court stated:

> [The] plaintiff was fully justified in refusing to surrender possession of the X-ray negatives. In the absence of agreement to the contrary, such negatives are the property of the physician or surgeon who has made them incident to treating a patient. It is a matter of common knowledge that X-ray negatives are practically meaningless to the ordinary layman. But their retention by the physician or surgeon constitutes an important part of his clinical record in the particular case, and in the aggregate these negatives may embody and preserve much of value incident to a physician's or surgeon's experience. They are as much a part of the history of the case as any other case record made by a physician or surgeon.

The court went on to state:

> ...there is every good reason for holding that X-rays are the property of the physician or surgeon rather than of the patient or party who employed such physician or surgeon, notwithstanding the cost of taking the X-rays was charged to the patient or to the one who engaged the physician or surgeon as part of the professional services rendered.[2]

The court also indicated that the x-rays should be kept by the physician as a possible defense in a malpractice suit. One wonders if the decision of the court would have been the same if office duplicating equipment for records and x-rays had been available in 1935. However, the case firmly established the absolute right, if not the responsibility, of the physician to exercise exclusive rights to the records of patients, notwithstanding the fact that the patient paid for the services that generated the information on the record.

The McGarry decision continued undisturbed by the courts until a case was decided in New York in 1968. The chipping away by the courts of the exclusive ownership rights of the physician began with the case, *In re Culbertson's Will*. Dr Culbertson, a physician, directed in his will that his executor "burn and destroy all of his records and files without opening or examining same." He was concerned about the confidentiality of the information given to him by his patients in the course of their treatment. Several of his former patients petitioned the Court to compel delivery to them of their personal medical records in the possession of the executor. As an alternative, they requested permission to examine and make copies of their records.

In deciding the case, the court took note of the McGarry case in stating:

> The question raised herein is unique. This court is satisfied, however, that records taken by a doctor in the examination and treatment of a patient become property belonging to the doctor.

The court went on to raise and answer the following question:

> Under the circumstances, should the patient be deprived of the benefit of whatever notes and records that were maintained by an attending physician in those situations where the patient seeks the services of another physician? In this regard, the urgency of certain situations, and particularly the best interest of the patient, must be considered.

The court took judicial notice of the Principles of Professional Conduct of the American Medical Association and concluded that:

> Based upon general considerations of public policy, together with a recognition of the principles of procedure of the American Medical Association, it is the opinion of this Court that Paragraph Tenth of testator's will is invalid as against public policy.
>
> Unquestionably these records might be of extreme value to a subsequent examining physician. Their destruction could have grave consequences.
>
> It is, accordingly, the decision of this Court that the specific relief demanded by the petitioners be denied in that the records and notes requested by petitioners will not be delivered to them personally. The executors should make available the records and notes pertaining to the petitioners to the succeeding physician of the petitioners upon the authorized request of the petitioners.[3]

In summary, although the court did not disturb the exclusive ownership of patients' records by the doctor, it did provide the patient with some limited rights to the information contained in the record.

The next chipping away occurred in New York. The case was decided in 1977 and was concerned with the records of a dentist. In the *Application of Susan Streigel*, a demand was made to have her dental records produced for discovery and inspection for the purpose of determining by her attorney if the records contained sufficient grounds to sustain an action against the dentist for malpractice. No legal action was pending at the time. The *Civil Practice Law and Rules* (CPLR) of the State of New York provides for the discovery of records in contemplation of litigation only by court order. This procedure was not invoked by the patient. The court was faced with determining the rights of the patient to the record in the absence of a pending action and a court-ordered discovery procedure.

The court stated:

> Upon balance of petitioner's (patient's) need for access against the minimal inconvenience to respondent (dentist) which would be entailed, I conclude that petitioner has shown a sufficient factual basis for pre-litigation discovery of her dental records. Stated another way, the supporting papers demonstrate 'some probability' that petitioner may have a good cause of action and that she is not 'merely taking a stab in the dark.'

Of more significance, the court went on to say:

> More importantly, although a doctor or dentist may well have the primary custodial rights to the treatment records of his patients, it does not follow that his rights are exclusive and that the patient has no rights with respect thereto. To the contrary, in my view, the patient has a 'property' right sufficient to afford her the privilege of reasonable access to her medical and dental records. The existence of such right does not depend upon the provisions of CPLR 3102 (subd. [c]) or upon whether or not litigation is even contemplated.[4]

A similar situation was litigated in Illinois several years before the Streigel case. In *Connell v. The Medical Surgical Clinic S.C.*, decided in 1974, the court, faced with almost identical facts as the Streigel case, came to the same conclusion.[5]

And so we have witnessed in a period of about 40 years the evolution of patients having no rights to their personal medical or dental records to having property rights sufficient for them to discover and examine the records, even in the absence of litigation. Conversely, the rights of doctors diminished from exclusive control to limited custodial rights.

OWNERSHIP: BLACK LETTER LAW*

Many states have enacted legislation, or rules and regulations, affecting the rights of patients to their medical and dental records. The right of access to the information, or to a copy of the record, may appear in the Dental Practice Act, the rules of the administrative agency regulating the practice of dentistry, the public health law, the rules of a public health agency, or in some legislation or rules relating the patients' rights. It is the responsibility of the dentist to determine if such law exists, where it can be found, its provisions, and the penalty for noncompliance.

---

* Black letter law is a term used to describe laws enacted by elected bodies (eg, congress, legislatures). Included are statutes, ordinances, and rules and regulations of administrative agencies (eg, dental boards, the Food and Drug Administration, Internal Revenue Service) created by these elected bodies.

Insurance companies are of little assistance to the dentist in this matter. On many occasions, they advise not giving the patient access to the record. Their presumption is that the reason for the request is with litigation in mind. The state dental association may be of assistance. An attorney would provide the most reliable information.

The laws of California and New York serve as examples of how states may deal with the ownership and access to patients' records. California enacted a law, which became effective on Jan 1, 1983, relating to patients' records. The major provisions include:

1. The patient has a right to inspect his or her dental record within 5 days after a written request is delivered to the dentist, and after the payment of a reasonable clerical fee for making the records available.
2. The patient has a right to obtain copies of records and radiographs within 15 days after a written request. The dentist may charge 25 cents per page, plus a reasonable clerical charge for preparation. The charge for copies of radiographs may not exceed their actual cost.
3. The dentist is allowed the option of providing a summary of the records to the patient within 10 days, instead of allowing inspection or copying of the records.

In New York, the Board of Regents (the administrative agency regulating all licensed professionals within the state) adopted the following rule in 1977 and amended it in 1978. Unprofessional conduct is defined as:

> ...upon a patient's written request, failing to make available to a patient... copies of the record...and copies of reports, test records, evaluations or X-rays relating to the patient which are in possession...of the licensee... Reasonable fees may be charged for such copies...but prior payment for the professional services to which such reports relate may not be required as a condition for making such reports available.[6]

Because of a conflict in a related statute, an appellate court in New York ruled that the unprofessional conduct requirement does not apply to physicians or hospitals. They are only required to send a copy or summary of the patient's record to another physician or hospital upon the request of the patient.[7]

Even in those states where there is no legal requirement to provide patients with their records, or the information contained therein, it is advisable to do so. The trend in case law is to provide patients with access to their records. However, when the dentist is aware that the patient has litigation in mind in making the request, the professional liability insurance company should be contacted for their advice and guidance.

RECORD CONTENT AND FORM

There are no laws on the specifics of record-keeping. Perhaps the rule of the New York Board of Regents comes closest in stating that the records of the diagnosis and treatment of the patient be accurate.[8] There are, however, certain standards accepted by the profession that provide specifics about record content. Information on the treatment record may be divided into the following components: (1) demographic and personal data; (2) chief complaint(s); (3) histories (medical and dental); (4) diagnostic tests and results; (5) consultation requests and reports; (6) the diagnosis; (7) treatment plan(s); (8) treatment and outcomes; (9) home care instructions; (10) prescriptions and medications administered; (11) consents to care; (12) cancellations and no-shows; and (13) conversations held with patients regarding their care. Things that should not be on the treatment record may be as important as what should be on it, eg, financial information (charges, payments, and balances), subjective evaluations of the patient that are outside the scope of practice of the practitioner, and conversations held with attorneys and professional liability insurance companies.

Entries should be made in blue or black ink or ball-point pen. Where more than one individual is authorized to make entries, it should be signed. To correct errors on the record, it is best to draw a single line through the entry, write "error" above it, and enter the correction on the next available line. To completely obliterate the error raises a suspicion in the eyes of the court and jury that the entry was damaging to the case of the defendant-dentist. Your attorney will wish you had not done it.

As a general rule, the test of the thoroughness of the record is that any other dentist should, by reading the record and without the assistance of the treating dentist, know the total dental experience of the treating dentist's patient. To accomplish this minimal goal, the record should be complete, accurate, and legible, and the author of all entries should be easily identified.

A landmark case was decided in New York in 1982. Herbert Schwarz, a practicing physician, was accused of violating a rule of the Board of Regents that required that health practitioners "keep patient records which accurately reflect the evaluation and treatment of the patient."[9]

The petitioner, Dr Schwarz, defended his record-keeping by stating that the records were his, they were about his patients, he understood his entries, and it was his policy to note "only unusual and exceptional matters on the record," thus accounting for the blanks on the medical history form. Few practitioners would disagree with the arguments Dr Schwarz presented to the court. However, the court disagreed by stating:

> The purpose of the record-keeping requirement is, at least in part, to provide meaningful medical information to other practitioners should the patient transfer to a new physician or should the treating physician be unavailable for any reason.

The court continued:

> Thus, for the foregoing reasons, a patient record so sparce as to be accurate and meaningful only to the recording physician fails to meet the intent of the requirement to maintain records which 'accurately reflect the evaluation and treatment of the patient.'[10]

It should be noted that the rule of the Board of Regents, upon which the court relied, places the same level of responsibility for record-keeping on dentists as it does on physicians.

It is reasonable to expect, even in those states that have no legal requirement that records be kept, that case law will support the idea that, in accepting a patient, one of the implied duties of the practitioner is that accurate records be maintained of the patient's treatment.

In looking at both the decision of the court in the Schwarz case and the right of the patient to access to the record or its contents, it is of particular importance to the dentist that what is written on the record may be seen by the patient or the patient's attorney. Inappropriate notes that reflect subjective conclusions by the dentist may turn an innocent request for the record into a lawsuit.

RETENTION OF RECORDS

There are two major considerations in deciding how long to retain the patient's record after the patient leaves the practice. Legal requirements may establish the minimum length of time patient records must be kept. If such requirements exist, the exact wording of the law should be carefully examined by the dentist. As an example, the Board of Regents in New York rules that all patient records must be retained for at least 6 years. Records of minors must be retained until the minor patient reaches the age of 21 years.[11] Availability of the record may not satisfy the rule. This law may affect the sale of a practice if the contract of sale includes delivery of the records to the purchaser. Suggestions on how to manage this problem and other problems associated with the transfer of records will be discussed later in this chapter.

The other consideration that contributes to deciding how long to keep the patient's record relates to civil actions alleging malpractice or breach of contract. The statute of limitations for each provides guidance. The longer of the two should be the rule. If the statute of limitations for each is shorter than the time period required by law, the rule of law should prevail. The problem, however, is complicated by the fact that there are many situations in which the statute of limitations on malpractice actions may be tolled. If it is alleged that the dentist was guilty of fraudulently concealing information from the patient for the purpose of depriving him of his rights, the statute may be extended.[12] Also, in third party practice, a practitioner may have to produce the patient's record years after the statute of limitations on malpractice has run. In one such case, tried in New York, two physicians and the hospital were required to defend a case and were in need of their records years after the treatment was performed and the statute on malpractice had run.[13]

The best advice is to keep the patient's original records, including the radiographs, forever.

RECORDS AND THE SALE OF A PRACTICE

The transfer of records to a purchaser-dentist, without taking several legal precautions, brings with it many risks, some of which may be serious. If the law in the jurisdiction requires or implies that records be retained, the law has been violated by turning the records over. In addition, if the records are transferred without the patient's permission, confidentiality has been breached. To avoid these problems, Steiner[14] suggests that the parties to the sale form a partnership and announce the relationship to all patients of record. When the seller or retiring partner leaves the practice, he or she is relieved of the requirement to retain the records; the partnership retains them. This procedure should satisfy the law. In addition, unless a patient objects at the time of the partnership announcement, confidentiality may be waived.

The solution proposed by Dr Steiner does not take into account the problem of a suit being instituted by a patient years after the sale of a practice, when the records of the patient are no longer available to the defendant-dentist. Perhaps the only low-risk solution for the retiring dentist, after announcing the partnership arrangement and before leaving the practice, is to duplicate all records and radiographs and leave the copies with the purchaser. This is expensive, time consuming, and inconvenient for both parties, but it is the only way a seller-dentist can be fully protected. To some dentists, particularly those in high-risk practices, the inconvenience might prevent future legal problems. In a

54

case decided in California, the court commented on the absence of the original record by stating:

The inability of the physician to produce the original of the clinical record concerning his treatment of the plaintiff creates a strong inference of consciousness of guilt.[15]

SUMMARY

1. Accurate records must be kept of all treatment provided to the patient, including diagnosis, treatment plans, consultation reports, radiographs, consents, treatment outcomes, and conversations held with the patient.
2. If possible, records should be kept forever.
3. If the records are to be transferred as a result of the sale of the practice, consult an attorney about matters of confidentiality and any law relating to the requirement to retain patients' records.
4. Make certain that entries on the record are legible and the author of the entry is easily identified. Entries should be made in blue or black ink or ball-point pen. Avoid the use of pencil.
5. Personal subjective statements should not be entered on the treatment record, nor should financial information or conversations held with the insurance company or attorneys.
6. Never completely block out an entry so that it cannot be read.
7. Use standard abbreviations and avoid the use of cryptic notes and symbols.
8. It is of the utmost importance that the original records of the patient's treatment, the radiographs, study casts, and any other records relating to the care of the patient never be surrendered by the dentist to anyone, except by court order — not to another dentist, your insurance company, their attorney, your attorney, and, most certainly, not to the patient.
9. Never tamper with a record once you are aware that a lawsuit is contemplated.
10. Provide safeguards to maintain confidentiality.

REFERENCES

1. Louisell, D.W., Williams, H. *Medical Malpractice*. Vol. 1. New York: Matthew Bender, 1985, p. 7–36.

2. *McGarry v. J.A. Mercier Co.*, 272 Mich. 501 (1935).
3. *In re Culbertson's Will*, 292 N.Y.S.2d 806 (1968).
4. *Matter of Streigel v. Tufano*, 92 Misc. 2d 113 (1977).
5. *Connell v. The Medical and Surgical Clinic S.C.*, 315 N.E.2d 278 (1974).
6. *Rules of the Board of Regents*, Section 29.2 (6).
7. *Denton v. The Board of Regents of the State of New York*, 452 N.Y.S.2d 861 (1982).
8. *Rules of the Board of Regents*, Section 29.2 (3).
9. *Id*
10. *Schwarz v. Board of Regents of the State of New York*, 453 N.Y.S.2d 836 (1982).
11. *Id*
12. *Simcuski v. Saeli*, 44 N.Y.S.2d 442 (1978).
13. *Musco v. Conte et al.*, 254 N.Y.S.2d 589 (1964).
14. Steiner. Dental malpractice, in Louisell, D.W., Williams, H. (eds): *Medical Malpractice*. Vol. 2. New York: Matthew Bender, 1985.
15. *Thor v. Bosca*, 38 Cal.App.3d 558 (1974).

6 The Insurance Contract: Professional Protector Plans, Professional Liability Insurance

Oliver C. Schroeder, Jr.
Burton R. Pollack
Morton Glick

Newly licensed practitioners as well as established practitioners need to understand the legal implications and practical applications of dental insurance, including professional liability insurance (malpractice insurance).

Your first consideration is whether to obtain any insurance. For most of your practice activities, you will have little choice. Property insurance protecting your office leasehold and the chattel mortgage your lending agency holds on the dental equipment, as well as employer liability for employee injury, are types of insurance required either by state law or by private contract.

With professional liability insurance, you have a choice. You can be a self-insurer ("going bare"), carrying the risk yourself against a patient's claim of substandard practice. The personal economics of this approach are dubious at best. When a patient sues alleging malpractice, you must defend yourself at your expense or risk a default judgment. You must pay litigation expenses — lawyers' fees and court costs. If a judgment is rendered against you, your property is subject to levy and sale if you have no insurance coverage to meet the judgment.

Although bankruptcy is an option, whereby certain items necessary for living expenses would be exempt from levy and sale, no person ever emerges from bankruptcy with an enhanced economic position or an improved professional reputation. If you place assets in your spouse's or children's exclusive control to shield them from judgment creditors, intricate tax problems arise at both the federal and state levels. The tax and legal complications that such a move necessitates may well be more of a financial burden than the annual malpractice insurance premium. Many courts have expressed the notion that professional liability insurance carried by a health practitioner serves the purpose of protecting the patient rather than the doctor. This view is supported by hospitals that require attending staff members to insure themselves against claims of malpractice. Therefore, doctors who divest themselves of their assets and go bare to avoid compensating patients injured as a result of their negligence are not likely to be treated with much compassion by the courts.

In addition, any attempt to explain to patients that you have no insurance for any negligent act could easily generate a psychological barrier interfering with the dentist-patient relationship. Legally, you cannot contract with a patient and exculpate yourself from malpractice liability. Exculpatory language (ie, language that relieves a party from liability due to negligence) is against public policy and will not be supported by the courts.[1]

In simple terms, insurance is part of the cost of practicing dentistry. It is recognized as such by the Internal Revenue Code, which permits the deduction of the premium expense for income tax purposes. Accept and use insurance, not only for economic protection but also for peace of mind in practice.

An insurance policy is a contract enforceable at law. It not only specifies the types of property, people, and conduct it covers, but it also states the obligations the insured (eg, the dentist) must meet before any money will be paid by the insurance company. These obligations may be simple, such as notifying the insurance company of loss within a certain period of time, or they may be more complex and subtle.

Insurance companies may try to limit the scope of coverage so that they are not insuring everything that appears at first glance to be insured. The most obvious method of limiting coverage is the exclusion clause, in which the company lists losses for which it shall not be liable. The policy will also have a clause stating exactly what types of property and/or conduct are covered. The more a policy covers, the less protection the insured is receiving, because a court may construe such a list as exclusive, ie, what is not mentioned will not be covered. A more subtle method used to limit the scope of coverage is the insurance company's use of definitions. In defining a term, such as personal property, the company may limit the meaning the words have within the policy to the exact definition stated in the contract. Unless dentists carefully note the exact definition, they may later find that what they thought was personal property is not, according to the insurance policy. Dentists may thereby be precluded from recovering money under the policy. While it is becoming fashionable to write and organize insurance contracts that are easier for the layman to read, do not be fooled by a simple format. The insurance company that uses a simpler style has not made a single concession that it did not intend to make without your paying for it. It is important to read every word and phrase of the insurance contract.

Insurance is a necessary cost of doing business as a dentist. The complexities of today's practice necessitate an in-depth study of the individual needs of the practitioner. In addition, former standard insurance policies, particularly professional liability policies, are now complex in many of their terms. Each practice must assess its needs, and each policy offered must be examined carefully. Each plan has its good and bad points; you must choose a plan based on your personal insurance needs. In most cases, the average dentist is not equipped to evaluate the coverage necessary and the policies offered. Assistance should be obtained from an attorney and from someone who is experienced in insurance.

CHOICE OF POLICY

Your next major decision is which kind of insurance to procure. In most states, there are two major policies available. One is sponsored by the American Dental Association (ADA) or your local dental society, and the other is provided through a local agent of a private company. Both policies offer protection beyond malpractice coverage; they cover many risks dentists may encounter in their offices and in the course of their practices. While these insurance policies are both package policies, designed to cover all aspects of personal and professional liability as well as property damage to the dentist's equipment and office, the basic approach of each insurance policy may be entirely different.

The crisis in dental malpractice insurance that surfaced in the early 1980s had a major effect on the availability and cost of professional liability insurance. Additional effects of the crisis and a detailed review of professional liability insurance will be presented later in this chapter.

Traditional Policies

The privately sponsored plan is traditional in its approach. It offers basic coverage and allows the dentist to decide on the type and amount of extra coverage. The advantage of this system is that dentists buy and pay for the exact amount of insurance that they have decided is necessary to meet their specific needs. The danger of this plan is that dentists may end up underinsured in certain areas, overinsured in other areas, and perhaps not insured at all in areas that they should be insured. Lack of foresight and experience, oversight, or inadequate guidance may mean that dentists are spending money for inadequate plans, the dangers of which they may not discover until they try to make claims.

ADA Policy

The ADA plan offers a comprehensive package plan that has all types of coverage deemed necessary for the adequate financial protection of the dentist. In most geographical areas, the ADA package offers a set amount of coverage that the dentist must accept if he or she wants the policy. The premium for the ADA plan varies according to the amount of protection provided for total loss of equipment. Essentially, this plan attempts to offer the greatest good for the greatest number of policy holders. The ADA plan is the best policy for dentists who have neither the time nor the inclination to analyze all professional risks and how and to what extent they should be protected against those risks.

The ADA plan requires accepting all of the types of coverage that are offered. In doing so, the dentist is provided with adequate amounts of insurance. It is always better to pay more and be overinsured than it is to be underinsured and sorry about it when it is too late. Realistically, a dentist can afford the higher premium. Even if the premium is $1000 more a year, it is worthwhile to know that the insurance company will be handling any $1 million legal action. Saving $100 a year on premiums and getting only $300,000 of coverage does not pay — if the patient sues for an amount exceeding the coverage, you will have to retain an attorney at your own expense to represent your interest in the suit. If the patient gets a judgment in excess of the coverage, you will be personally responsible for paying the additional amount. The same reasoning applies to the forced coverage in the ADA's package plan — it is better to spend the additional amount for coverage now and let the insurance company worry about the big damages later. In today's litigious environment, the general practitioner should have at least $1 million in professional liability coverage, and the oral and maxillofacial surgeon should have all that is available. The same applies to any dentist who uses general anesthetics or performs intravenous (IV) sedation in the office.

Currently, the ADA-endorsed policy is written by CNA and referred to as the Professional Protector Plan. It insures about 50,000 dentists. Prior to April 1984, the ADA-endorsed policy was written by the Chubb Group.

The American Society of Oral and Maxillofacial Surgeons entered into a contract with the St. Paul Company to provide professional liability insurance for its members until 1990. In 1985, Aetna refused to cover dentists for malpractice, as did St. Paul for all dentists except the oral surgeons. The ADA-endorsed policy is available in all states except California and New York. However, not all state dental associations endorse the ADA policy.

The value of the ADA plan, ie, forced coverage for adequate amounts, is also its weakness. By providing the greatest good for the greatest number, the ADA plan is not necessarily the best insurance policy for the dentist who has a competent, qualified insurance agent. Such an agent can spot needs and write a policy to fit them. For example, a solo practitioner with a small office and no secretary or assistants will not need the employee liability coverage required under the ADA plan. In choosing an insurance plan, only the dentist can balance the security and convenience of the package plan with professional risks and financial demands.

Basic Insurance Contract of the ADA Professional Protector Plan
Coverage is provided for:

1. Dentist's insurance schedule
   personal and professional property losses
   practice interruption
   accounts receivable
2. Extra expense schedule
   due to loss or damage of property
3. Blanket employee fidelity insurance schedule
   employee dishonesty
4. Insurance against all-risk
   any direct loss or damage
5. Comprehensive liability insurance including written contracts schedule
   professional liability insurance
   products liability
   damage to property owned by landlord
   hired automobile

Professional Liability Insurance

The early and mid-1980s saw a crisis in dental malpractice insurance unlike anything that had occurred before. The crisis in medical malpractice of a decade ago had little, if any, effect on dentistry. Although most states modified their tort laws in the mid-70s to control the runaway malpractice crisis affecting physicians and hospitals, the crisis returned 10 years later.

In many respects, the crisis of the 1980s had a greater effect on dentistry than on medicine. Within a period of 3 years, insurance premiums for general practitioners rose as much as 300% in some areas of the country. For oral and maxillofacial surgeons, premiums rose as much as 3000%. One major company refused to cover surgeons who provided general anesthesia in the office. Within a period of 4 years, six different insurance companies were endorsed by the Dental Society of New York. Some remained in the business of writing dental professional liability policies for only 2 years. The premium for oral and maxillofacial surgeons practicing in New York City, who were insured by the company endorsed by the Dental Society of the State of New York, was in excess of $60,000 and only provided coverage for the restricted use of general anesthesia in a hospital. The premium for oral and maxillofacial surgeons practicing in Dade County, Fla, in 1986 for coverage by the ADA-endorsed policy was $93,000.

The crisis was not solely the fault of the dentists, although malpractice claims against dentists rose sharply from 1975. Jury awards increased dramatically, as did settlements. A major contributing factor was a crisis in the general insurance industry, caused in some measure by the fall in interest rates. Together, the result had a major effect on the cost of doing business as a dentist.

Contributing to the increase in the vulnerability of dentists and in awards and settlements are:

1. An awareness on the part of the public of its right to recover for the negligence of the dentist;
2. the general litigious environment, stimulated by the media and economic considerations;
3. attorneys, whose level of sophistication in suits brought against dentists has increased;
4. advertising practices of attorneys who encourage litigation by patients against health practitioners (the practice was supported in a decision by the US Supreme Court in 1985[2]);
5. dentists who criticize other dentists in an attempt to fill their appointment books during difficult economic times, and patients who are unwilling to pay twice for the same service;
6. insurance companies that are anxious to settle claims because of the rising costs of defending them, and the risk of loss with an excessive award by a jury.

The broadening scope of dental practice also contributed to the malpractice insurance crisis by enabling dentists to provide patients with procedures of high legal risk, such as the use of general anesthesia in the office and the hospital, the use of IV sedation, orthognathic surgery, extensive treatment of temporomandibular problems, and the use of blade implants. Insurance companies became reluctant to cover dentists who engaged in these professional treatment modalities. Those companies that continued to cover them reflected the increased risks in their markedly increased rates.

Dentists in general became high-liability risks because claims against them are difficult to defend, often as a result of poor office practices (see chapter 5).

The crisis led to several major problems for practicing dentists:

1. *Affordability of professional liability insurance.* The rapid and precipitous rise in premiums has dramatically increased the overhead of doing business. For young practitioners in some specialties, particularly oral and maxillofacial surgery, it has become prohibitive.

2. *Availability of professional liability insurance.* In some areas of the country, dentists have had their policies cancelled in the middle of the term. Companies have refused to renew high-risk practitioners at the end of the term. Others have stopped writing professional liability insurance. Dentists and state dental associations have had to shop around to find a company willing to write policies, no matter what the terms.

3. *Insurance companies, because of lack of effective competition and experiences of loss, have been able to dictate the terms of the policies to their own advantage and to the major disadvantage of dentists.* Policy terms have, in some cases, dictated scope of practice. Terms may prohibit the use of blade implants, temporomandibular treatment, the use of general anesthesia in the office, the use of IV sedation, etc. Some policies are based upon "occurrences" while others are "claims-made." Other terms relate to settlement clauses, scope of coverage, reporting requirements, etc.

TERMS OF THE PROFESSIONAL LIABILITY POLICY

Occurrence *v.* Claims-Made Policies

In some states, insurance carriers involved in writing dental professional liability insurance are switching coverage from the previously used occurrence form to the less-desirable claims-made form.

Unfortunately, many dentists who have switched to the claims-made form have not been made aware of the significant disadvantages of this type of coverage — specifically, the built-in annual premium increase for each of the first 5 years and the need to purchase additional insurance coverage when changing carriers or leaving this type of program.

In simple terms, the occurrence form policy protects the dentist against claims occurring during the policy period, regardless of when the claim is presented to the insurance company and whether or not the policy is still in force at the time the claim is made. Therefore, there is no need to purchase additional insurance coverage to cover past acts when changing carriers, leaving the program, selling the practice, or retiring. Premiums also remain level from year to year (except for general rate increases).

By contrast, the claims-made policy requires that the incident both occur and be reported during the insured's continuous coverage with the same carrier. If the incident is reported after the policy period and discovery period have expired, the insurance company has no obligation to the insured. An example of such requirements in the policy states:

> The Company will pay on behalf of the insured all sums ... for which claim is first made against the insured and reported to the company during the policy period ...

Statistics indicate that most dental claims are not reported in the year in which treatment takes place. If the dentist had a claims-made policy when the incident occurred and is no longer insured by that carrier at the time the claim is reported, the dentist will not be covered unless additional insurance called "tail coverage" (also known as extended reporting endorsement) is purchased.

The purpose of tail coverage is to provide against claims that occurred during the policy period but were not reported until after the policy had terminated. Such coverage can be necessitated if the carrier terminates the program (as has often been the case in recent years), if the dentist desires to change to another carrier, relocate to another area, etc. The tail coverage premium is a one-time charge based upon the number of years in which you were insured in that program. It can cost as much as 130% of the final year's premium.

The insured dentist should also be aware that the claims-made policy has an annual built-in premium increase for each of the first 5 years (not including any general rate increase that the carrier might request). In some cases, the second-year premium may be more than double the first-year premium, and by the third year it may triple.

While it is obvious that the claims-made form of policy is of considerable benefit to the insurance companies because they can more accurately predict their losses and may attract more policy holders because of the lower initial premium, it presents many problems for the insured dentist.

Settlement Clauses

One of the important terms of the professional liability insurance policy is the settlement clause. Until recently, the clause in policies written for physicians provided that the insurance company was precluded from entering into settlement negotiations with the patient-plaintiff without the written consent of the assured. Insurance companies found this provision to be against their financial interest. Too often, physicians refused to permit the insurance company to open settlement negotiations with the plaintiff, based on principle and professional ego rather than the merits of the case. The trial of a suit in malpractice is costly, and juries are unpredictable. Insurance companies often find it more expedient to settle a claim rather than to go to trial and risk large awards. Gradually, the insured physicians were deprived of the right to control the company in settlement negotiations.

Policies written for dentists, however, continue to give the dentist the right to dictate whether the insurance company can offer settlement to the plaintiff. The typical clause reads:

> No claims covered by this policy shall be settled by the Company without the written consent of the insured.

Many policies, although providing this option to the insured, add a significant risk when the insured elects not to have the company enter into settlement negotiations by further stating:

> If, however, the insured shall refuse to any settlement recommended by the Company and shall elect to contest the claim ... then the Company's liability for the claim shall not exceed the amount for which the claim could have been so settled plus claim expenses incurred up to the date of such claim refusal.

As the insurance companies increase their control over the market, it is expected that the right of the insured to dictate whether the insurance company may enter into settlement negotiations will be lost. Many state dental associations are losing their ability to dictate to insurance companies the terms of professional liability insurance policies. The result is that there is a trend to completely divest the dentist of control whether the company defends a suit or tries to settle the claim.

New York is unique in that companies endorsed by the State Dental Society must submit claims to a committee of the society for the committee's recommendation as to whether the suit should be defended or attempts to settlement should be made by the company. A typical clause states:

> No claims covered by this policy shall be settled or compromised by the Company except with the written consent of a majority of a committee or committees authorized by the Dental Society of the State of New York.

Both the company and the defendant-dentist are bound by the decision of the committee. This system represents a reasonable middle ground between having either the company or the dentist exercise exclusive control over the settlement-or-defend option. How long the dental society in New York will be able to maintain this type of settlement clause is speculative.

Policies in which the insured has no control over the right of the company to enter into settlement negotiations typically state:

> The insured shall cooperate with the Company and, upon the Company's request, shall assist in making settlements ...

Reporting Incidents and Claims

All policies require that unusual incidents be reported to the insurance company at the earliest possible time. The use of terms such as "unusual incidents," "unusal occurrences," and "occurrences" leads to much confusion as to what constitutes an incident that must be reported. Failure to report may lead to the refusal of the company to defend the suit and the refusal to indemnify the defendant-dentist for losses resulting from an unfavorable decision by the court. It is clear that, if a patient or lawyer threatens suit, or if service of suit is made on the dentist, it must immediately be reported to the insurance company. But it is not at all clear as to what constitutes an unusual occurrence. Polarized examples present no difficulties. For example, if a patient aspirates a bur, it must be reported. A patient who feels faint momentarily, following an injection of an anesthetic, need not be reported. The gray areas between these examples present the problem. There is no simple answer. However, the consequences of not reporting when a report is called for may lead to a major financial loss for the dentist. It seems better to overreport than to underreport.

Other Terms of the Professional Liability
Insurance Policy

Scope Some policies that were on the market several years ago, and might still be available, provided the dentist with much-needed extensive coverage. Included in addition to coverage for negligence were the defense and indemnification from losses resulting from claims of breach of contract, defamation, assault and battery, and, in some rare policies, undue familiarity and payment for the awards of punitive damages. When cases involving the latter two occurred, an insurance company denied coverage although the policy provided for such coverage. In both cases, the courts held the company to the terms of the policy.[3,4]

Today, it is almost universal in professional liability insurance policies to cover the insured only for negligence in the performance of dental services.

Persons Covered A policy issued to a dentist may, in addition to covering the dentist, cover his or her employees. Some policies exclude employees who are licensed; in this type of policy, hygienists and assistants (in those states where assistants are licensed) would not be covered. Although the licensed hygienist and assistant may not be covered by the policy, the dentist may be covered, depending on the terms of the policy, if sued for their negligent acts.

Good Samaritan Acts Professional liability insurance policies generally cover dentists who provide services in emergency situations.

Service on Peer Review Committees Coverage is usually provided for the insured dentist who serves as a member of a peer review committee of a dental society or on a comparable committee of a hospital.

What Is Not Covered Except for the special situation noted above, the professional liability insurance policy will not pay awards of punitive damages or undue familiarity. Acts that are illegal will also relieve the company of liability. Although the company may defend a suit based on negligence during the performance of a service that may be illegal, the company is precluded from paying the claim if the service is determined to be illegal because of strong public policy. If the act is clearly illegal, they may not enter into the defense. Allegations of criminal fraud also relieve the insurance company of responsibility.

ATTEMPTS AT SOLVING THE CRISIS

Reforms in tort law, eagerly sought by the medical profession and obtained during the crisis of the mid-1970s, did little to stem the rise in awards and settlements of medical and dental malpractice claims. The crisis of the 80s stimulated another wave of pressure on legislatures to make recovery by injured patients more difficult, to punish lawyers and their clients for initiating "frivolous suits," to place caps on pain and suffering, to reduce awards when collateral sources of recovery are available to the injured party, to limit the fees of plaintiffs' attorneys, to structure awards for pain and suffering, and to require judges and juries to itemize verdicts.

Caps on Pain and Suffering (noneconomic losses)

The purpose of this legislation is to limit the amount that a jury can award to a plaintiff for noneconomic losses resulting from injury due to medical malpractice. In 1975, California enacted such legislation, placing the cap at $250,000. The law was challenged. The United States Supreme Court, in a decision reached in 1985, declared the cap as legislated in California to be constitutional.[2]

New York, in its Malpractice Reform Act of 1985, did not place a cap on pain and suffering.[5]

Itemized Verdicts

The rule for courts or juries to itemize verdicts is to force placement of an exact amount of compensation for each of the specific areas in which an injured patient is entitled to be compensated. Lump sum verdicts, to many in the field of litigating malpractice claims, are thought to bring higher awards. In those jurisdictions that have enacted legislation requiring structured awards and modified the collateral source rule, itemized verdicts are essential.

Structured Awards

Structured awards require a court or jury to apply the injured patient's award money to the payment of future expenses incurred as a result of the injury and for future pain and suffering over a period of years. The stated purpose is to avoid the depletion of funds made possible if the money is turned over to the plaintiff in one lump sum at the time of the award.

Opponents of the rule feel that the party that is made to pay in a structured award is able to use the money that is due to the plaintiff during the delayed payment to reduce their own losses, and, should the injured party die before all payments are made, the defendant or the insurance company would not have to continue payments. An additional problem, evident in the New York legislation of 1985, is that the insurance company of the defendant-doctor *and the doctor* must guarantee, through the purchase of an annuity policy, that money is available during the entire period of the structured award.

Collateral Source Payment Rule

The proponents of this change, which provides for the reduction in the award by an amount equal to any financial benefit the injured plaintiff receives from outside sources (such as insurance for medical care, workmen's compensation, etc), feel that it will prevent double financial compensation for the plaintiff and will reduce the amount of money paid out by the insurance company or the defendant-doctor.

The Incompetent Practitioner

One of the major goals of proposals under consideration in many states is the achievement of an effective way to deal with the incompetent and impaired practitioner. Many proposed laws include reporting by the insurance companies to licensing agencies of payments made to patients as a result of claims of malpractice. In some proposals, a considerable burden would be placed on hospitals and health facilities to report acts of negligence, incompetence, and impairment of its medical and dental staff to the licensing agency.

Miscellaneous Legislation

Other forms of state legislation aimed at curbing malpractice litigation include limiting plaintiff's contingency fees, reducing the statute of limitations, creating panels to fix liability, requiring pretrial hearings, punishing patients and/or attorneys for instituting frivolous suits, etc.

Professional liability insurance companies have not escaped proposed malpractice reform legislation. Increasing the state insurance department's control over premiums and coverage appears in many bills before legislatures.

In 1985, 20 states passed some form of legislation aimed at curbing malpractice litigation. As of February 1986, according to a report in the March 3 *American Dental Association News*, 25 states were considering malpractice reform legislation. The same issue reported that federal legislation was introduced in both House and Senate committees designed at tort reform. New York passed its Medical Malpractice Reform Law in July 1985.[5]

Summary and Recommendations

Many of the so-called tort reforms are designed to limit the money received by both the injured party and his or her attorney. The proponents feel that this approach will reduce the number of malpractice claims by making them less attractive financially to the plaintiffs' bar and their clients. The malpractice legislation of the early and mid-70s appears not to have stemmed the rising tide. We have yet to evaluate the legislation of the 80s.

The future of malpractice litigation is difficult to predict. While the professions are demanding effective changes, the legislatures seem slow to respond, and the courts are reluctant to support legislation that limits the right of injured parties to sue. For dentists, the lesson to be learned from the events of the early 80s is that as the scope of practice expands, the cost of malpractice insurance increases.

These rules for conducting the professional practice of dentistry have emerged over the centuries from judicial decisions. The court cases have produced clearly defined legal rights and duties for both the dentist and patient. By knowing the legal rights set forth in specific cases, a dentist can compare his or her daily practice to the professional performance that has been found legally acceptable or unacceptable. A further instructive guide for the professional dentist can be found in the jury verdicts, court awards, and litigants' settlements that affix dollar evaluations to dental acts legally identified as unacceptable dental practice. Dollar amounts are rough indicators of the legal importance attached to acts of dental malpractice. The competent dental practitioner should not fear malpractice law. The competent dentist should understand the rules of conduct for professional practice and adjust his or her daily practice to conform to the legal rules governing the dentist-patient relationship.

CONCLUSION

Insurance is a necessary cost of doing business as a dentist. All-protection insurance is essential in today's litigious society. The risk of suit for providing substandard care has increased dramatically in the past decade, as have the awards by courts and juries. All aspects of professional liability insurance have increased the cost of doing business for the dentist. Insurance is the only way to protect the assets of the practitioner. The selection of the right kind of insurance is essential to adequately protect these assets. Terms of the contract of insurance should be carefully studied by the practitioner, and advice should be sought from competent insurance agents and attorneys before embarking on a program of insurance protection.

70

REFERENCES

1. *Porubiansky v. Emory University et al.*, 282 S.E.2d 903 (1981).
2. *Zauderer v. Office of Disciplinary Counsel of the Supreme Court of Ohio*, Supreme Court of the United States, Slip Opinion 83–2166, May 28, 1985.
3. *Public Service Mutual Insurance Company v. Goldfarb*, 430 N.Y.S.2d 72, 442 N.Y.S.2d 422 (1981).
4. *Public Service Mutual Insurance Company v. Levy*, 87 Misc.2d 924 (1981).
5. Analysis of new comprehensive Medical Malpractice Reform Law. *NY Law J.* August 13, 1985, p1.

7 Dental Malpractice: Laws for Conducting Professional Practice

Oliver C. Schroeder, Jr.
Burton R. Pollack

The basic principles of tort law are the foundations for the malpractice rules applied to dentistry. Consideration of these rules requires an investigation of four areas: (1) the standard of care owed to a patient; (2) additional sources of a dentist's liability to a patient; (3) recent examples of specific acts or omissions that produced malpractice litigation; and (4) damages.

STANDARD OF CARE

General Rule

The rules governing the duty of care a dentist owes a patient are identical to those applied to physicians and surgeons.[1] The dentist must possess and exercise that level of skill and judgment prevailing in the dental community.[2] A dentist representing himself as a specialist is held to a higher standard of care with respect to that specialty, as measured by the level of care offered by similar specialists. One of the earliest

71

cases establishing a dentist's standard of care concerned a suit brought by a dentist to recover the price of dentures he had prepared. The patient, claiming the dentures did not fit properly, refused to accept or pay for them. At trial, the jury's verdict was in favor of the patient, based on the judge's instruction that the dentist was required to use the highest degree of skill attainable at that time. On appeal, the verdict was reversed on the ground that the standard of care imposed on a dentist was a reasonable level of care and skill, not the highest degree of care available.[3]

A more recent case involved a hypodermic needle that broke off in a patient's tissues during the administration of a local anesthetic. Because no evidence was presented to indicate the dentist had failed to exercise that level of ordinary and reasonable care practiced in the community, the dentist was not held liable for the injury to the patient.[4] Consistent with the decision, courts have held that dentists are not liable for latent defects in instruments not discoverable at the time of use.

Governed by Locality

Traditionally, because of the differences in education and practice prevailing in various localities, courts required the dentist to conform only to that standard of care exercised in his particular locality. This traditional rule was recently applied when a dentist was found not liable for failing to refer a patient to a periodontist.[5] Because dentists in the locality were accustomed to treating periodontal disease themselves, the dentist was not required to refer the patient to a specialist.

The trend toward standardization of dental and medical education, plus the numerous opportunities available to dentists to keep abreast of developments in the profession, have prompted some courts to abandon the strictly local rule in favor of either a standard of care based on practices prevailing in similar localities or a nationwide standard. For example, in a case where brain damage resulted from a general anesthetic administered during surgery to repair a fractured jaw, a court held that the standard of care was not measured by the immediate locality; instead, the applicable standard was what a competent practitioner would do under the same, or similar, circumstances in an area readily accessible to the patient for appropriate treatment.[6] In another case in which a dentist was allegedly negligent in failing to diagnose and treat periodontal disease, the court held the governing standard of care was determined by the practices of the dental profession at large.[7]

The adoption of nationwide or similar-locality standards to gauge the dentist's performance has several significant effects. First, a lower standard of care for rural areas with limited access to dental teaching and treatment facilities is no longer permitted. Second, patients are able to obtain dentists from areas outside that of the defendant-dentist's immediate area to testify as experts. Under a strictly-local rule, the plaintiff must find a local dentist to describe the standard of care in the immediate area. As might be expected, it is often difficult to find a professional who is willing to testify against a fellow practitioner from the local community. The problem is described as the "conspiracy of silence." The nationwide or similar-locality rules circumvent this problem.

Implicitly Warranting the Results of Treatment

When the standard of reasonable and ordinary care as practiced in the community is applied, unless the dentist expressly promises results from a proposed treatment, he or she does not guarantee the success of such treatment.[8] This general rule holds regardless of how broadly the community may be defined. Under this standard, without a promise of success, it has been held that an orthodontist does not warrant a perfect result in correcting malocclusion.[9] Similarly, it has been held that a periodontist does not warrant complete success in trying to correct a potentially traumatizing malocclusion.[10]

Burden of Proving Malpractice

As a general rule, a patient must prove the following elements to recover on the basis of malpractice: (1) that a duty of care arose from a dentist-patient relationship; (2) that a specific standard of care existed for the treatment involved; (3) that the dentist departed from that standard of care; (4) that the patient suffered an injury; and (5) that the departure was the direct cause of the injury. If the conduct of the patient contributed to the injury, in some jurisdictions the dentist is relieved of liability (contributory negligence rule); in others, the damages are assessed based on the degree of fault of each party (comparative negligence rule).

These requirements for recovery represent the burden of proof the plaintiff must bear in a malpractice action. They may present serious obstacles to the patient's success. Assuming that a plaintiff can prove that he or she was the defendant-dentist's patient, and that an applicable standard of care exists, the plaintiff may be unable to prove exactly which of the dentist's acts or omissions caused the injury. The patient is rarely aware of the dentist's actions during the course of treatment.

Judicial Doctrines Aiding the Malpractice Plaintiff

To aid the plaintiff when the allegedly negligent act cannot be proven by facts within his or her knowledge, courts have applied a presumption of negligence under certain conditions. To rebut this presumption, the burden of presenting evidence shifts to the dentist, who is better able to explain what actions were taken. The dentist must then prove that his or her actions conformed to the standard of ordinary and reasonable care, or that the injuries were not a result of his or her acts.

The doctrine allowing the rebuttable presumption of negligence or inferred negligence is called the common knowledge doctrine, or *res ipsa loquitor* ("the facts speak for themselves"). Essentially, this doctrine allows the finder of fact (either the jury or a judge) to presume negligence if: (1) the testimony of experts (or, where expert testimony is not required, the common knowledge of the layman) indicates that the plaintiff's complaints usually would not have arisen without negligence, and (2) the defendant was the sole potential source of the injury.

The doctrine of *res ipsa loquitor* is not a recent development in the law; according to one commentator, it was first applied to a dental malpractice case in 1882.[11] In that case, the court held that a rebuttable presumption of negligence was raised when an extracted tooth fell into an anesthetized patient's bronchial tube. Courts are divided on whether to presume negligence when fractured jaws result during tooth extractions.[12] However, negligence has been presumed when injuries to the patient's lip and chin[13] or tongue and throat[14] result from slipped drills. While negligence has been presumed in one case in which a nerve was injured during oral surgery,[15] the presumption has not been applied in other cases involving nerve injuries from drilling,[16] injections,[17] or oral surgery.[18] In spite of vigorous opposition, courts have applied the presumption of negligence when injuries and death resulted from general anesthetics[19] or from local anesthetic solutions containing vasoconstrictors.[20] On the other hand, the doctrine has not been applied when idiopathic infections were diagnosed subsequent to dental treatment.[21]

Contributory Negligence as a Bar to Recovery

The courts have traditionally denied relief to patients who have negligently contributed to the cause or the extent of their injuries (contributory negligence rule). To mitigate harsh results, some states have modified this rule. A New York court has held that when a patient failed to follow the dentist's advice on oral hygiene and exacerbated the injury complained of, the patient's contributory negligence merely reduced the amount of damages awarded rather than precluded recovery (comparative negligence rule).[22]

ADDITIONAL SOURCES OF LIABILITY

Informed Consent

The doctrine of informed consent has been applied to dentistry in the same manner that it has been applied to the other healing arts. Essentially, the doctrine requires that the patient provide an informed consent before receiving treatment. If the dentist fails to obtain a valid consent, he or she may be liable for assault and battery, even though performing with the highest degree of care and skill. The issue that usually arises in connection with this doctrine involves the extent to which the dentist must disclose the possible risks of the procedures to be performed so that the patient's consent is be based on an intelligent choice.

Courts have traditionally treated informed consent cases and malpractice cases similarly, holding that patients must prove the standard of disclosure in the dental community and the dentist's failure to meet that standard.[23] In a case involving a sinus infection that resulted from impression material which had lodged in a fistula between a root canal and a sinus cavity, the court held that the standard of disclosure did not relate to all possible risks involved in such a procedure. Instead, the dentist had a duty to disclose only those risks a dentist in the community would reasonably expect the patient to be made aware of in order for the patient to make a reasoned consent.[24]

Informed consent cases usually involve patients who consent to a procedure but then allege that they would not had consented if they had been informed of the possibility of the consequences that had occurred. However, informed consent has also been an issue in cases involving unauthorized treatment. For example, recovery has been permitted for failure to obtain informed consent when a dentist decided to extract additional teeth while the patient was under general anesthesia,[25] or when the dentist inadvertently extracted the wrong teeth.[26]

For a more detailed discussion of informed consent, see chapter 10.

Products Liability

In products liability cases, purchasers of defective products sue to recover damages for injuries resulting from the defect. While some states have expanded the category of persons who may be held liable for injuries from defective products, one court did not impose such liability on a dentist in a case involving injuries resulting from an allegedly defective hypodermic needle that broke in the patient's jaw.[27]

Breach of Contract

The liability of the dentist stems not only from the dentist-patient relationship but also from the contract between dentist and patient. Although dentists do not implicitly warrant complete satisfaction with their treatment, they may be liable for breach of any express warranties or promises that they make. Thus, when a dentist assured a patient that the dentures he prepared would please her, and the patient was not pleased, she was permitted to rescind her contract for dentures and recover her payment.[28]

Cruel and Inhuman Treatment

In at least two reported cases, prison inmates have attempted to sue prison dentists for cruel and inhuman treatment, denial of equal protection under the law, and violation of federal civil rights statutes. In both, the courts refused to recognize these claims.[29] In a recent case decided in the Federal Court, Southern District in New York, the court found that denial of treatment to prison inmates deprived them of their civil rights.[30]

Property Lost in Waiting Room

Another potential source of liability was recognized in an early New York case involving a patient who lost property in a dentist's waiting room.[31] The court held that when the dentist or his assistant knew the patient left her coat in the waiting room and failed to protect the coat, the dentist assumed liability for its loss.

Liability for the Acts of Others

The general rules of employer liability for the acts of employees are applied to dentists. Therefore, dentists may be held liable for the intentional or negligent acts of nurses, dental assistants, or other dentists they employ when such actions occur during the course of employment and injure patients.

This theory of *respondeat superior*, or vicarious liability, is generally justified on the basis of the dentist's right to control the actions of his or her employees.[32] Under this theory, a college of dentistry was held responsible for the negligence of a dental student and an attending dentist.[33] A dentist was also liable for injuries that resulted when his assistant spilled acid on a patient's leg.[34]

When an employee-dentist failed to use a rubber dam or other safety procedures during the course of root canal treatment, and a reamer was dropped into the patient's throat, the court held the employer-dentist liable.[35] Liability for the patient's injury was imposed on the employer-dentist despite the court's refusal to find that the employer had a duty to supervise the treatment of the employee-dentist.

Duty to Maintain a Skilled Staff

When the activities of a dentist require support services or staff with special training, failure to maintain a properly trained staff may give rise to liability. Thus, when a patient's death resulted from general anesthesia, the oral surgeon's failure to maintain staff properly trained in the administration of general anesthesia constituted grounds for liability.[36]

SPECIFIC ACTS OR OMISSIONS PRODUCING MALPRACTICE LITIGATION

Medical History

The dentist's failure to obtain a patient's medical history prior to treatment, and the use of procedures and substances that would have been contraindicated had such a history been obtained, have led to liability for a patient's injury or death. In one case, a dentist did not obtain a medical history that would have revealed his patient suffered from hypertension. The dentist administered a local anesthetic with a vasoconstrictor, which, according to the package insert, was contraindicated for use in hypertensive patients. The dentist was held liable for the patient's death from a cerebral hemorrhage induced by the epinephrine.[37] Major losses have occurred in general practice for failure to discover, through the medical history, that the patient suffered from rheumatic fever.[38]

Diagnosis

A number of cases have involved the negligent failure of a dentist to diagnose a serious medical or dental condition that could have been detected with reasonable care. Liability has been imposed for the failure to diagnose cancer when the oral surgeon suspected a malignancy and did not perform a tissue biopsy,[39] or the failure to extend the surgical procedure when the biopsy was positive.[40] In another case, a dentist was held liable for the failure to diagnose cancer in the face of two indicators: the patient's repeated complaints of soreness that prevented the proper fitting of dentures, and a white spot on the patient's tongue.[41]

Other courts have found negligence in the failure to diagnose periodontal disease[42] or a fractured jaw.[43]

Failure to Refer

Dentists have been held liable for injuries resulting from the failure to refer patients to physicians or dental specialists when the standard of care in the community would require such referral. When dentists in the community traditionally treated periodontal disease themselves, a dentist was not held liable for failure to refer a patient suffering from periodontal disease to a periodontist.[44] With the proliferation of community periodontists, recent cases have held that failure to make appropriate referrals for specialty care constitutes negligence.

Consistent with liability for failure to make a timely referral, a dentist was found negligent in failing to refer a patient suffering from pansinusitis to a physician.[45] In another case, a dentist who after performing a full mouth extraction failed to refer a patient suffering from a lung abscess to a physician was held liable.[46]

Administration of General Anesthetics

Several cases have arisen concerning death or brain damage resulting from the use of general anesthetics. In one such case, an oral surgeon failed to provide for resuscitation as the patient was transported to the hospital, and the patient was pronounced dead on arrival.[47] The court held the oral surgeon liable for failure to employ resuscitation procedures and failure to maintain staff properly trained in the administration of general anesthetics.

In a case involving oral surgery to reduce a fractured jaw, the patient did not awake from general anesthesia for nearly 1 month. When the patient regained consciousness, he had sustained brain damage. The court applied the presumption of negligence in the face of this unusual occurrence.[48] Liability has also been imposed when, in the course of a tooth extraction, the oral surgeon and anesthesiologist failed to suspend procedures and revive a patient who showed signs of cardiac arrest.[49]

Administration of Local Anesthetics

Claims against dentists have frequently involved injuries from hypodermic needles breaking in the patient's jaw when local anesthetics were administered. Although one court found negligence when too short of a needle was used and another court imposed liability when the portion of a broken needle embedded in the patient's jaw was not surgically removed,[50] the breaking of the needle alone is insufficient to establish liability.[51,52] In general, a dentist is not held liable for latent defects not discoverable at the time the needle is used.

Several cases have involved untoward effects of injections. In general, negligence has not been presumed from such abnormal occurrences. When continued pain allegedly resulted from an injection,[53] or when a patient complained of headaches following mandibular block injections,[54] negligence was not presumed. However, negligence was presumed when a patient complained of pain following an injection that was not administered in the region (mandibular foramen) preferred by local practitioners for the procedure involved.[55]

Tooth Extractions

Tooth extractions can generate numerous problems that may lead to malpractice suits, such as fractured jaws, incomplete or mistaken extractions, or infection.

Courts have been divided in their approach to jaw fractures that occur during the course of tooth extractions. A presumption of negligence was applied when a fracture occurred while a dentist used a surgical elevator to twist and pry out a broken root portion of a molar,[56] and when an oral surgeon testified that extractions of third molars normally do not result in such fractures.[57] However, other courts have refused to apply a presumption of negligence in this situation[58]; these courts require patients to prove negligence — a burden of proof that is difficult to meet.

The failure to remove all tooth and root fragments has not been held negligent in itself,[59] nor has liability been imposed for problems arising from subsequent surgery to remove the remaining fragments.[60]

In one case, a Florida appellate court reversed a decision for a dentist when an infected palatal root remained in the patient's jaw during the extraction of an infected molar.[61] The reversing court found that an issue of negligence arose concerning whether due care would have revealed the root in the patient's jaw.

In contrast to cases involving incomplete extractions, at least one case involved the removal of too much bone from the patient's jaw. In this case, some bone process adhering to the root of the tooth was removed with the root.[62] On the basis of the defendant's testimony that such a problem was not uncommon, the court refused to apply a presumption of negligence.

One relatively recent case concerned an infection of unknown origin following a tooth extraction.[63] The court refused to presume negligence in such a case. However, when a dentist extracted an abscessed tooth before treating the infection, a presumption of negligence was recognized.[64]

There have been a number of cases about the mistaken extraction of the wrong tooth or the extraction of more teeth than the patient requested be removed. Because these suits involve action taken without consent, or a battery upon the patient's body, the patient is generally awarded damages.[65]

In two cases decided in New York, the court ruled that in certain situations involving surgical procedures, the jury, without benefit of experts, could judge whether the dentist departed from an acceptable standard of care.[66]

One unreported extraction case highlights the importance of determining whether the patient can pay for dental services before such services are performed. In this case, the dentist prepared 14 of the patient's teeth for crowns before the patient indicated that financing could not be arranged for the treatment. Because the patient could not finance the care, the 14 altered teeth had to be extracted. The patient was awarded $300,000, presumably for the pain and suffering caused by the dentist's negligent failure to ascertain whether the treatment could be financed.[67]

Nerve Injury

A common source of dental litigation is unexplained anesthesia or paresthesia following dental treatment. In such cases, the plaintiffs usually allege that the dentist injured a nerve in the course of treatment, and such injury resulted in the loss or alteration of sensation. It is generally difficult to prove or disprove negligence in these cases. However, not informing the patient of the possibility of paresthesia following the extraction of an impacted lower third molar may support a claim of lack of informed consent.

When a patient alleged the dentist severed two nerves by allowing the drill to penetrate the lingual periosteum, and the dentist testified that he worked from the other side of the tooth involved, the patient was denied recovery.[68] However, when a dentist allegedly severed the mental nerve while performing an alveolectomy and subsequent procedure to remove a sequestrum before fitting the patient with dentures, the court permitted the jury to find negligence based on the testimony of the dentist.[69] The court held that the dentist's explanation would be construed in the plaintiff's favor, if such a construction were possible.

In the District of Columbia, a patient suffered paresthesia following an operation to remove a root fragment left in his jaw after an extraction, but he was denied recovery.[70] Yet, a California court permitted a patient suffering from paresthesia following the extraction of a molar to recover.[71]

Other Acts

A large number of malpractice cases arise when dentists drop reamers into the throats of patients during root canal treatment. These reamers usually end up on a bronchus or in the patient's gastrointestinal tract. Because using rubber dams or other procedures can prevent this problem, courts have little difficulty in finding negligence in such cases.[72]

In one case, the dentist dropped a reamer into the patient's throat, informed the patient that he had dropped something, and said it would pass through the patient's system if she ate roughage. The patient visited a hospital for radiographs. Surgery was necessary to remove the reamer. The jury was permitted to find negligence without the aid of expert testimony.[73]

"Runaway drills" represent another category of cases where negligence is generally found with little difficulty. Recovery has been permitted when a disk attached to a drill jumped a safety guard and cut through the patient's lower lip down to the point of the chin,[74] and when a drill slipped and lacerated a child's mouth, leaving permanent scar tissue.[75] In another case, as the dentist drilled one of the patient's lower left molars, the drill slipped off the tooth, causing the dentist to lose his balance and fall into the patient's lap. The drill then cut through the patient's tongue and into his throat. The jury needed no expert testimony to find negligence.[76]

Patients have recovered damages in a variety of cases involving chemical or thermal burns. In one such case, a patient brought suit to recover damages related to a tissue burn caused by hot impression material.[77] Recovery has been permitted when patients suffered burns from carbolic acid spilled on them by dental assistants,[78] and when bleaching fluid was dropped on the patient's lip and mouth during the course of treatment.[79]

A number of cases have concerned burns from other sources. A patient recovered damages for burns from electrosterilization following root canal treatment.[80] Other cases have permitted recovery for burns from overexposure to radiation from x-ray machines,[81] or from electric shocks caused by x-ray machines.[82]

Malpractice litigation has involved infections in the patient's mouth or respiratory system following treatment. The usual allegations of the dentist's negligent failure to sterilize equipment or disinfect the treated area of the body are often difficult to prove. For example, when a patient died of tetanus diagnosed after the patient had undergone tooth extractions and the fitting of dentures, the court did not permit an inference that the dentures were improperly sterilized and carried tetanus spores to the wounds left by the extractions.[83]

In another case, a 14-year-old boy visited a dentist complaining of swelling and pain associated with a tooth. The dentist removed a crown, inserted an antiseptic, and cemented the crown. The boy's condition deteriorated, however, and he lost sight in the eye on the swollen side of his face. The boy's physician diagnosed the condition as maxillary and ethmoid sinusitis with secondary orbital cellulitis and edema. At trial, the plaintiff attempted to prove that the dentist's actions had prevented the infection from draining, and, as a result, caused gases to enter the boy's sinus to create the condition. However, the jury did not find the dentist negligent.[84]

Cases involving sinus conditions are illustrated by two fairly recent decisions. In one case, some impression material entered a fistula between the patient's sinus cavity and a root canal of a tooth extracted preparatory to fitting dentures. The material entered the sinus cavity and caused a sinus infection. The jury found the dentist was not negligent in failing to discover the fistula, and the verdict was affirmed on appeal.[85] In the other case, the dentist was found negligent in creating an opening between the root canal and a sinus cavity.[86] Although it was unclear whether the condition was created in the course of the tooth extraction or during the subsequent procedure to remove a remaining root fragment, the dentist's negligence was presumed to be the cause of the patient's injuries.

The foregoing cases represent common grounds for malpractice litigation, but the examples do not provide exhaustive coverage of the variety of claims made. Dentists have also been held liable for improperly fitting bridges,[87] for negligently capping teeth,[88] and for injuring a patient's neck during the course of tooth extractions.[89]

DAMAGES

Award Trends

Malpractice verdicts against dentists indicate the recovery rate is slightly higher than that for medical malpractice cases: 40% for dental malpractice as compared with 33% for medical malpractice.[90] The rate of recovery and amount of awards appear to be increasing in dental malpractice cases.[91] The range of awards for a study period from 1967 to 1975 was $300 to $40,000, with two verdicts in the $300,000 to $400,000 range.[92] Although 48% of the awards were above $10,000, the average award (it is not clear whether this is the mean, median, or mode) was $11,270.[93]

The above data reflect the situation as of 1971 and 1975. The latest data, collected from the same source, indicate a dramatic increase in jury reaction to dental malpractice. Data collected until 1977 showed that only 25% of dental malpractice cases resulted in a verdict for the plaintiff. However, the results of a survey conducted in 1983 revealed that, for a period of 18 months prior to October 1983, plaintiff's verdicts rose to 56%. Further, in 1981 the average jury award was $50,000. By 1983, it rose to $93,266.[94]

How Recent Awards Were Calculated

The following cases are illustrative of jury awards in dental malpractice cases.

Generally, in situations involving the negligent failure to diagnose a dangerous medical or dental condition, the condition progresses and the extent of the injury increases. When a dentist failed to diagnose cancer, despite the patient's repeated complaints of soreness and the white spot that appeared on the patient's tongue, the patient was awarded $40,000.[95] Similarly, when a dentist failed to diagnose advanced periodontal disease in the course of treatment spanning 7 years, the patient recovered $15,000.[96] The delay caused deterioration in the patient's gums, which required upper and lower gum resection, splinting, and bridge work, at a cost of $1,500.

Related to the failure to diagnose is the failure to refer a patient for treatment by a medical or dental specialist. The patient who developed a cough after a full mouth extraction was awarded $3,000 for the dentist's negligence in failing to refer the patient for treatment of lung abscess.[97] Fortunately, the patient recovered without residual lung damage, with total medical expenses of only $1,050.

In malpractice cases involving general anesthesia, death or brain damage have often resulted. The defendant is subjected to a large verdict based, in part, on the loss of future earnings by the patient. During an extraction performed under general anesthesia, when the oral surgeon and anesthesiologist failed to suspend procedures and revive the patient showing signs of cardiac arrest, the patient's estate was awarded $359,333.[98] The patient, president of a data processing corporation, could have earned a substantial future income, and this factor was taken into account in determining the award.

When a dentist is found negligent for fracturing a patient's jaw during tooth extractions, health complications may have a bearing on the award. A patient who contracted osteomyelitis as the result of a negligent fracture was awarded $12,500.[99] Another patient was awarded $10,000 following the extraction of an impacted wisdom tooth when she developed an abscess. Her jaw was fractured and had to be wired. A patient who claimed to have requested the extraction of all of his upper teeth and one of his lower teeth received $20,000 when the dentist mistakenly removed all of the patient's lower teeth.[100] The defendant in this case claimed he no longer employed the dentist who performed the treatment. Nevertheless, the employer-dentist was held liable for the total damage figure, of which $15,000 constituted punitive damages for the intentional battery stemming from the lack of consent.

In another case involving unauthorized extractions, the dentist's attempt to correct his error only served to complicate matters further. After extracting the wrong tooth, the dentist proceeded to extract the proper tooth. However, in the course of the second extraction, the nerve of an adjacent tooth was severed, resulting in the loss of a third tooth and orthodontic complications. The $1,500 verdict seemed to reflect the mitigating fact that all of the teeth involved were deciduous molars.

The following cases may provide some insight into the manner in which malpractice damages are calculated. When an opening was negligently made between a root canal and a sinus cavity, and this condition could not be corrected by two operations, the patient was awarded $8,800. Of this amount, $3,900 constituted past and estimated future medical expenses, $500 constituted lost earnings, and $4,400 constituted compensation for pain and suffering.[101]

When an improperly fitted bridge caused the protrusion of the patient's two front teeth and upper lip, and the patient waited 2 months before the dentist replaced the bridge, the patient was awarded $850 for pain and suffering, offset by $69 for radiographs, an extraction, and a prosthetic device.[102]

A patient claiming a neck injury suffered during an extraction of five teeth under general anesthesia was awarded $40,000. Of this figure, $4,000 represented medical expenses, $10,000 constituted compensation for earnings lost before the time of the award, and $26,000 was compensation for the loss of future wages.[103]

The following sums were awarded in other recent verdicts: $12,500 for a nerve injury and resultant paresthesia suffered during an extraction;[104] $4,080 for lacerations from a drill that slipped during a tooth preparation;[105] $5,000 for burns from bleaching fluid dropped on the patient's mouth;[106] $1,500 for negligence in improperly capping a patient's teeth;[107] and $15,000 for severe burns of the gum and bone and the loss of two teeth after electrosterilization following root canal treatment.[108]

Damages are affected not only by malpractice rules, but also by the mores, customs, and attitudes of the decision-makers in the community. The social values of these decision-makers, whether judge or jury, are important determining factors for malpractice awards or settlements.

Both patient-plaintiff and dentist-defendant must be sensitive to what is occurring in the community where the malpractice claim is made. *Personal Injury Valuation Handbooks*, a unique service provided by Jury Verdict Research, Inc, of Solon, Ohio, has provided much of the information previously set forth. If one turns to the timely *Verdict Reports* circulated nationwide weekly by this corporation, the verdicts and settlements in specific communities provide interesting material for analysis.

Salt Lake City, September 1976   A dentist placed a rubber band around the upper incisors of a minor patient in order to close the gap in the front teeth. The patient contended that the dentist was negligent in follow-up care and had never obtained the patient's informed consent. The patient established special damages of $1,500 for past and future dental care costs and demanded $10,000 damages. A verdict was rendered in favor of the defendant-dentist.

Rockville, Md, July 1976   The dentist allegedly administered anesthesia improperly when providing root canal therapy, resulting in a prolonged recovery from the anesthesia. The patient demanded $12,000 to settle; the dentist offered $6,000. The jury awarded $9,000.

Cleveland, April 1976   A 21-year-old female fainted and then died while a tooth was being extracted. The decedent patient's representative claimed the dentist had failed to monitor her adequately after injecting a drug. In addition, the dentist allegedly failed to administer first aid when the patient lost consciousness. The dentist countered that fear had caused the patient to faint. The patient had two minor children. The dentist offered to pay $15,000 after the patient's representative had demanded $100,000. The jury awarded $90,000 for the wrongful death caused by the dentist.

Miami, March 1976   When a 59-year-old female visited a dentist because of a mouth irritation, the dentist referred her to a second dentist, who performed a root canal procedure without completing an oral examination. Both dentists claimed that a lesion on the patient's tongue was not visible in the early months when the patient was being treated. The patient claimed she had a visible irritation on her tongue and had told both dentists about it on several occasions during the 1973 to 1974 period of treatment. The patient had a cancer on the tongue, necessitating partial removal of the tongue and a left radical neck dissection at a cost of $2,483. A settlement of $100,000 was negotiated between the parties.

Chicago, February 1976   Following reconstruction work on 22 of her teeth, a 55-year-old woman contended the dentist reduced her teeth size by drilling. He used silver points instead of gutta percha as root canal filling material and he generally performed in a professionally unorthodox manner. The patient lost 15 teeth as a result. The dentist responded that the damage had occurred before he treated her, and that he used techniques which had been successful for the past 25 years. Medical expenses for the patient were $14,000. A demand for $50,000 brought a settlement offer of $25,000 for this incident in 1970. At trial, the jury awarded the patient $55,000.

Seattle, January 1976 A patient visited a dentist for an upper molar extraction. A piece of the bone remained attached to the root of the extracted molar, causing a fistula to the sinus area. The patient alleged that the dentist had failed to warn of the risk of the sinus opening, and that he was negligent in the extraction as well as the postoperative care. The dentist contended he had warned of the possible risk to the patient. The patient had medical expenses of $600 and had demanded $5,000; the dentist had offered to settle for $1,500. The jury verdict was rendered in favor of the dentist.

Los Angeles, September 1975 A 48-year-old patient was treated with penicillin injections for a painful lesion on the right lower jaw. After a period of time, the physician told the patient he was concerned about the malignancy. The patient entered the hospital for a biopsy, and the physician removed the crown of a third molar. After surgery, the lesion did not heal. The patient claimed that roots of the third molar had been left in the jaw. Five months later, a dentist removed these roots. The patient sought damages for loss of the tooth, for anxiety and distress over fear of possible cancer, for medical costs of $200, and for loss of earnings of $500. The patient offered to settle the case for $1,500, but the defendant-physician and hospital refused to submit an offer. During the trial, the hospital settled its claim for $2,500. The patient's jury verdict of $62,500 was reduced to $61,250 under a comparative negligence law requiring that the value of any of the plaintiff's contributory negligence be deducted from the full value of the defendant's negligence.

Yreka, Calif, April 1975 A 21-year-old woman visited her dentist to have an impacted third molar removed. The lingual nerve was severed during the extraction. The patient, claiming permanent numbness of the tongue and cheek on the right side of her face, contended that no informed consent was given and that the surgery was performed negligently. The dentist replied in defense that no such consent was required for this procedure, and that no negligence of permanent injury existed. Plaintiff's medical expenses were less than $200. A jury returned a verdict for the dentist.

San Jose, Calif, July 1974 A family of four contended that the dentist had treated the family for many years without full mouth radiographs; without administering local anesthetics to remove deep tooth decay, so that restorations were placed over the remaining decay; and that root canal therapy and substantial restorations were needed as a result of these omissions. Prophylaxis was allegedly below the proper standard, and oral hygiene instruction was also omitted. The father claimed failure to diagnose his periodontitis. The dentist responded that the family was apprehensive about local anesthetics and x-ray over-exposure, and that the father refused treatment for periodontitis. Dental costs of $5,000 arose from these acts of omission and commission. A settlement of $20,000 resulted.

Fort Lauderdale, Fla, June 1975 A 23-year-old mother died from cardiac arrest while in the dentist's office for extensive oral surgery. Allegations against the dentist included improper pretreatment pre-paration, negligent administration of sedatives and anesthetics, abandonment of the patient after sedatives and anesthetics were administered, and inadequate observation and monitoring of the patient, causing delay in recognition of the patient's cardiac arrest. A settlement of $250,000 was negotiated.

Redwood City, Calif, July 1971 A 35-year-old woman who had been treated by her dentist for 10 years claimed that poor dentistry caused her periodontitis, which the dentist never diagnosed or treated. Periodontal surgery was required, and one tooth was lost. Hypersen-sitivity to hot or cold food resulted. Medical expenses amounted to $3,951. The patient demanded $8,387, and the dentist offered $5,000. The award adjudicated was $20,000.

Los Angeles, April 1977 Employees of the defendant-dentist administered to a 33-year-old patient two applications of RC2B root canal filling manufactured by the defendant drug company and unapproved by the US Food and Drug Administration. The filling extended past the root canal into the underlying mandibular nerve canal. The plaintiff-patient contended that the dentist negligently used the drug and that the drug company negligently marketed the drug, failing to warn of its risk, causing paresthesia of lip and chin with pain behind ear. Loss of patient's earnings was $3,500; medical expenses were $100. In the $80,000 settlement, the dentist contributed $67,500.

Rockville, Md, October 1977 A 22-year-old patient consulted an oral surgeon for removal of her third molars. During anesthesia, signs of oxygen deficiency appeared. The dentist administered what he thought was oxygen. Actually, it was nitrous oxide. The patient lapsed into coma, dying several days later. The oxygen and nitrous oxide lines had been crossed in their pathways from tanks to outlets. The surviving husband sued the dentist, the dental equipment supply company, and the plumbing contractors for negligent acts causing the patient's death. A settlement of $750,000 was negotiated.

Denver, November 1977 A 36-year-old patient sought treatment from a dentist for two infected teeth. The dentist extracted one tooth. The patient was referred to a physician when his condition worsened.

The infection was then treated as a medical problem. The second tooth was finally extracted when medical treatment failed. The patient claimed that negligent delay in the dentist's treatment caused toxicity and alleged medical expenses of $4,400 and loss of earnings of $1,200. A settlement of $4,000 was negotiated.

Mississippi, 1984 Following the extraction of two third molars, the patient suffered numbness and loss of sensation of the lips and face. The dentist had left a packet of gauze in the socket. An infection of the area followed. The patient subsequently died of an unrelated cause; however, the suit was continued by heirs in behalf of the patient. The jury awarded $20,000. It was affirmed on appeal.

Massachusetts, 1984 The patient suffered a permanent lingual nerve injury following the removal of impacted third molars. Immediately following surgery, the patient experienced loss of sensation. On exploratory surgery, it was discovered that the lingual nerve had been severed. The patient sued the two dentists who performed the surgery. Their defense was that damage to the lingual nerve is a known risk of the surgery. A structured settlement was reached with a total payment of $360,000.

Dade County, Fla, 1985 During the extraction of a maxillary right premolar, the root fractured and had to be removed in fragments. After the surgery, the patient experienced numbness of the right side of the face and alleged damage to the right infraorbital nerve during the surgery. The case was settled before trial for $75,000.

New York, 1984 Following three injections of local anesthetics to the lower right jaw, the patient experienced a tingling sensation of the jaw. A tic later developed on the right side of the face. Plaintiff sued, alleging that three injections constituted negligence and increased the risk of striking a nerve. The lack of informed consent was also alleged by the plaintiff. The dentist admitted he had not discussed the risks to the patient. The jury found for the defendant.

Houston, 1983 The patient had 17 teeth extracted over a period of 2 days and claimed the dentist did not prescribe antibiotics as part of follow-up care. The result was massive infection and some loss of tissue. Verdict was for the plaintiff in the amount of $5,000.

Tampa, Fla, 1983 A 12-year-old girl was referred to an oral surgeon by her orthodontist for the extraction of four deciduous teeth. The surgeon inadvertently extracted the permanent molar, which he immediately reimplanted. He allegedly told the mother he had "loosened" the tooth. Endodontics was required and was successful. Settlement was made in the amount of $4,900.

Minnesota, 1982 A 24-year-old woman had a lower right incisor erupt and occupy the same space as a deciduous tooth that had not exfoliated. Her dentist referred her to an oral surgeon for the extraction of the deciduous tooth and four third molars. The surgeon extracted the permanent tooth instead of the deciduous tooth. Settlement was made in the amount of $6,000.

San Diego, 1983 A 21-year-old patient suffered from diabetes since the age of 3. A lower molar was extracted by an oral surgeon. Three days later, the surgeon performed an incision and drainage due to a spreading infection. Seven months later, the patient suffered renal failure. Award was made in the amount of $800,000.

Los Angeles, 1982 The patient suffered a fractured jaw during the extraction of a third molar. The dentist admitted that the consent was signed after surgery and that the patient was still under the influence of the general anesthetic. Award was made in the amount of $75,000.

SOURCES OF FUTURE LITIGATION

Transmission of communicable diseases, such as hepatitis, herpes, and possibly acquired immunodeficiency syndrome (AIDS), in the dentist's office may represent a potential source of malpractice litigation against dentists. In addition, with the expansion of services rendered by the dental profession has come an increase in the risk of allegations of malpractice. Oral surgeons are now oral *and maxillofacial* surgeons, extending their scope of practice to facial cosmetic reconstruction (orthognathic surgery — repositioning of the bones of the face). More dentists are holding themselves out as specialists in the treatment of temporomandibular and nutritional disorders. The use of blade implants has increased vulnerability to allegations of malpractice. The practicing dentist should keep in mind that as the scope of practice increases, the risk of allegations of malpractice also increases. New and experimental techniques should be avoided until sufficient data are available to support their use in everyday practice. Some state laws have been changed to include permitting the dentist to complete physical evaluations of patients.[109] The change in law that extends the scope of practice brings with it increased opportunities for dentists to commit acts of negligence and, thus, increased sources of possible litigation.

REFERENCES

1. *Shoumatoff v. Wiltbank*, 226 N.Y.S.2d 208 (1962).
2. *Watkins v. Parpala*, 2 Wash. App. 484, 469 P 2d 974 (1970), discussed infra.
3. *Simonds v. Henry*, 39 Me. 155, 63 Am. Dec. 611 (1855)
4. See reference 1, supra.
5. *Brock v. Gunter*, (La, App. 1974) 292 So.2d 328.
6. *Pederson v. Doumoushel*, 72 Wash.2d 73, 431 P.2d 973 (1967).
7. *Sanderson v. Moline*, 7 Wash. App. 439, 499 P.2d 1281 (1972).

8. *Robins v. Nathan*, 179 N.Y.S. 2d 281 (1919).
9. *Phelps v. Donaldson*, 243 La. 1118, 150 So.2d 35 (1963).
10. *Viland v. Winslow*, 34 Mich. App. 486, 191 N.W.2d 735 (1971).
11. W. Morris, "Dental Litigation," 76 *W. Va. Law Rev.* 153, 157 (1973), citing *Keily v. Colton* (N.Y. Marine ct. 1882) 1 City Ct. Rep. 439.
12. In recent cases, courts have applied a presumption of negligence to jaw fractures relating to extractions in *Eugene v. Douglas*, (La. App. 1972) 260 So. 2d 69, Writ refused, 261 La. 1044, 262 So. 2d 35 (1972); and *Raza v. Sullivan*, (D.C. App. 1970) 432 F. 2d 617, cert. denied, 400 U.S. 992,27 L. Ed. 2d 440, 91 S. Ct. 458 (1971). Courts have held such presumption inapplicable to jaw fractures in *Brown v. Keaveny*, 117 App. D.C. 117, 326 F. 2d 660 (1963); *Hayes v. Hulswit*, 73 Wash. 2d 796, 440 P. 2d 849 (1968); *Negaard v. Estate of Feda*, 152 Mont. 47, 446 P. 2d 436 (1968); and *Trotter v. Hewett*, (Fla. App. 1964) 163 So. 2d 510.
13. *Merold v. Stang*, (Fla. 1961), 130 So. 2d 119, discussed infra.
14. *Neal v. Wilmotg*, (Ky. 11961), 342 SW 2d 701, discussed infra
15. *Myers v. Ross*, 216 Cal. App. 2d 645, 31 Cal. Rptr. 110 (1963), discussed infra.
16. *Cassano v. Hagstrom*, 5 N.Y.2d 643, 159 N.E. 2d 348, 187 N.Y.S.2d 1 (1959), discussed infra.
17. *Lambert v. Soltis*, 422 Pa. 304, 221 A. 2d 173 (1966), and *Surabian v. Lorenz*, 229n Cal. App. 2d 462, 40 Cal. Rptr. 410 (1964), both discussed infra.
18. *Smith v. Reitman*, 128 App. D.C. 352, 389 F. 2d 303 (1967), discussed infra.
19. *Pederson v. Dumouchel*, 72 Wash.2d 73, 431 P.2d 973 (1967)
20. *Sanzari v. Rosenfeld*, 34 N.J. 128, 167 A. 2d 625 (1961), discussed infra.
21. *Germann v. Matriss*, 55 N.J. 1193, 260 A. 2d 825 (1970), and *Pfeifer v. Konat*, 181 Neb. 30, 146 N.W. 2d 743 (1966), both discussed infra. *Russo v. Rifkin*, New York Supreme Court, Appellate Division, Second Department, *New York Law Journal*, p.1, January 13, 1986.
22. *Morse v. Rapkin*, 24 App. Div. 2d 24, 263 N.Y.S. 2d 428 (1965), *Zito v. Friedman*, 430 N.Y.S.2d 78 (1980).
23. E.g., *Petterson v. Lynch*, 59 Misc. 2d 469, 299, N.Y.S. 2d 244 (1969).
24. *Watkins v. Parpala*, 2 Wash. App. 484, 469 P 2d 974 (1970).
25. *Ober v. Hollinger* (Oh. Apps. 1933) 14 Oh. L. As. 514, wherein the court held that, in the absence of a situation endangering the life of the patient or an agreement by the patient to the contrary, the oral surgeon was not authorized to extract additional teeth found to be infected.
26. *Day v. Bernard*, No. 317081 (Portland, Ore., Nov., 1966).
27. *Magrine v. Spector*, 100 N.J. Super. 223, 241 A. 2d 637 (1968).
28. *Rosenblum v. Cherner*, (D.C. App. 1966) 219 A. 2d 491.
29. *Stokes v. Hurdle*, (D. Md. 1975) 393 F. Supp. 757, and *Isenberg v. Prasse*, (3d. Cir. 1970) 433 F. 2d 449.
30. *Dean v. Coughlin*, U.S.S.D., *New York Law Journal*, P.2, February 5, 1986.
31. *Webster v. Lane*, 125 Misc. 868, 212 N.Y.S. 298 (1925).
32. Liability of employers for the acts of their employees has also been justified on the grounds that they can insure against the harm caused by such acts and spread the cost of indemnifying injured parties by increasing fees or prices charged to all consumers of their products or services.
33. *Blair v. N.Y. Univ. College of Dentistry*, 15 A.D. 2d 211, 222 N.Y.S.2d 1 (1961), discussed infra.

34. *Richardson v. Parker*, 38 Misc. 2d 36, 237 N.Y.S. 2d 495 (1963).
35. *Cohen v. Weber*, 36 App. Div. 2d 921, 320 N.Y.S. 2d 759 (1971).
36. *Barnes v. Tenin*, (2d Cir. 1970) 429 F. 2d 117.
37. *Germann v. Matriss*, 55 N.J. 1193, 260 A. 2d 825 (1970), and *Pfeifer v. Konat*, 181 Neb. 30, 146 N.W. 2d 743 (1966).
38. *Rosso v. Rifkin*, Supreme Court, Appellate Division, New York, *New York Law Journal*, P.1, January 13, 1986.
39. *O'Brien v. Stover*, (8the Cir. 1971) 443 F. 2d 1013.
40. *Engstrand v. Friedman*, 488 N.Y.S.2d 202 (1985).
41. *Engstrand v. Friedman*, 488 N.Y.S.2d 202 (1985). 41. *Hawthorne v. Campbell*, No. 592355, (San Francisco, Cal. March, 1973).
42. *Soulin v. Manchester*, No. 363–66 (Washington, D.C. April, 1968).
43. *Waters v. Dana*, 348 Mass. 800, 206 N.E. 2d 87 (1965).
44. *Brock v. Gunter*, (La. App. 1974) 292 So. 2d 328.
45. *Graham v. Roberts*, (D.C. App. 1970) 441 F 2d. 995.
46. *Higgins v. Pease*, No. 63–3618. (New York, N.Y., June, 1969).
47. *Barnes v. Tenin*, (2d Cir. 1970) 429 F. 2d. 117.
48. See reference 6, supra.
49. *Forman v. Spiro*, No. 63–C–3618. (New York, N.Y., June, 1969).
50. See reference 33, supra.
51. See reference 1, supra.
52. See reference 27, supra.
53. *Lambert v. Soltis*, 422 Pa. 304, 221 A. 2d 173 (1966), and *Surabian v. Lorenz*, 229n Cal. App. 2d 462, 40 Cal. Rptr. 410 (1964).
54. Ibid.
55. *LaRocque v. LaMarche*, 130 Vt. 311, 292 A. 2d 259 (1972).
56. See reference 12, supra.
57. Ibid.
58. Ibid.
59. *Weeks v. Heinrich*, (Tex. Civ. App. 1969) 477 S.W. 2d 688.
60. *Gorsalitz v. Harris*, (Tex. Civ. App. 1966) 410 S.W. 2d 956.
61. *Furnari v. Lurie*, (Fla. App. 1971) 242 So. 2d 742.
62. *Brown v. Swindal*, (Fla. App. 1960) 121 So. 2d 38.
63. *Brown v. Swindal*, (Fla. App. 1960) 121 So. 2d 38.63. *Germann v. Matriss*, 55 N.J. 1193, 260 A. 2d 825 (1970), and *Konat*, 181 Neb. 30, 146 N.W. 2d 743 (1966).
64. *Wilson v. Kornegay*, 108 Gas. App. 318, 132 S.E. 2d 791 (1963).
65. *Day v. Bernard*, No. 317081 (Portland, Ore., Nov., 1966).
66. *Zettler v. Reich*, 11 N.Y.S.2d 85 85, aff'd 281 N.Y. 729 (1939), and *Lawrence v. Bluestone*, *New York Law Journal*, p.13, col.2, February, 15, 1978.
67. *Wilson v. Kornegay*, 108 Gas. App. 318, 132 S.E. 2d 791 (1963).
68. *Cassano v. Hagstrom*, 5 N.Y.2d 643, 159 N.E. 2d 348, 187 N.Y.S.2d 1 (1959).
69. See references 13 and 64, supra.
70. *Smith v. Reitman*, 128 App. D.C. 352, 389 F. 2d 303 (1967).
71. *Garban v. Weiss*, No. 130784 (Redwood City, Calif., March, 1969).
72. E.g., *Cohen v. Weber*, op. cit., and *Dufrene v. Faget*, (La. App. 1972) 260 So. 2d 76, writ denied, 261 La. 1043, 262 So. 2d 35 (1972).
73. See references 13 and 64, supra.
74. *Thomas v. Schonfeld*, No. 636563 (Boston, Mass., March 1971).
75. See reference 14, supra.
76. Ibid.

77. *Newport v. Hyde*, 2454 Miss. 870, 147 So. 2d 113 (1962).
78. *Richardson v. Parker*, 38 Misc. 2d 36, 237 N.Y.S. 2d 495 (1963).
79. *Martell v. Meyer*, No. 8186 (Flint, Mich., March 1968).
80. *Martell v. Meyer*, No. 8186 (Flint, Mich., March 1968). 80. *Mehall v. Sherman*, (Los Angeles, Calif., August 1968).
81. E.g., *Coover v. Painless Parker, Dentist*, 105 Cal. App. 110, 268 p. 1048 (1930).
82. E.g., *Curley v. McDonald*, 263 Mass. 285, 160 N.E. 796 (1928).
83. *Germann v. Matriss*, 55 N.J. 1193, 260 A. 2d 825 (1970), and *Konat*, 181 Neb. 30, 146 N.W. 2d 743 (1966).
84. *Buffo v. Page*, No. 95498 (Martinez, Calif., May 1968).
85. See reference 1, supra.
86. *Howard v. Bekier*, No 63S–39590 (Chicago, IL, December, 1968).
87. *Aden v. Pickett*, No. 47423 (Fairfield, Calif. Super. Ct., June 1970).
88. *Cooper v. Thompson*, No. 115359 (Martinez, Calif., February 1971).
89. *Pyatt v. Ruff*, (Perth Amboy, N.J., November, 1966).
90. Jury Verdict Research, Inc., III-A *Personal Injury Evaluation Handbooks* 698, Special Research Report No. 130 (1971).
91. Ibid.
92. Ibid. Vol. II at 1108, Injury Valuation Report No. 181 (1975).
93. Ibid.
94. *Personal Injury Verdict Reviews*, Issue 1, October 17, 1983, Jury Verdict Research, Solon, Ohio.
95. *Hawthorne v. Campbell*, No. 592355, (San Francisco, Cal. March, 1973).
96. *Soulin v. Manchester*, No. 363–66 (Washington, D.C. April, 1968).
97. *Higgins v. Pease*, No. 63–3618. (New York, N.Y., June, 1969).
98. *Forman v. Spiro*, No. 63–C–3618. (New York, N.Y., June, 1969)
99. *Blunt v. Stewart*, No. 62C–9025 (Chicago, I11., September 1967).
100. *Day v. Bernard*, No. 317081 (Portland, Ore., Nov., 1966).
101. *Howard v. Bekier*, No. 63S–39590 (Chicago, I11., December 1968).
102. *Aden v. Pickett*, No. 47423 (Fairfield, Calif. Super. Ct., June 1970).
103. See reference 89, supra.
104. *Garban v. Weiss*, No. 130784 (Redwood City, Calif., March, 1969).
105. *Thomas v. Schonfeld*, No. 636563 (Boston, Mass., March 1971). *Thomas v. Schonfeld*, No. 636563 (Boston, Mass., March 1971).
106. *Martell v. Meyer*, No. 8186 (Flint, Mich., March 1968).
107. *Cooper v. Thompson*, No. 115359 (Martinez, Calif., February 1971).
108. *Mehall v. Sherman*, (Los Angeles, Calif., August 1968).
109. New York State Education Law, Article 133, Section 6601.

8 Evidence in Law: Legal Protection for Malpractice Lawsuits

Bernard D. Katz
Burton R. Pollack

In deciding a case, the first step is to determine the facts. The next is to apply legal precedent or the appropriate law to the facts. Legal precedent is established when a decision is reached by a court. Once established, it gives the court guidance when other cases with the same or similar facts come before the court. By this process, legal precedent is established and is then used by an attorney to predict the outcome of a particular case.

It is essential, in the conduct of a case, that all facts relating to the situation are presented. However, not all the facts may be admitted into evidence, and those that are admitted may be given different weights. For instance, hearsay evidence (evidence of conversations overheard, when the party that was overheard is available) is generally inadmissible. Statements made in books and in guidelines of professional organizations are often considered as hearsay, and therefore are inadmissible. A textbook cannot be cross-examined.

The weight given to evidence generally applies to facts that are disputed. Facts submitted by the employee of the dentist may be given

94

little weight because the court recognizes that the employee is likely to support the employer. The court must also weigh the opinions of experts. The professional opinion of an expert who has little experience would be given less weight than one with impressive credentials.

In addition to the process of admission of evidence and weighing facts, the courts apply legal principles to the facts. These rules have developed over a long period of time. They decree that in our system of justice the facts of the individual case must be applied to the relevant rules of law. This occurs in a procedure described as the adversary process. To prevail in a civil suit, the plaintiff must produce evidence in excess of 50% (by a preponderance of the evidence) supporting the claim. In criminal matters, the prosecution (government) must provide evidence that proves beyond a reasonable doubt the guilt of the accused. It is a significantly more difficult burden of proof to sustain. In administrative law, the administrative agency has the least burden to hold a defendant in violation of its rules or regulations. Thus a state board of dentistry need only show by substantial evidence (may be less than 50%) that the dentist violated its rules or regulations.

In civil malpractice cases, the dentist must seek facts to provide a preponderance of the evidence and credible witnesses to support his or her position or to undermine the position of the plaintiff-patient. Therefore, the dentist must conduct his or her practice so as to assure the best defense against malpractice claims.

There are legitimate malpractice cases. Dentists are not free of fault. However, the chief concern here is with frivolous lawsuits. These cases are burdensome and troubling to conscientious practitioners. The problem is compounded by the fact that, although many situations arise leading to a suit having no basis in law, the suit may be lost or settled because the defendant-dentist was unable to support his or her position because of negligent office practice rather than negligent care.

LEGAL AND PROFESSIONAL RESPONSIBILITY

A dentist must understand the concepts that are involved in legal matters, principally, how the law looks at one person's civil duties in relation to another's. Our system attempts to resolve disputes among people, after the machinery of compromise and negotiation has broken down, by using well-developed legal principles and processes. The acts that one may perform, or their omissions, involve duties to another person imposed by law. If you performed a service that did not meet the standard established by the community, you are liable for the injury caused by the departure. Civil law is comprised of duties imposed (by the doctor-patient relationship), duties breached (departure from the standard), and remedies for the person injured by the breach.

Once dental care has begun, the dentist has a legal and professional duty to provide the patient with that standard of dental care which a reasonably prudent dentist would give to that patient. Deviation from that standard of care, by either act or omission, may result in a claim of malpractice. Perfect dental treatment is not required. Dental practice can go wrong. However, legal problems occur only when you practice what you know, or should know, by education, training, and experience, to be substandard dentistry.

What can you do to prevent malpractice pitfalls? First, when you assume a duty to a patient, be sure it is carried to completion. Completion does not necessarily include achieving a satisfactory result. It is a reasonable result that is expected from the practice of dentistry in the community, or a similar community, in which the dentist practices. Second, when you treat a patient, an important protection is honesty. If something goes wrong, you must inform the patient. If something is beyond your competency, if an accident occurs, or if the patient's health has been placed in jeopardy, either directly by your treatment or by some omission, you must inform the patient. You should do everything within reason to inform your patient what has happened. A third level of protection concerns your records. Telling the patient of an accident in treatment is not enough. More weight will be given by the court to an entry made on the patient's record in the usual course of practice than to evidence presented of conversations held with the patient. Courts hold to the theory that the shortest written word lasts longer than the longest memory. Remember that no amount of documentation is too much, and no detail is too small to be recorded. The outcome of a malpractice suit may depend on the records of the practitioner. More on records below.

MALPRACTICE CHARGES

Let us examine the legal elements involved in a claim of malpractice. It will lead to an understanding of the process followed by plaintiffs' lawyers.

Proximate Cause

First, it is important to define the word "proximate." It describes the legal boundaries within which one is responsible for his or her acts or omissions. Suppose you cause an automobile accident. The injured person is taken to a hospital. On the way, another accident occurs as the result of another person's act. Who is responsible for the injury to the patient? Your negligent act set up the opportunity for the second act to occur. If you had not been negligent, the second act would not have occurred. To cause an injury proximately means to cause that injury legally. Therefore, your act was the proximate cause of injury to the patient. The second event was foreseeable in that it could not have occurred if the first act had not occurred.

Cause In Fact

Second, you should understand the meaning of "cause in fact." When a lawyer puts together a case, he or she must include all the elements required to prove the case. If you are charged proximately for an injury, then you are charged legally for what has occurred. Unforeseeable events are not within the proximate cause required by law. You cannot be charged for an "act of God," or something that happened beyond your control as a reasonably prudent dentist. Such acts are unforeseeable. The following case is directed solely toward this aspect of law.

A Cook County, Illinois dentist was served with the following charges:

> . . .Carelessly and negligently failing to review the previous medical history of the patient prior to performing dental procedures; carelessly and negligently failing to diagnose the prior medical history of the patient prior to an extraction of a tooth; carelessly and negligently failing to take the necessary precautions for the health and well-being of the patient; carelessly and negligently making an injection into an area that was infected; and as a direct or proximate result of one or more of the foregoing wrongful acts or omissions, the patient has been severely injured both internally and externally, suffering severe shock to her nervous system, swelling and lacerations to her body and more particularly to her neck, becoming sick, and disabled, and suffering since the injury and will suffer in the future, preventing her from attending to her normal duties.

For these injuries, directly caused by the dentist's acts or omissions, the plaintiff demanded $75,000 in damages. An additional claim in this case stated:

> . . .direct and proximate result of her dental injuries an aggravation of her pre-existing diverticulosis was caused which made her sick, sore, lame and disordered, and unable to tend to her ordinary duties.

The plaintiff has the burden to prove, by a preponderance of the evidence presented to the court, that these alleged facts are true.

Contributory Fault

Illinois and some other states are known as contributory fault states. If the plaintiff negligently performs any act or omission that causes, or contributes to, the injuries, the defendant is not legally liable. Therefore, if the plaintiff contributed 1% to the injury by his or her own acts, the defendant is relieved of liability. For example, in postoperative treatment, if the patient sticks a finger into the wound or does something that was not within reason, then the patient's negligent act contributed to the injury and the defendant is absolved of legal liability. In some states, the patient must be entirely free of contributory negligence to prevail in an action based on the negligence of the health provider.

In other states the rule of comparative negligence applies. In those states, when the patient negligently contributes 1% to the cause of the injury and the defendant is 99% responsible, legal decision-makers, jury or judge, can reduce the award to the patient by 1%.

Contributory negligence states are more helpful to defendants. Only a few facts may be needed to prove contributory negligence on the part of the plaintiff, thereby totally absolving the defendant from liability. However, the trend in most states is to apply comparative negligence in malpractice cases. Until recently, New York was a contributory negligence state. By a change in the civil court practice rules, it is now a comparative negligence state.

DEFENSIVE MEASURES (RISK MANAGEMENT)

How can we protect ourselves against cases such as the one described above? In every lawsuit, there is real evidence: written records, radiographs, and similar items that speak for themselves. Real evidence is mostly demonstrative evidence. The jury can examine such evidence and see the facts. The other type of evidence is testimonial evidence: things people know about and tell to the jury.

What does a jury do when the testimonies of the practitioner and the patient are in conflict? How can the jury decide who is telling the truth? What lawyers try to do is to build up a truth image. An adroit lawyer can draw out the discrepancies in what has been said by the use of cross-examination, a most powerful legal weapon. The lawyer attempts, in the courtroom setting, to impeach a witness; to prove the doubtfulness of what the witness is saying; or to attack the credibility of the witness.

Records

How can you prove that what you say, or what the patient told you, is true? Your records, radiographs, and documents are sources of facts for your defense. Proper office procedure requires that you write down, as legibly as you can, everything that occurs in the treatment of your patients. Longhand entries, rather than symbols or something only another dentist could understand, are much more valuable legally for your defense. Professional jargon helps defeat a cause. Abbreviations are not understood by laymen. However, the jury can read a well-constructed sentence with ease.

If some untoward event does occur, you must never erase, completely block out, or omit the entry on the record, no matter how damaging you think it might be. To do so may serve as an admission. When you perform a service, you do not have to admit that it is right or wrong; just indicate what had occurred. If, however, a reasonable person under the same circumstances would make a statement, then you are held to that standard and should speak, either orally or in writing.

Patient records, made in the usual course of business, are admitted into evidence as an exception to the hearsay evidence rule. Oral statements, made against self-interest and at the time of the occurrence of the incident (*res gestae*) may also be admitted into evidence by another party as an exception to the hearsay evidence rule. Therefore, if you should say, "Oops, I slipped and cut your tongue; I'm sorry for the injury I caused," the statement may be admitted into evidence by the patient over your objection.

Auxiliaries

Another defensive point relates to assistants in the dental practice. The actions of auxiliary help are included under the doctrine of *respondeat superior*. The dentist is liable for negligent acts performed by employees within the course of their duties. Careful employment procedures that assure reasonably prudent dental assistants are a major means of avoiding legal litigation. In addition, auxiliaries may testify directly about controversial matters to support the dentist's versions of the incidents.

Dentist-Patient Privilege

Another area requiring careful attention is the dentist-patient privilege. The dentist is not allowed to repeat information obtained as a result of the dentist-patient relationship. In many jurisdictions, this requirement to remain silent extends to judicial proceedings. On the other hand, persons who work in offices tend to talk about patients and their problems to others, in and out of the office. They may be overheard. Auxiliaries must be reminded not to repeat what they have heard or learned in the office. Inform auxiliaries that they must tell you whatever they do, whatever occurs, and whatever a patient says. Reinforcement by constantly admonishing auxiliaries to keep silent about patient matters and constantly reminding them to report their acts to you is an important aspect in the supervision of employees.

Treatment Provided by Other Dentists

A final preventive measure centers on remarks to patients about treatment provided by other dentists. This is a very delicate matter. You are often called upon to make a judgment. If something you see needs care, you should correct the problem, but do not make gratuitous statements. It is not likely that you know all the circumstances that surrounded the provision of the prior care. You may explain what the current condition is and what you think should be done to correct it. If the patient wants to follow that new course of treatment, or corrective measures recommended by you, it is the patient's decision. But do not ever, from both a legal and a professional standpoint, make statements that tend to incriminate other dentists unless you are certain about all the facts related to the care. Not only do you risk being wrong, but you may be the subject of a suit in defamation brought by the dentist you criticized.

THE DEEP POCKET DOCTRINE

A full appreciation of the need to reduce legal risks in the practice of dentistry may be realized when the deep pocket doctrine is understood. Courts look to the one with the deepest pockets to pay for the injury to an innocent party. Deep pocket means that the one who can afford to pay should pay. The average patient knows that a health practitioner has malpractice insurance and that the insurance company can pay for any injury, no matter how large the amount. Because the dentist has the deepest pockets in the dental office, in the assessment of liability the dentist becomes the one must vulnerable.

CONCLUSION

Defensive treatment practice results in overtreatment — a waste of office resources, time, and the patient's financial resources. It should be avoided because defensive treatment or diagnostic practices may be considered malpractice. However, defensive practice management (risk management) is essential in today's litigious environment. Because of the rules of evidence, much of what goes on the dentist's office — much of what is said, overheard, and written in the patient's record — may be introduced into evidence during the trial of a malpractice suit. Some of the information may be damaging to the defendant-dentist, while some may be helpful. These facts should be kept in mind by the practitioner during the course of the patient's treatment.

9 Legal Hygiene for Dental Practice

Thomas H. Lawrence

The onrush of consumerism during the 1970s has for many reasons, some sound and some unsound, spilled into the field of professional services. The liability of the practitioner has somehow become separated from the dedication to ethical and professional relationships.

PROBLEM OF MALPRACTICE

Malpractice has long been a part of the physician-patient relationship. The question today is why this concept of malpractice has snowballed to the point that insurance protection, staff functions, and patient services themselves have been deeply affected. Many assert that the legal profession is responsible; that the impact of law on clinical dentistry has taken on new meanings. At any rate, the whole field of dental jurisprudence is expanding, leading to apprehension on the part of the practitioner and uncertainty concerning relationships with the patient.

Studies of doctor-patient relationships have established that most legal actions have developed from emotional breakdowns between the dentist and the patient. These generally have evolved because the dependency relationship normally established between the dentist and the patient creates certain expectancies on the part of the patient. Dependency leads to conflict — between the parent and the child, the boss and the subordinate, and the dentist and the patient. Often this feeling of dependency on the part of the patient takes on strong emotional tones: authority figure, love, reliance, and even the dependency of despair. The critical problem appears to be that the dentist, because of the pressures of time and circumstances, can give the patient the impression that the original individual care, attention, and concern have somehow lapsed, that the dentist has become gradually unconcerned, has let down the very strong emotional figure on which the patient has become dependent. When such a lapse in patient communications and interpersonal concern occurs, there is clear evidence from many studies of legal action that the patient is asserting emotional needs: the reestablishment of personal importance and status in the eyes of the dentist.

There will always be some basis for asserting malpractice against any practitioner. The extent to which people wish to press suits can be measured, in a high percentage of cases, by the degree to which the people feel they must reestablish the personal attention and importance that they feel, whether rightly or wrongly, has been treated inconsiderately by the practitioner.

LEGAL HYGIENE

Apart from all considerations of insurance, professional liability, and legal trends, the dentist today must concentrate on a fundamental concept: legal hygiene. The term relates to a concept similar to preventive dentistry: it relates to sharing with the patient his or her expectations of dentistry, the relationships and concerns of the dentist, and the inseparable responsibilities of the dentist and the patient.

When a patient is admitted to a practice, it is essential that a positive approach be developed concerning the patient's needs and expectations. Following diagnosis, there should be open and directed discussion concerning what the professional clinical competence of this office can do to fulfill the needs of this particular patient. The case presentation is no longer a sales process in which the dentist attempts to secure the approval of the patient for a particular treatment program. The case presentation is looked upon today as a case conference in which there is an open exchange of information, ideas, and plans that affect both the patient and the dentist.

As a starting point, the dentist must understand that every patient brings four fundamental needs to the practice. These needs are the needs of all human beings under all circumstances. It is the fulfillment of one or more of these needs that causes the patient to seek dentistry; it is the fulfillment of one or more of these needs that the patient expects this dental practice to achieve. Every member of the dental staff should be aware of these four basic needs of the patient and, even more, how every action and activity within the dental office can affect them:

1. *Physical needs:* those needs that have to do with health, well-being, and the preservation of dental hygiene as a key factor in general health and care.
2. *Social needs:* what dentistry can do to improve the patient's acceptability to others; to improve personal relationships, romance, and marital happiness. The cosmetic contribution of dentistry is often directly related to these expectancies.
3. *Ego needs:* those needs that have to do with the contribution of dentistry to job success, to self-image, and to that sense of personal poise and confidence that comes from good dental condition and appearance.
4. *Spiritual needs:* that sense of self-fulfillment that can come from achievement in other areas of need. Dentistry is often greatly underestimated in the fulfillment of patient needs in this area.

Perhaps the most important part of legal hygiene is the ability of the dental practitioner to evaluate these needs properly with the patient, and then to express them during the case consultation in a meaningful and pragmatic manner that will create the proper expectancy in the mind of the patient. Legal hygiene means establishing a mutuality of understanding between the patient and the dentist. It means that a closeness must be developed, that the dentist must express a caring attitude which demonstrates that the real purpose of dentistry is to fulfill the human needs of the individual rather than just the dental needs of the patient.

CONSULTATIVE TREATMENT

Experience has shown that attention to these basic human needs by the truly professional practitioner has elevated the image of dentistry from one of mechanics to one of true health care delivery. The future of private practice will depend a great deal upon the dentist's ability to develop consultative treatment, the kind of communication with the patient that enables the proper expectancies to be identified and all elements of treatment and posttreatment to meet those expectancies.

Consultative treatment means that the dentist and the patient become mutually involved in the case. The clinical needs of the patient should be interpreted in a manner than enables the patient to develop realistic expectancies from the treatment program. The acceptance of the treatment program should be further developed in a consultative manner that involves a sharing of logic and fact, an examination of any prejudicial barriers to dentistry, and a close sensitivity to the feelings and emotions of the patient as they are expressed during this consultation.

It is more important today then ever before that the dentist gain knowledge in the behavioral sciences. In addition to clinical skill, it becomes imperative that the dentist comprehends the total patient and total patient needs. The consultative dentist can detect quite readily whether a patient, during the patient history phase of entering the practice, is expressing certain kinds of needs. Patients who talk continually about their health, digestion, headaches, or other physical ailments, may be saying in loud clear terms, "I hope your dentistry can make me feel better." The relationship between good dental health and good general health then becomes part of the dentist's consultation.

The patient entering the practice who talks of family, friends, club activities, and a broad range of interpersonal contacts, may be saying, "I hope your dentistry can make me to be more acceptable to other people; to improve my appearance and my confidence in relating to others." Another patient may remark, "My husband has been after me for a long time to make this appointment." In such a case, the dentist must be sensitive to the probability that this patient is saying, "I hope dentistry can improve my romance, my domestic situation, and cause me to be more attractive to those I love." Another patient may strongly express the importance of his or her position on the job, and show a strong sense of ego and importance. Often, this patient is expecting dentistry to improve job confidence, result in a greater sense of ego satisfaction, and even bring success.

Consultative treatment is directed toward examining these human needs, along with the clinical needs, of the individual. When the case conference can clearly identify which of the needs is most important to the individual, then proper expectancies can be established. Proper time frames for achieving those expectancies can also be structured. Perhaps most important, a proper posttreatment follow-up will ensure that the individual's expectancies have been reasonably attained.

When clinical care neglects these emotional needs, the patient can become resentful. A patient may feel emotionally abandoned, and the dependency that has been developed between the dentist and the patient becomes an unfulfilled contract. Legal hygiene can prevent this from happening. Once these concepts are properly understood in the dental office, all members of the auxiliary staff can assist in the proper emotional support of the patient. Indeed, it becomes imperative that staff members both understand and fulfill their responsibilities in this area of patient relations.

CONSIDER THE WHOLE PATIENT

The preventive aspects of legal hygiene become increasingly important as pressures in the American society move more strongly toward human rights. The rights of individuals are gaining increasing visibility; whether at the consumer level or at the clinical level, they must be given genuine concern and consideration. Accordingly, the dentist must develop plans for the future needs of practice management, rather than reacting to the conditions and problems that will develop through shifts and changes in social values.

The following concepts will be important in the development of practice management in the 1980s and 1990s:

1. A far greater emphasis on teaching the behavioral sciences in the dental college;
2. continuing postgraduate study by the dentist to update behavioral concepts in practice management;
3. training auxiliary staff in specific areas of contribution to patient attitudes and behavior;
4. research and continuing study of consultative roles *v* authoritative roles by the practitioner;
5. Broader public relations programs designed to improve the image of dentistry as a positive contributor to individual health and social welfare.

CONCLUSION

The profession of dentistry has come far. The practitioner will need to adjust to many elements of change in the period ahead. A positive starting point is the practice of consultative dentistry and the application of legal hygiene. These are not merely defensive tools to fend malpractice lawsuits and claims from dissatisfied patients. They are basically positive concepts that help us to integrate dentistry with all the health sciences and to practice dentistry on the whole person.

10 Consent: The Patient's Right to Self-Determination

Burton R. Pollack

A dentist who treats a patient without the patient's consent may be liable for committing the civil wrong of battery — the unlawful touching of another person without consent. Although the aggrieved individual may have benefited from the encounter, the mere touching in the absence of permission may lead to liability. In some jurisdictions, even though intent to harm is absent, such unauthorized touching of the patient also may be criminal. For consent to be valid, it must be both informed and granted voluntarily. If circumstances permit, the patient must be told in understandable language (1) the nature of the prescribed procedure; (2) the material risks, complications, and benefits involved; (3) the prognosis if the treatment is not carried out; and (4) alternative methods of treatment, if any, and their benefits and risks. The patient also must be given the opportunity to ask questions concerning the treatment and have their questions answered.

As long as the above elements are present, the consent may be oral. In many states, the elements required for a valid consent are established by statute, in others, by case law. In special situations involving research, experimental procedures, or the use of new techniques, some states have required that the consent be in writing and signed by the patient. When federal financial assistance is used for experiments or studies on human subjects, the guidelines for obtaining consent are carefully set out and require a written and signed consent statement. When research is carried out in an institutional setting, such as a hospital, health center, or dental clinic, institutional rules, state laws, or administrative regulations governing consent may have to be followed. Such requirements are designed to protect the institution and the patients, as well as the providers of care. Those who provide care in institutions under these circumstances should become familiar with the rules and follow them carefully.

In true emergencies, when consent is impossible to obtain, it is implied by law. When minors or mentally incompetent patients are to be treated, consent must be obtained from the parent or guardian. Minors 14 years of age or older, as well as their parents, should sign consent forms. Telephone consent is valid when it is properly obtained and appropriate notes are recorded.

The case law in each jurisdiction determines how much information the practitioner is required to disclose to the patient about the risks of treatment. Currently, there are two schools of thought concerning the standard by which to judge the scope of disclosure. One view, the community professional standard, is judged against what the physicians or dentists practicing in the same or a similar community tell their patients under similar circumstances.[1] However, the current trend in the courts is to apply the reasonable person standard. The scope of disclosure is measured by how much a reasonable person must be told to enable him or her to make an intelligent decision about whether to proceed with the treatment, postpone it, or seek other advice.[2] Regardless of which standard is applied by the court, a doctor is usually not required to reveal any information that would jeopardize the mental health or well-being of the patient.[3]

The trend in federal rules and regulations, state statutes, and case law is to limit the latitude of health providers in obtaining consent. Courts are requiring practitioners to provide patients with more detailed information about the risks and benefits involved in a recommended course of treatment and to disclose alternative forms of treatment.

EVALUATION OF THE LAW OF CONSENT

Many recent cases in professional responsibility have focused on the issue of informed consent. Lack of valid consent to care may lead to allegations by the patient of malpractice, battery, breach of contract, or deceit on the part of the practitioner. These cases may involve (1) total lack of consent on the part of the patient; (2) failure to obtain proper consent in the treatment of minors; (3) consent that is too vague; (4) extension of treatment beyond that for which consent was obtained; (5) performance of a service different from that for which consent was obtained; (6) consent that is involuntary; or (7) consent granted, but based upon inadequate information.

Courts have stressed the patient's right of self-determination in making decisions about how his or her body should be treated. Providers of health care may not adopt a paternalistic attitude toward their patients. The idea that the doctor knows best is not the basis of the doctor-patient relationship in this country. Trust alone will not substitute for the patient's intelligent consent to submit to the suggested treatment.

The move away from the paternalism exercised by the medical profession began with the famous case of *Mohr v. Williams*[4] in 1905. In that case, although the medical treatment was necessary, properly performed, and beneficial to the patient, the court found that proper consent for the operation was not obtained. The patient had consented to an operation on the right ear; however, when she was anesthetized, the surgeon found that the condition of the left ear was worse and proceeded to operate on it. The Minnesota Supreme Court, in finding that the physician had committed a battery, stated:

> Under a free government, at least, the free citizen's first and greatest right, which underlies all others — the right to the inviolability of his person; in other words, the right to himself — is the subject of universal acquiescence, and this right necessarily forbids a physician and surgeon, however skillful or eminent ...to violate, without permission, the bodily integrity of his patient...[5]

The court further stated:

> The patient must be the final arbiter as to whether he will take his chance with the operation, or take his chances of living without it. Such is the natural right of the individual, which the law recognizes as a legal right.[6]
>
> If [the act] was unauthorized, then it was within what we have said, unlawful. It was a violent assault, not a mere pleasantry; and even though no negligence is shown, it was wrongful and unlawful. The case is unlike a criminal prosecution for assault and battery, for there an unlawful intent must be shown. But that rule does not apply to a civil action, to maintain which it is sufficient to show that the assault complained of was wrongful and unlawful or the result of negligence.[7]

In awarding damages, however, the court considered the benefit to the patient and the good faith of the surgeon.

Some important and far-reaching principles were established in this early case. Basic to the decision is the precept that patients have an unchallenged right to decide the nature and extent of the care they receive. A physician, even with the most benevolent intentions, cannot substitute his or her judgment for that of the patient. Neither negligence on the part of the physician nor a bad result need to be shown to hold the physician responsible for battery.

Another important case in the development of informed consent is *Schloendorff v. Society of New York Hospital*, in which Justice Cardozo established the basis of the modern theory of consent:

> Every human being of adult years and sound mind has a right to determine what shall be done with his own body; and a surgeon who performs an operation without his patient's consent, commits an assault, for which he is liable in damages. This is true except in cases of emergency where the patient is unconscious and where it is necessary to operate before consent can be obtained.[8]

The Schloendorff case established additional elements to be considered in evaluating the validity of consent: the consenting party must be of adult years and of sound mind. Minors and mentally incompetent patients could not give a valid consent to treatment.

Thus, the laws of the United States are based on the assumption that a legal right of individuals is the right of self-determination: individuals of adult years and sound mind will determine what is best for themselves. This basic concept, initially stated in the Mohr case in 1905, has been consistently reinforced in cases, statutes, and regulations. *Natanson v. Kline*, decided in 1960, echoes the law established in Mohr:

> Each man is considered to be the master of his own body, and he may, if he be of sound mind, expressly prohibit the performance of life-saving surgery, or other medical treatment. A doctor might well believe that an operation or form of treatment is desirable or necessary but the law does not permit him to substitute his own judgment for that of the patient by any form or artifice or deception.[9]

Therefore, before a dentist or other treating health professional initiates treatment of any kind, consent of the patient is essential. A provider of care who ignores this admonition places himself at considerable legal risk.

Since the Nathanson case, case after case, statute after statute, and regulation after regulation have reinforced the right of self-determination and, in most cases, extended it.

NATURE OF CONSENT

A patient may indicate consent in several ways. A written and signed consent that sets out all the details of the agreement is the most reliable way, and it facilitates proof, if proof becomes an issue. However, in the absence of special circumstances, as may be required by statute or regulation, oral consent is valid. Both written and oral consent are termed actual or express consents.

Consent may also be apparent or implied from the behavior of the patient, as illustrated in the celebrated case of *O'Brien v. Cunard*[10] in 1891. In that case, the plaintiff stood in a line of people waiting to be vaccinated. She observed the vaccination of others standing in front of her and even received a vaccination. No questions were asked, and no statements were made as to the matter of consent. The court ruled that the conduct of the plaintiff implied consent to the vaccination. Thus, by entering a dentist's office, completing pretreatment office procedures, and sitting in the dental chair, a patient is implying consent to some form of examination and/or treatment. Courts take the position that if patients are aware of the need for treatment and the general nature of the treatment, and if they permit the treatment to begin without objection, they have granted consent implied by their actions.

Another form of consent is one implied by law. This is applicable to emergency situations when treatment cannot be postponed without jeopardizing the life or well-being of the patient, and the patient is unable to grant consent because of physical impairment. Consent may also be implied as a matter of law in situations in which a patient is under a general anesthetic and there is an unanticipated need for more extensive surgery. In the case of *Kennedy v. Parrott*[11] in 1956, the North Carolina court said that the following conditions imply consent as a matter of law: (1) the condition encountered cannot reasonably have been diagnosed prior to surgery; (2) the surgery in question has not been expressly proscribed by the patient; (3) the more extensive surgery is in the area of the original incision; (4) sound medical practice dictates such an extension; and (5) neither the patient nor a surrogate is immediately available to give the necessary consent.

In other emergency situations, such as when care is rendered at the scene of an accident, courts have applied the following criteria in implying consent as a matter of law: (1) actual consent was not obtainable; (2) immediate action was necessary to protect the life or well-being of the injured party; (3) consent would have been granted if the victim had been able to; and (4) a reasonable person would have given consent under the same set of circumstances. These criteria are applicable to Good Samaritan situations. Most states have enacted Good Samaritan statutes to cover such circumstances; many have imposed other conditions that must be met before protecting a Good Samaritan from suit, eg, that no financial remuneration was expected and that the care was rendered in a carefully described situation defined as an emergency. However, none of these statutes would protect the provider of emergency care from a suit for gross negligence.

CONSENT OF MINORS

As established in the case *Schloendorff v. Society of New York Hospital* in 1914, only adults may give a valid consent. At common law, the age at which one reaches majority is 21 for males and 18 for females; however, for most purposes this has been modified by statute. In contract law, one who has reached the age of 18 may execute a contract that is not voidable at the minor's option. The basis of the law of consent is found in contract law because the granting of consent is itself a form of contract. Therefore, where the age of majority is established as 18, anyone who reaches that age may grant consent to treatment on his or her own behalf, and neither parents nor guardians need to be consulted. Many states have enacted special statutes relating to consent by minors for health care.

When the patient is below the age of 18, or below the statutory age of majority in the specific locality, the health practitioner may be faced with issues involving the emancipated minor, the mature minor, emergency situations, students living away from home, children of divorced or separated parents, and responsibility for payment for the minor's care.

The Emancipated Minor

An emancipated minor is one who is not subject to parental control or regulation, or not dependant on the parent for maintenance. An emancipated minor may independently grant consent to care, and parental consent is not required. Should disputes arise between the emancipated minor and the parent as to whether consent should be given, the doctor has only two protected choices: to refuse to provide the care if there is no legal requirement to do so, or to provide the care consented to by the emancipated minor. If the practitioner follows the treatment consented to by the parent but in conflict with that of the minor, he places himself in legal jeopardy. Considering the emancipated minor as an adult will serve to guide the treating doctor into a legally defensible position in virtually all situations.

The definition of emancipation differs among jurisdictions. Generally, the emancipated minor is one who is not living at home and is self-supporting. Pregnancy and marriage are also conditions that establish emancipation. Married minors may grant consent for themselves and for their minor children; divorce does not change the consent status. Minors in military service are also emancipated.

Many jurisdictions have enacted statutes concerned with treatment for venereal disease, abortion, and birth control that grant minors independent consent status and ensure privacy of such information from parents. Although such statutes do not directly affect dentists, they do protect the confidentiality of any such information obtained by a dentist in taking the history of a minor patient.

The Mature Minor

To date, no parent has been successful in a suit against a doctor when the suit involved treatment of a minor without the parent's permission when the minor was over the age of 14, which is considered the age of discretion. The mature minor rule, which recognizes the consent of a minor in the absence of parental consent, is applied to the minor who is capable of understanding the nature, extent, and consequences of the treatment. However, there is some question as to whether the mature minor rule would attach to serious procedures when the parent is available. When an emergency exists and the parent is inaccessible, treatment may be initiated without parental consent based upon the emergency, rather than the mature minor rule. Dentists are cautioned to secure the consent of any child between the ages of 14 and 18, as well as that of the parent, preferably in writing. When the parents are not present, attempts should be made to locate at least one of them before treatment is begun.

Emergency Situations

True emergencies are rare in denistry; most involve cases of facial trauma that require oral surgery. There are, however, situations in which prompt action must be taken by the dentist in the treatment of children. The case of an evulsed tooth represents the typical situation. Often, a school teacher or neighbor brings the injured child to the dentist's office. Neither is in a position to grant valid consent. If the child is 14 years of age or older, the mature minor rule may be applicable. If the child is under the age of 14, the need for actual consent may give way to the exception for an emergency, and thus protect the dentist from suit by the parent. In all cases, efforts should be made to locate at least one of the parents and secure telephone consent.

A New York court has defined a medical emergency as a situation in which the life or health of the patient is endangered or in which suffering or pain may be alleviated.[12] The state of New York, by statute, recognizes an emergency in the following terms:

> ...an emergency exists and the person is in immediate need of medical attention and an attempt to secure consent would result in delay of treatment which increases the risk to the patient's life or health.[13]

Similar definitions exist in many jurisdictions, either by case law or statute. In general, if a dentist, in the treatment of a minor, is of the opinion that any delay would compromise the dental health of the patient, he or she may institute the necessary treatment without obtaining parental consent, but only after attempting to locate parents. The individual who escorted the child to the office should be considered a witness to the facts, including the attempts to locate the parents, and appropriate notes and signatures should be secured. These rules of conduct would also apply in cases where the child and/or family are patients of record of the dentist.

Obtaining a consent by telephone is not difficult. Once the parent is located and the call placed, one of the office personnel, after informing the patient, should listen in on the conversation as a witness. The parent should be positively identified and informed of the situation. Following the oral telephone consent, suitable notes should be entered into the patient's record. The notes should be dated, timed, and signed by the dentist, the third party, and the child, if 14 years of age or older. A follow-up written and signed consent should be obtained from the parent as soon as possible after the telephone consent.

In providing nonemergency care to a minor child, the usual consent principles apply. In providing any unexpected care not covered in an original consent for treatment, a special consent to deliver the un-anticipated treatment procedure must be obtained, even if the care must be delayed. This applies even in treating the families of long-standing patients. Remember, telephone consents, if properly executed, can cover nonemergency situations.

Minors Away From Home

A student living away from home, although financially dependent on the parent, may be considered an emancipated minor. However, in most situations the dentist can and should contact the parent before initiating treatment. Written consents can be negotiated through the mail; telephone consents would also be valid. College and school officials may also have the power, granted by the parent, to sign in loco parentis. In all cases, the child should also execute the consent.

The runaway child presents some unique concerns. First, the parent has not agreed to the separation, as in the college or boarding school situation. Second, the child is not likely to reveal the location of the parent. Given such a situation, a dentist may administer care to a runaway without fear of punitive action. The dentist should have the child sign a consent and a statement reflecting the refusal to reveal the location of the parent.

Divorced or Separated Parents

In the case of divorce or separation, the parent with legal custody of the child has the right to consent to medical treatment without the need to consult and obtain the approval of the other parent. As a practical matter, the dentist may look to actual custody in identifying the parent from whom consent should be sought. The dentist is under no duty to examine the separation agreement or the divorce decree to make a determination as to legal custody. It would be best to obtain the consent of both parents; however, this presents considerable difficulty because interpersonal relationships may be strained, and locating both parents may be difficult.

Responsibility for Payment

In the absence of an express agreement, the rendering of professional services to a minor with the actual or apparent consent of the parent implies an obligation on the part of the parent to pay for the services rendered. When emergency care is administered, even without parental consent, the parent is responsible for the professional fee. Courts would probably apply this principle even in cases where necessary treatment was administered to a mature minor. However, it is likely that emancipated minors would be held responsible for payment of fees for their own care, even when the care was given in an emergency situation.

In cases of separation or divorce, in most states, in the absence of an arrangement to the contrary, the father is responsible for the necessary expenses of his child. Because the dentist is not privy to any private agreements, he may logically hold as liable for payment the parent who has apparent custody and who grants consent to treatment. The parents must then settle between themselves on the basis of a court order or a private agreement. Parents who are neither separated nor divorced are jointly liable for payment of any care.

NEW TECHNIQUES AND EXPERIMENTS

Generally, when experiments are being conducted on human subjects, the individual receiving the treatment must be informed that it is experimental. In the absence of this information, the consent is not valid. Although it is unlikely that dentists in private office practice would be conducting experiments on their patients, they should be familiar with any state statutes that cover the subject. A situation might arise in which it becomes difficult to separate a new technique in treatment from an experiment. As a rule, state statutes[14] and federal regulations[15] that cover human experiments or studies require, in addition to the usual elements of informed and voluntary consent, that: (1) the consent be in writing and signed by the patient; (2) the procedure be identified as an experiment or study; (3) any inquiries relating to the procedure be answered; (4) the person be free to withdraw at any time without prejudice; and (5) no exculpatory language be included in the consent.

The courts have taken a different view in considering new techniques that have clearly developed beyond the experimental stage. Because the modern construction of consent includes the need to identify alternative methods of treatment, courts accept the fact that differences in opinions regarding treatment procedures occur among practitioners. In establishing standards of care relative to deciding cases of alleged malpractice, courts have accepted those treatment techniques approved by a "respectable minority of the medical community." Thus, courts have not discouraged innovation in health practice. Where these latter principles apply, special provisions need not be included in the consent agreement.

CONCLUSION

The health practitioner must satisfy legal requirements in obtaining informed consent from his patients in all professional endeavors. Recognition of the patient's right to self-determination is the first step. Establishment of routine consent procedures, either oral or written, is next. Finally, the actual voluntary consent of the patient to a certain course of treatment must be obtained, based upon the patient's informed understanding of the diagnosis, the nature of the prescribed procedure, the risks and complications involved as well as the benefits that may result, the prognosis if the treatment is not effected, and what alternative methods of treatment, if any, are available. A valuable by-product of this legal procedure is often the enhancement of the dentist-patient relationship through the clarification of the expectations of both parties concerning the delivery of professional services, a factor that may also reduce exposure to malpractice charges. The law of informed consent not only ensures the patient's right to determine what course of treatment is to be undertaken, but also elevates the professionalism of every practicing dentist.

REFERENCES

1. *Bly v. Rhoads*, 216 Va. 645, 222 S.E. 2d 783 (1976).
2. *Canterbury v. Spence*, 464 F. 2d 772 (D.C. Cir. 1972); *Zeleznik v. Jewish*

Chronic Disease Hospital, 47 App. Div. 2d 199, 366 N.Y.S. 2d 163 (1975).
3. *Roberts v. Wood*, 206 F. Supp. 579 (S.D. Ala. 1962).
4. *Mohr v. Williams*, 95 Minn. 261, 104 N.W. 12 (1905).
5. Id. at 268; 104 N.W. at 14.
6. Id. at 268; 104 N.W. at 14–15.
7. Id. at 271; 104 N.W. at 16.
8. *Schloendorff v. Society of New York Hospital*; 211 N.Y. 125, 129–30, 105 N.E. 92, 93 (1914).
9. *Natanson v. Kline*, 186 Kan. 393, 406–407, 350 P. 2d 1093, 1104 (1960).
10. *O'Brien v. Cunard Steamship Co.*, 154 Mass. 272, 28 N.E. 266 (1891).
11. *Kennedy v. Parrott*, 243 N.C. 355, 90 S.E. 2d 754 (1956).
12. *Sullivan v. Montgomery*, 279 N.Y.S. 575, 577 (1935).
13. New York Pub. Health Law §2504 (McKinney).
14. New York Pub. Health Law §2441 and §2442 (McKinney).
15. 40 *Fed. Reg.* 11854–58 (1975); 21 C.F.R. §310.102.

11 The Dentist and State Law

Oliver C. Schroeder, Jr.
Burton R. Pollack

Historically, state law has been the primary legal system to affect dentistry. The state has legally defined the practice of dentistry and the rules regulating it, and has served as the public agency controlling the dentist in his or her professional practice. Because the American system of jurisprudence is a composite of 50 sovereign states, its territories, and the District of Columbia, each has exercised its legal authority to enact and enforce the dental practice laws for its specific jurisdiction. It is helpful for the dental student and practitioner to be exposed to these laws in order to compare the definitions of dentistry, the dental licensing requirements, and the various state boards of dentistry. Thus, a legal spectrum is available to students and practitioners by which their particular states can be compared and by which the general law of the United States can be understood.

DEFINITION OF DENTISTRY

Each state defines dentistry by listing what the practice of dentistry includes and what practices or operations are exempted. The lists

116

appear endless and somewhat repetitious, but there does not seem to be a better way to define the profession. Four examples of state definitions of the practice of dentistry follow.

Colorado

12–35–110. What constitutes practicing dentistry. (1) Any person shall be deemed to be practicing dentistry who:

(a) Performs, or attempts or professes to perform, any dental operation or oral surgery or dental services of any kind, gratuitously or for a salary, fee, money, or other remuneration paid, or to be paid, directly, or indirectly, to himself or to any other person or agency;

(b) Is a proprietor of a place where dental operation, oral surgery, or dental services are performed; except that nothing in this section shall be construed as prohibiting a dental hygienist or dental auxiliary from performing those tasks and procedures consistent with section 12–35–5 (2) and (3);

(c) Directly or indirectly, by any means or method, takes impression of the human tooth, teeth, or jaws or performs any phase of any operation incident to the replacement of a part of a tooth or supplies artificial substitutes for the natural teeth;

(d) Furnishes, supplies, constructs, reproduces, or repairs any prosthetic denture, bridge, appliance, or any other structure to be worn in the human mouth other than on the written laboratory work order of a duly licensed and practicing dentist, or professionally places such appliance or structure in the human mouth, or adjusts or attempts or professes to adjust the same, or delivers the same to any person other than the dentist upon whose laboratory work order the work was performed;

(e) Professes to the public by any method to furnish, supply, construct, reproduce, or repair any prosthetic denture, bridge, appliance, or other structure to be worn in the human mouth;

(f) Diagnoses or professes to diagnose, prescribes for or professes to the public to prescribe for, treats or professes to treat disease, pain, deformity, deficiency, injury, or physical condition of the human teeth or jaws or adjacent structure;

(g) Extracts, or attempts to extract, human teeth, or corrects, or attempts to correct, malformations of teeth or of the jaws;

(h) Repairs or fills cavities in the human teeth;

(i) Uses a roentgen or X-ray machine for the purpose of taking dental X-rays or roentgenograms;

(j) Gives, or professes to give, interpretations or readings of dental X-rays or roentgenograms;

(k) Uses the words dentist, dental surgeon, oral surgeon, or the letters D.D.S., D.M.D., or any other words, letters, title, or descriptive matter which in any way represents to the general public that he is able to diagnose, treat, prescribe, or operate for any disease, pain, deformity, deficiency, injury, or physical condition of the teeth or jaws or adjacent structures; or

(l) States, permits to be stated, or professes by any means or method whatsoever that he can perform or will attempt to perform dental operations or render a diagnosis connected therewith.

12–35–111. Persons exempt from operations of this article. (1) Nothing in this article shall apply to the following practices, acts, and operations:

(a) Practice of his profession by a physician or surgeon licensed as such under the laws of this state unless he practices dentistry as a specialty;

(b) The giving by a qualified anesthetist or registered nurse of an anesthetic for dental operation under the direct supervision of a licensed dentist;

(c) The practice of dentistry in the discharge of their official duties by graduate dentists or dental surgeons in the United States armed forces, public health service, coast guard, or veterans administration;

(d) Dental interns regularly employed by a private hospital or by a city, county, city and county, or state hospital under an internship approved by the council on dental education of the American Dental Association and registered as such by the board;

(e) The practice of dentistry by instructors and students in schools or colleges of dentistry or schools of dental auxiliary education accredited by the American Dental Association while participating in programs of such schools or colleges;

(f) The practice of dentistry by dentists of other states or countries while appearing in programs of dental education or research at the invitation of any group of licensed dentists in this state who are in good standing;

(g) The filling of laboratory work orders of a licensed and registered dentist, as provided by section 12–35–130, by any person, association, corporation, or other entity for the construction, reproduction, or repair of prosthetic dentures, bridges, plates, or appliances to be used or worn as substitutes for natural teeth or for regulation of natural teeth; or

(h) The performance of acts by a person under the personal direction of a dentist licensed in Colorado when authorized pursuant to the rules and regulations of the board or when authorized under other provisions of this article.

Hawaii

§448–1 Dentistry defined; exempted practices. A person practices dentistry, within the meaning of this chapter, who represents himself as being able to diagnose, treat, remove stains and concretions from teeth, operate or prescribe for any disease, pain, injury, deficiency, deformity, or physical condition of the human teeth, alveolar process, gums, or jaw, and who offers or undertakes by any means or methods to diagnose, treat, remove stains or concretions from teeth, operate or prescribe for any disease, pain, injury, deficiency, deformity, or physical condition of the same, or to take impressions of the teeth or jaws; or who owns, maintains, or operates an office for the practice of dentistry; or who engages in any of the practices included in the curricula of recognized and approved dental schools or colleges. The fact that a person uses any dental degree, or designation, or any card,

device, director, poster, sign, or other media whereby he represents himself to be a dentist, shall be prima facie evidence that the person is engaged in the practice of dentistry. The following practices, acts, and operations, however, are exempt from the operation of this chapter: (1) The rendering of dental relief in emergency cases in the practice of his profession by a physician or surgeon, licensed as such as registered under the laws of this State, unless he undertakes to reproduce or reproduces lost parts of the human teeth in the mouth or to restore or replace in the human mouth lost or missing teeth;
(2) The practice of dentistry in the discharge of their official duties by dentists in the United States Army, the United States Navy, the United States Air Force, the United States Public Health Service, or the United States Veterans Administration;
(3) The practice of dentistry by licensed dentists of other states or countries at meetings of the dental society of Hawaii or component parts thereof, alumni meetings of dental colleges, or any other like dental organizations, while appearing as clinicians;
(4) The use of roentgen and other rays for making radiograms or similar records of dental or oral tissues;
(5) The making of artificial restorations, substitutes, appliances, or materials for the correction of disease, loss, deformity, malposition, dislocation, fracture, injury to the jaws, teeth, lips, gums, cheeks, palate, or associated tissues, or parts, upon orders, prescription casts, models, or from impressions furnished by a licensed and registered dentist.

New York

§6601. Definition of practice of dentistry. The practice of the profession of dentistry is defined as diagnosing, treating, operating, or prescribing for any disease, pain, injury, deficiency, deformity, or physical condition of the human mouth, including the teeth, alveolar processes gums, or jaws, and adjacent tissues; or, except by the use of impressions or casts made by a licensed dentist and on his written dental laboratory prescription, furnishing, supplying, constructing, reproducing, or repairing prosthetic dentures, bridges, appliances, or other structures to be used and worn as substitutes for natural teeth, or in the treatment of abnormal conditions of the teeth or jaws or adjacent tissues; or, placing such devices in the mouth or adjusting the same. The practice of dentistry may include performing physical evaluations in conjunction with the provision of dental treatment.
§6610. Exempt persons. Nothing in this article shall be construed to affect or prevent:
1. An unlicensed person from performing solely mechanical work upon inert matter in a dental office or on a dental laboratory prescription of a dentist holding a license or limited permit;
2. A student from engaging in clinical practice as part of a registered program operated by a school of dentistry under supervision of a dentist holding a license or limited permit for instructing in dentistry in a school of dentistry;
3. A student from engaging in any procedure authorized under section sixty-six hundred six of this article in clinical practice as part of a

registered program in dental hygiene under supervision of a dentist holding a license or a limited permit for instructing in dentistry in a school of dental hygiene;

4. An employee of a federal agency from using the title of and practicing as a dentist or dental hygienist insofar as such activities are required by his salaried position;

5. A dentist or a dental hygienist licensed in some other state or country from making a teaching clinical demonstration before a regularly organized dental or medical society or group, or from meeting licensed dentists in this state for consultation, provided such activities are limited to such demonstration or consultation.

Ohio

§4715.01 **Definitions.** Any person shall be regarded as practicing dentistry, who is a manager, proprietor, operator, or conductor of a place for performing dental operations or who, for a fee, salary, or other reward paid or to be paid either to himself or to another person, performs, or advertises to perform, dental operations of any kind, or who diagnoses or treats diseases or lesions of human teeth or jaws, or attempts to correct malpositions thereof, or who takes impressions of the human teeth or jaws, or who constructs, supplies, reproduces, or repairs any prosthetic denture, bridge, artificial restoration, appliance, or other structure to be used or worn as a substitute for natural teeth, except upon the order of a licensed dentist and constructed upon or by the use of casts or models made from an impression taken by a licensed dentist, or who advertises, offers, sells, or delivers any such substitute or the services rendered in the construction, reproduction, supply, or repair thereof to any person other than a licensed dentist, or who places or adjusts such substitute in the oral cavity of another, or uses the words "dentist," "dental surgeon," the letters "D.D.S.," or other letters or title in connection with his name, which in any way represents him as being engaged in the practice of dentistry.

Manager, proprietor, operator, or conductor as used in this section includes any person:

(A) Who employs licensed operators;

(B) Who places in the possession of licensed operators dental offices or dental equipment necessary for the handling of dental offices on the basis of a lease or any other agreement for compensation or profit for the use of such office or equipment, when such compensation is manifestly in excess of the reasonable rental value of such premises and equipment;

(C) Who makes any other arrangements whereby he derives profit, compensation, or advantage through retaining ownership or control of dental offices or necessary dental equipment by making the same available in any manner for the use of licensed operators; provided that this section does not apply to bona fide sales of dental equipment secured by chattel mortgage.

Whoever having a license to practice dentistry or dental hygiene enters the employment of, or enters into any of the arrangements described in this section with, an unlicensed manager, proprietor, operator, or conductor, or who becomes mentally incompetent, or is committed by a court having jurisdiction for treatment of mental illness, may have his license suspended or revoked by the state dental board.

§4715.34 Provisions not applicable to physicians and surgeons; exception Sections 4715.01 to 4715.35, inclusive, of the Revised Code do not apply to a legally qualified physician or surgeon unless he practices dentistry as a specialty, or to a dental surgeon of the United States army, navy, public health service, or veteran's administration; or to a legal practitioner of dentistry of another state, making a clinical demonstration before a dental society, convention, association of dentists, or college.

Commentary

It is obvious that each of the four states represented above elects to define dentistry somewhat differently, as do all the other states in the nation. The same is true of the laws that control the practice of dental hygiene, and, in those states where applicable, the laws that regulate dental assistants. What appear to be slight differences in wording may result in major differences in practice. Ultimately, the courts interpret the laws that regulate dentistry and dental assisting. Regarding the latter group, the state of New York does not recognize dental assisting as a legal professional occupation.

STATE DENTAL BOARDS

All states, the District of Columbia, the territory of the Virgin Islands, and Puerto Rico maintain dental boards to administer their respective licensing and regulating statutes. However, in each jurisdiction, the role of the dental board may be different. As an example, in Colorado, under §12–35–107, Powers and duties of the board, the board shall:

1. conduct examinations to ascertain the qualifications and fitness of applicants for licensure in dentistry and dental hygiene;
2. adopt rules and regulations related to the conduct of the licensing examination, the practice of dentistry and dental hygiene, tasks and procedures which may be assigned to dental auxiliaries and dental hygienists, and essential instructions to be included in a laboratory work order;
3. conduct hearings to revoke, suspend, or deny the issuance of a license;
4. conduct investigations and inspections for compliance with the provisions of the article;

5. make rules and regulations designed to govern the conduct of its business;
6. employ hearing or law officers to conduct any hearings required by the article.

The Colorado board has subpoena power to enable it to carry out its duties under the law.

In New York, the powers of the board are quite different, and, as compared with those of Colorado, are severely limited. Many of the powers in New York that are vested in the Colorado Board are granted to the Commissioner of Education and the Board of Regents. Neither of these administrative bodies are required to have dental representation. Thus, while the board that regulates the practice of dentistry and dental hygiene in Colorado is made up of dentists, hygienists, and public the body with comparable regulatory powers in New York may be completely devoid of representatives of dentistry and dental hygiene. The power granted by statute to the State Board for Dentistry in New York is limited to "assisting the board of regents and the state education department on matters of professional licensing and professional conduct." To carry out this function, the statute grants additional powers to the Board in delineating its mandate to "assist." These are that the Board shall:

1. conduct examinations for licensure;
2. assist the Department of Education and the Board of Regents on matters of licensure;
3. conduct disciplinary proceedings;
4. adopt rules to fulfill its mandate.

It should be noted that although the State Board for Dentistry in New York may advise the State Education Department and the Board of Regents on matters of licensure, it has no statutory authority to regulate the practice of dentistry or dental hygiene through the mechanism of rules and regulations. That power rests with the State Education Department and the Board of Regents. The State Board for Dentistry in New York has no subpoena power. Few states follow New York's pattern in the regulation of the dental profession. The Colorado model is by far the most representative of other states.

Requirements for Licensure

All jurisdictions have established rigid requirements for the licensure of health professionals. These requirements specify age, education, the successful completion of an examination, and good moral character. The minimum age for licensure varies between the ages of 18 and 21 years.

Reciprocity

A comparison of the laws of Ohio, Colorado, Hawaii, and New York demonstrates the variety of ways that states address the issue of reciprocity.

The key difference in the licensing statutes among these states concerns the issue of reciprocity. Colorado and Hawaii have no reciprocity. In Colorado, a licensee from another state must begin the application process from step one; no provision is made for previous years of experience. Many states have no provision for reciprocity. New York is an exception. It has such an informal system that it probably benefits an out-of-state practitioner. In New York, licensure by endorsement is authorized by statute and by regulations of the Commissioner of Education. Most of the application requirements are waived for experienced practitioners. Certainly this was a trend that Colorado investigated before writing its statute. In all probability, a reciprocity section was left out because of Colorado's attractiveness as a retirement haven or living place.

Ohio provides for what it calls a license by endorsement. It lists seven steps that place no great burden on an out-of-state dentist. The out-of-state dentist must have practiced in the other state for 5 years and must take an exam, but this can be waived by the board. It is assumed that if a reputable Ohio dentist vouches for the candidate, the exam will be waived. The other requirements then become mere formalities. Of course, Ohio will not accept anyone who has lost his or her license because of malpractice in another state.

The trend is to provide for reciprocity, encouraging an excess of dentists in one area to move to other sections of the country. On just that rationale alone, it is easy to see why Ohio favors reciprocity.

In 1986, 21 states, including Puerto Rico, had some form of recognition of licensure by other states.

In an article written by Waldman and Pollack, a case was made for state reciprocity of professional licensure on a constitutional basis.[1]

THE REGULATION OF DENTAL AUXILIARIES

Dental Hygienists and Dental Assistants

All states recognize the legal existence of dental auxiliaries, although there is wide disagreement as to their legally permissible duties. All recognize dental hygienists, but New York does not include dental assistants as a regulated profession. Although dentists may employ an individual to act in the capacity of a dental assistant, there are no laws directly related to their activities. The regulation of their activities is controlled as a result of defining the practice of dentistry and dental hygiene, and thus precluding anyone from engaging in any activity falling within the scope of practice of either profession. However, the law in New York permits "a person acting as a dental assistant" under the direct supervision of a licensed dentist to take radiographs, "limited to the patient's head." Based upon the size of the x-ray beam, they are permitted to take panographic films but are precluded from taking cephalometric films.[2]

The assignment of duties permitted by state law may either be by *open provisions* or by *listing*.

In the open provision approach, the dentist may assign to the auxiliary any duty the dentist feels the auxiliary can perform by training or experience. The law states what cannot be delegated, such as any function that "requires the knowledge and skill of the dentist."

In the listing approach, the law specifically lists those duties that are permitted to be delegated by the dentist. This method permits only those services listed, and a dentist who permits or directs an auxiliary to perform a service not listed is guilty of violating the law. The same is true of the auxiliary who performs the illegal act. The listing approach is more restrictive than the open provision approach.

It is essential that the practicing dentist become familiar with the law as it relates to regulating auxiliaries. A dentist who permits or authorizes the performance of an illegal duty by a dental auxiliary may be inviting serious trouble by the state agency regulating the practice of dentistry. If in the commission of an illegal act there is an allegation by a patient of negligence, the dentist may find himself in difficulty with his professional liability insurance company. Unfortunately, many dentists direct or otherwise permit dental auxiliaries to engage in illegal activities in the practice of dentistry.[3,4]

Laboratory Technicians

All states regulate, to some extent, the dental laboratory technicians as their activities relate to the practice of dentistry. Some states permit dental laboratories to provide direct services to patients. In those states, the laws regulating their activities are extensive, detailed, and vary from state to state. Currently there are six states that permit direct services to the public: Maine, Oregon, Montana, Arizona, Colorado, and Idaho. In the following seven states, legislation is proposed to permit the activity: Washington, Illinois, Mississippi, Michigan, New Jersey, California, and Indiana.[5] In states where direct services are prohibited, there are laws regarding work authorizations by dentists. Laws state how long the laboratory and the dentist are to retain the authorizations, and their form and content.

OTHER LAWS REGULATING DENTAL PRACTICE

Many statutes, rules, and regulations buried in state and federal laws affect the practice of dentistry. Unfortunately for the practitioner, these rules are not assembled in one volume or in one place, and therefore are not readily available for the dentist to study. To collect them represents a major undertaking by persons experienced in legal research. Some of the more important laws concern reporting child abuse, drug prescription writing and control, and issues of confidentiality. Although the specific laws are difficult to find, the dentist is responsible for their compliance. The phrase "ignorance of the law is no excuse" is not to be taken lightly.

CONCLUSION

Whenever legislation is enacted, the intent of the legislative body is paramount in determining the purposes for which the statute was adopted. Dental practice acts should be no exception, although in most jurisdictions the declaration of legislative purposes is not found in dental practice acts.

An understanding of the purposes set forth by the legislature will go a long way toward assuring proper judicial interpretation, better state board administration, and a higher level of individual performance by dentists to provide the best in dental health. For that reason, the Colorado legislative declaration is exemplary:

> **12-35-102.** Legislative declaration. The practice of dentistry in this state is declared to affect the public health, safety, and welfare and to be subject to regulation and control in the public interest. It is further declared to be a matter of public interest and concern that the dental profession merit and receive the confidence of the public and that only qualified dentists be permitted to practice dentistry in this state. It is the purpose of this law to promote the public health, safety, and welfare by regulating the practice of dentistry and insure that no one shall practice dentistry without qualifying under this article. All provisions of this article relating to the practice of dentistry and dental hygiene shall be liberally construed to carry out these objects and purposes.

126

REFERENCES

1. Waldman, H.B., Pollack, B.R. The developing legal basis for reciprocity. *NY State Dent J*, p. 624, November, 1982.
2. New York Public Health Law, Article 35, Section 89.4.
3. Waldman, H.B. The illegal delegation of duties to dental auxiliaries. *J Am Coll Dent* 48:246–264, Winter, 1981.
4. Waldman, H.B., Pollack, B.R. The illegal delegation of duties to dental auxiliaries in New York State: Some changes, but it continues. Accepted for publication, *NY State Dent J*, 1986.
5. Kettenbach, D. Denturists target 7 more states. *Modern Dentalab*, Vol. 4, No. 1, p. 1, Dec/Jan 1986.

12 The Professional Dentist Corporation: Contract Planning for Tax and Pension Benefits

Philip Glaser
Oliver C. Schroeder, Jr.

For years, the medical, dental, and legal professions have justifiably complained of the inequity of laws that allowed a private businessman to incorporate, thereby qualifying his business for the many tax and non-tax advantages available to corporations, while the professional person has been unable to enjoy these same corporate benefits. Finally, in 1969, the Internal Revenue Service conceded that it would recognize professional corporations as valid corporations for federal tax purposes. The many tax reforms since 1969 have, however, severely narrowed some of the advantages of the professional corporation over the partnership or individual practitioner. Nevertheless, since 1969 there has been a surge by professionals to operate in the corporate form, thus availing themselves of some of the benefits traditionally realized only by conventional business corporations. However, many factors enter into the determination of whether a professional should decide to incorporate. The Tax Reform Bill of 1986 made the decision of whether to incorporate more difficult because the tax advantages over solo practice were severely curtailed. Now more than ever, consideration must be given to the advantages and disadvantages before deciding to incorporate the dental practice.

TAX ADVANTAGES

In the past, the most obvious advantage was that the corporation was taxed at a rate of 15% on the first $25,000 of corporate income, 18% on the next $25,000, 30% on the next $25,000, 40% on the next $25,000, and 46% on any excess, whereas the individual would have been taxed on his income at sharply graduated tax rates. Starting in 1988, the corporate tax rate is 15% on the first $50,000, 25% on the next $25,000 and 34% over $75,000. There is a 5% additional tax between $100,000 and $335,000. The personal tax rate for married taxpayers is 15% on the first $30,000, 28% on the next $42,000, 33% up to $150,000, and 28% thereafter, with some qualifications. It is obvious that the tax differences between corporate and personal have been severely narrowed. This factor must be dealt with in conjunction with other facts before any decisions can be made. Before the numerous tax reforms, especially that of 1982, the principal economic advantage of incorporating a professional practice was that the corporate employees, namely the practitioners, could qualify for the enormous tax-saving opportunities available through pension or profit-sharing plans authorized by the Internal Revenue Service. Now these advantages are available to the nonincorporated practice. Briefly, these corporate plans are designed to provide for the payment of benefits to the covered employees over a period of years, usually for life, after retirement. These payments are facilitated by the employer, ie, the corporate entity, making contributions to the pension or profit-sharing funds during the years of employment. Such contribution can be made in a definite amount, which is the more conservative pension plan, or on a percentage basis (up to 15% of salary), which is the less stable but potentially more lucrative profit-sharing plan. If a combination of both is used, a contribution of up to 25% of salary is permissible. With defined benefit and target benefit plans, contributions well in excess of 25% of salary are possible. These plans afford the professional employees the following tax benefits:

1. The amount contributed by the corporation to the fund is deductible, thereby immediately reducing the corporation's taxable income.
2. The employee is not taxed on the amount of money put into the fund for him, even though it is actually income to the employee and is merely being held for his future use.
3. The amounts accumulated in the fund may be invested; any income and earnings produced by these investments are tax-free. This feature is particularly important to professionals who may very likely become affluent. The effect of a fund earning compounded income tax-free over a number of years can be overwhelming. Furthermore, employees may voluntarily contribute up to an additional 10% of their

salaries to the plans, though this is not deductible. Thus, an excellent vehicle for investment is available to the professional who incorporates.

4. Payments actually made to the employee or his beneficiaries are taxed as ordinary income. However, the payments are likely to be received after retirement, when the employee's tax bracket may be considerably lower than it was when the contributions were originally made. There is also the possibility of lump sum (10-year averaging or 5-year averaging if age 50 occurs after January 1, 1986) distributions or annuity distributions, which reduce the ordinary income taxes. Furthermore, the fund may be free of the federal estate tax when paid to beneficiaries at the employee's death.

The best way to understand the effect of these tax benefits is through an illustration. Remember that one or more professionals who are 100% owners and officers of their corporation are still employees for the purpose of qualifying for the plans. Assume the professional is filing a joint return, thereby affording himself the lowest personal tax rates possible. Unmarried persons or individuals who file separate returns will pay a higher tax than the professional in Table 12-1.

In an unincorporated practice, the individual earns $60,000 and pays an ordinary tax of $12,900. He therefore retains $47,100 for himself.

In a corporation, the corporation, rather than the individual, is considered to have earned $60,000. The professional sets for himself a $50,000 salary. The corporation deducts this expense, and its resulting taxable income becomes $10,000 (there may also be other operating expenses that further reduce taxable income). The tax on $10,000 is 15%, or $1,500, leaving the corporation with $8,500. It is important to note that this money retained by the corporation is taxed again on withdrawal. This minor problem will be discussed later, but in the meantime, there is no immediate tax. Returning to the example, the practitioner is taxed $10,100 on his or her $50,000 salary, leaving $39,900. Thus, the total amount remaining to the shareholder and the corporation is $48,400, or $1,300 less tax than the unincorporated professional paid.

In a corporation with pension and profit-sharing plans, the individual contributes the allowable 25% of his or her salary to pension and profit-sharing plans. The corporation earns $60,000, but contributes $10,000 to the plans and pays $40,000 in salary. The corporation still deducts the total $50,000, so its income and tax remain at $10,000 and $1,500, respectively, leaving $8,500 in the corporation. The practitioner is taxed only on his or her salary of $40,000, for a total tax of $7,300, leaving the practitioner with $32,700. Thus a total of $51,200 is re-

Table 12-1
Comparison of Tax Benefits — 1988 Tax Rates

	Unincorporated Practice	Practice in Corporation	Practice in Corporation With Pension and Profit-Sharing Plans
Income	$60,000	$60,000	$60,000
Salary		50,000	40,000
Pension and profit-sharing plan			10,000
Taxable income to corporation		10,000	10,000
Corporate tax		1,500	1,500
Net to corporation		8,500*	8,500*
Taxable income to shareholder (practitioner)	60,000	50,000	40,000
Shareholder tax (practitioner)	12,900	10,100	7,300
Net to shareholder (practitioner)	47,100	39,900	32,700
Net to pension and profit-sharing plan			10,000†
Total after tax	47,100	48,400	51,200

* Taxed again on withdrawal.
† Same as *, but can be invested and income is tax-free.

tained by the corporation, the shareholder, and the retirement plan. In addition, the $10,000 contribution may be invested, and the earnings are tax-free. Thus, under both corporation plans, less total tax was paid on the $60,000 earnings; more importantly, the corporation with the retirement plans paid even less than the one without these plans.

Although the pension and profit-sharing plans are easily the most substantial tax-saving benefits available, there are, in addition, several provisions in the Internal Revenue Code designed to encourage the corporation to provide other fringe benefits for employees.

These provisions, like the retirement plans, enable employees to exclude the cost of such benefits from their income, while the cost to the corporation is deductible. Thus, if a practicing professional incorporates and therefore becomes an employee of his or her own corporation, the professional can pay for all of these benefits with tax-free dollars. The fringe benefits available on this basis include:

1. Group term life insurance with a principal sum up to $50,000. Employees may effectively assign their benefits of

ownership under the policy and thereby remove the insurance proceeds from their estates for federal estate tax purposes, provided either state law or the policy itself does not prevent assignment.

2. Reimbursement for all medical and dental expenses of employees and their dependents. Bills may simply be turned in to the corporation. The reimbursement must be non-discriminating to other employees.

3. Death benefits up to a maximum of $5,000 free of estate and income tax. This is in addition to any bona fide gift made for nonbusiness reasons to the widow or widower of a valued employee.

4. Deferred compensation plans.

5. Wage continuation plans, such as workmen's compensation and state disability insurance.

6. Accident and health insurance plans.

7. Wage continuation plans by the corporation.

Most of these expenses are normal and necessary expenses for a professional, regardless of his mode of business operation. Yet the tax-saving feature of the costs deductible by the corporation and not taxable to the employee are unavailable through the unincorporated form of business.

Other Tax Advantages for the Corporation

1. Retained Earnings. There is a general limitation of $150,000 in a professional corporation.

2. Corporation may purchase automobiles for employee use.

HAZARDS OF INCORPORATION

Unfortunately, despite the advantages outlined above, the corporate tax laws involve pitfalls. However, if the corporation is simply aware of the hazards, the problems discussed below can easily be avoided and the full benefits of the tax plans can be realized.

Compensation for Professional Employee

The first problem concerns setting the amount of compensation for the professional employee. Because most earnings of a professional corporation are usually attributed to personal services rendered by the professional shareholder-employees, all of these earnings can usually be paid out as salaries without any problem. However, particularly in larger corporations, part of the earnings may result from the services of nonshareholder employees or from capital investments. Such earnings are available as compensation though they are not, in fact, earned by the employee to whom they are paid. The corporation is allowed a deduction for its salary expense, but attempting to avoid the corporate tax by paying out all these excess earnings as salaries may cause problems. Shareholders are merely corporate employees and are entitled to salaries only as they earn them. Therefore, if the Internal Revenue Service decides that the amount paid in salary and deducted by the corporation exceeds what it considers a reasonable amount, the excess is disallowed and treated as a dividend. This results in an unfavorable double tax, because the professional is taxed at ordinary rates for dividends received and the corporation is taxed on the original earnings without an allowable deduction for dividends paid.

This problem is not so drastic, however, and can easily be prevented. Employees' salaries can simply be set at each employee's individual billings, or at a level equal to the compensation paid elsewhere for similar services. Either method, preferably the former, will satisfy the Internal Revenue Service. Furthermore, a hedge is available to an employee if he or she agrees in writing to return to the corporation any portion of the salary that was disallowed as unreasonable. This payment will be deductible, thereby diminishing the penalty, even though the salary was originally set too high and will have to be adjusted.

Accumulated Corporate Income

The second problem involves accumulated corporate earnings. Suppose that the corporation decides that, rather than paying out all of its earnings in the form of compensation, it will accumulate part of these earnings, thereby lowering the amount of income subject to the higher personal tax rates of the employees and maximizing the amount subject to the 15% and 25% corporate tax rates. This is a perfectly legal tax break to the extent that such accumulations do not exceed $150,000. Once this amount is exceeded, the corporation must prove there is a reasonable business need for the excess. Otherwise, it will be assumed that the corporation is avoiding ordinary income tax rates by retaining the unneeded funds rather than distributing them as dividends to the shareholders. This results in a penalty tax of 27.5% on the first $100,000 of accumulated taxable income and 38.5% on any excess. This penalty tax is especially troublesome in professional corporations in which there is usually considerably less overhead and inventory than in conventional corporations. Thus, in our earlier example, in which the corporation was retaining $8,500 each year, the corporation may accumulate this amount without any explanation for almost 18 years. However, it must be realized that most professional corporations have several employees who may each be retaining $8,500 per year in the corporation. For instance, a professional corporation with only five shareholders, each earning $50,000 per year, may be accumulating $8,500 each, or $42,500 total. In this case, it only takes about 3½ years until the accumulations must be explained or alleviated by distribution or investment.

However, if a corporation is simply aware of the consequences of unreasonable accumulations, such problems can be prevented. Most of a corporation's income can be distributed in the form of salaries (keeping in mind the reasonable salary limitations), thereby minimizing accumulation. There may actually be reasonable business reasons for accumulated earnings, such as acquisition of a new building, expansion of the old one, liquidation of a mortgage, or, of particular interest to a dental corporation, the acquisition or replacement of equipment.

Classification as a Personal Holding Company

A third possible danger of incorporating results if the corporation is classified as a personal holding company. This is a complicated and detailed area. It will be outlined here as simply as possible merely to provide an awareness of the problem. A personal holding company is a corporation that holds private money for an individual. In the past, an individual in a high tax bracket would have incorporated himself and thereby obtained the benefit of the lower corporate taxes on his high investment income. This method of tax avoidance is met by a highly punitive tax of 50% on all personal holding company income. The concept of personal holding corporations is no longer as desirable because of the new corporate and personal tax rates.

A stock ownership test and an income test are applied to determine whether the drastic penalty tax will be imposed. The stock ownership test is met if, at any time during the last half of the taxable year, more than 50% of the value of the corporation's stock is owned by not more than five individuals. In most cases, a professional corporation will have few enough shareholders to meet the stock requirements for applying the tax. Corporations with any number of shareholders could, in fact, meet the test, depending on how the stock is distributed.

If the ownership test is met, the income test must be considered, because the corporation will achieve personal holding company status only if both tests are met. The income test is met if at least 60% of the corporation's adjusted ordinary gross income is personal holding company income. Personal holding company income, according to the Internal Revenue Code, is compensation received for personal services of a corporate employee who owns 25% or more of the corporate stock, if someone other than the corporation (namely the patient, client, or customer to whom services are being rendered) has the right to designate the individual employee who is to perform the services. This provision was intended to disallow entertainers or artists to incorporate and thus shield their income from personal services in a corporate format that is subject to lower tax rates. For example, if a famous singer incorporated himself and was hired to perform, the customer hiring him obviously had the right to designate who would perform; the singer-corporation could not designate someone else to perform the services of entertaining. This income test, however, when applied objectively, appears to present quite a problem for the professional corporation because the very basis of most doctor-patient relationships is the right of the patient to select the professional person with whom he will deal. If the professional owns 25% or more of the stock, fees attributable to these services will be personal holding company income and may be subject to the penalty tax. The tests appear to present an even greater problem to the one-man professional corporation when it is quite obvious that the patient is selecting that professional as the one who will perform services.

However, the outlook is not as bleak as it seems. For several reasons, it is questionable whether the penalty tax need apply at all. First, the IRS has ruled that the personal holding company penalty tax does not even apply to one-man corporations. Second, a professional corporation may have a system whereby the patient is assigned to the professional employee whose expertise is needed for the particular services, or assigned to several professional employees to perform the services as a staff, or even assigned to whomever is available in the office at that time. This operation, where the corporation delegates work among its employees as it chooses, not only defeats the requirement that the patient has the right to designate the person to perform the services, but appears to be a more efficient system as well.

Third, it must be remembered that the corporate employee that performs the services must own 25% or more of the stock, and at least 60% of the corporation's adjusted ordinary gross income must be personal holding company income. Thus, the penalty tax cannot apply if none of the shareholders owns 25%, or even though some do, if more than 40% of the adjusted ordinary gross income is attributed to the services of the other employees who own less than 25%.

Finally, the 50% penalty tax, regardless of any of the above situations, applies only to corporate income that is retained and not distributed. Therefore, the simplest solution for a solo practitioner or group practitioners who incorporate is to distribute most of the income rather than to accumulate it in the corporation, thus avoiding the dangers of both the professional holding company tax and the accumulated earning tax previously discussed.

Tax Disadvantages

Another obvious disadvantage of a professional corporation is that of double taxation: on the original corporate earnings and on the earnings when withdrawn and distributed to the shareholders in the form of corporate dividends. However, the payment of salaries, bonuses, and contributions to the retirement and fringe benefit plans should not leave a sufficient amount of retained income to force the corporation to declare a dividend. Furthermore, any distributions that are made can probably be made in later years when the individual is in a lower tax bracket. Prudent tax planning with regard to compensation, expenses, and the time of distribution can greatly minimize the prospect of double taxation.

Incorporating has slightly increased the Social Security tax because the liability is imposed upon both the employer and the employee. The employer tax is a corporate deductible expense which mitigates the additional contribution. Incorporating will also result in higher state and federal unemployment taxes and increased workmen's compensation and state disability insurance rates. However, these increases seem to have little significance when compared to the overall advantages involved in corporate practice. Furthermore, they are expenses that eventually benefit the employee and may be personally borne by the practitioner at the present time as well. There are initial expenses of incorporating as well as ongoing additional accounting fees. Finally, other miscellaneous taxes, such as state and local income taxes, property taxes, or a corporate franchise tax, may result from incorporating. Again, these are not likely to be of great consequence when considered in the entire corporate tax plan.

Thus, while there are no clear and certain guidelines in weighing the tax factors, it nevertheless seems that the disadvantages are smaller relative to the advantages, particularly if the corporate employees and advisors are aware of the problems and how they can be avoided.

NONTAX ADVANTAGES

There are several nontax factors in favor of incorporating which, while not as important as the tax considerations, may still be quite substantial.

Limited Liability

The most significant nontax advantage is the limited degree of liability, which is not possible in a partnership. Presently, the members of a partnership are exposed to broad liability. All partners are personally liable for any loss or injury resulting from the malpractice of the other partners and for business debts and contracts entered into by the partnership. However, a shareholder in a corporation, as an employee of the corporation, has the available protection of the corporate shield. There is no personal liability for the conduct of the other professional employees performing services for the corporation; the corporation itself is the liable entity. Of course, the individual committing the wrongful act is personally liable under any circumstance. However, in these days of malpractice popularity, the importance of protecting the innocent practitioner may be a crucial consideration in the decision of whether or not to incorporate.

Centralized Management

Another nontax advantage of a corporation is the greater degree of centralized management that is possible. A corporation's important policies and decisions are determined by a small number of people, namely the board of directors and officers. Compared with a partnership, where authority is commonly divided or spread too broadly, the corporate form of management affords better control, especially when dentists practice as a group. By delegating management responsibility to a professional manager, the shareholder-dentists are free to devote more time and concentration to their professional practices. The larger the practice, the greater the benefit of centralized management, and hence the importance of this factor.

The professional corporation, as any corporation, has a continuity of life because, unlike a partnership, it does not dissolve when a partner leaves the corporation. A professional corporation is an entity and continues to exist regardless of death, resignation, retirement, or any other withdrawal from the corporation. This factor is particularly important in the case of a sole practitioner incorporating. Upon the death of the sole shareholder, the files and records of a patient will belong to the corporation, not to the estate of the deceased doctor, where they would come under the control of the court for probate purposes. When there are two or more shareholders, the continuity is further strengthened because the others simply carry on the corporation.

NONTAX DISADVANTAGES

Professional incorporation involves some nontax disadvantages that merit discussion. The key problems arise with respect to the attitudes of many professional people. Some professionals simply want or need their total earnings available to spend immediately, whether it be to achieve or maintain a high scale of living or to make personal investments. They do not want their money tied up and their spending limited by the various corporate programs, regardless of the attractive tax advantages and the benefits to be received upon retirement. This may be particularly true of young professionals whose education has been long and difficult and who want their income for the present, rather than making plans for the distant future.

Another attitude problem that may apply to older professionals is the change of status. Some professional practitioners do not wish to become corporate employees after operating in a partnership or as a solo practice for several years, regardless of the benefits available through incorporating.

Patients may feel that there is an increased distance between them and their dentist when corporate practice is announced and maintained.

A factor that could eventually cause problems is that the practice must actually be carried on in the corporate form. Such corporate formalities as board meetings, minutes, and record-keeping cannot be ignored. If statutory corporate procedures are disregarded, the government may not recognize the enterprise as a corporation. A loose alliance between individual professionals, whereby earnings are channeled through the corporation for tax benefits and then returned, will not suffice. In short, if professionals form a corporation, they must act as a legal entity. Although it may not involve changes in methods of operation, some sacrifices in independence and some additional legal and accounting expenses are required.

CONCLUSION

It is obviously impossible to give a clear answer to the question of whether or not it is advisable for a professional to incorporate. The decision will depend upon many factors, and all of them must be carefully weighed in light of the particular circumstances involved. It may be that in a certain situation nontax considerations may warrant incorporating, even though no tax benefits will be realized. On the whole, however, it clearly appears that the attractiveness of the many tax benefits will be the determining factors. Naturally, tax risks and nontax disadvantages exist and will have to be coped with. However, in light of the ever-increasing taxes on professionals, these hazards should not outweigh the decision to utilize all the legitimate opportunities to minimize the tax burden.

13 Person Identification Through Dentistry

Irvin M. Sopher

IDENTIFICATION OF A DECEASED PERSON

Contemporary advances in forensic odontology permit identification of the person for legal purposes. The law now accepts as positive evidence the identification of a deceased through his or her teeth and the identification of an assailant through his or her bite mark on a victim. Both the practicing dentist and the forensic odontologist are essential for the performance of these two procedures. The dental practitioner is required to have dental records of each patient. Poor dental records or, worse, no dental records at all can stymie the law and prohibit the achievement of justice. Poor scientific investigation by the dental expert in odontology can have the same effect.

The following legal cases are presented to demonstrate, first, how the legal issue requiring dental science can sometimes arise and, second, how a forensic odontologist determines dental facts upon which to establish his or her opinion on the dental identification either of a deceased person or of an assailant.

Determining the Dental Facts

To convict a defendant of murder, the identification of the victim is not a necessary legal requirement. However, to identify the victim is a major factor which can provide "proof beyond a reasonable doubt" that the defendant did indeed commit a murder. Prosecutors strive to prove the identity of a murder victim because it helps them greatly when trying to prove their case against the accused.

The law concerning this problem has been ably stated:

Defendant contends that his guilt was not proven beyond a reasonable doubt inasmuch as the body alleged to have been that of Harvey Weinstein was not proven to have in fact been his body. We disagree.

The argument is advanced that the dental chart comparison made by Dr. Zullo was insufficient to identify the burned body as being that of Harvey Weinstein. Although a question of first impression in this State, it cannot be seriously disputed that a dental structure may constitute a means of identifying a deceased person, otherwise unrecognizable, where there is some dental record of that person with which the structure may be compared. Comparison of dental structures falls within the category of circumstantial evidence and involves the question of weight and credibility, rather than that of competency.

. . .

The charts of Harvey Weinstein's dental structure compiled by Drs. Gelberd and Pallotto between 1957 or 1958 and February 1963, differed from each other in only one minor respect and substantially conformed to the chart made by Dr. Zullo of the dental structure of the burned body. All three charts showed the dental structure to have been missing six specific teeth, three upper and three lower; thirteen specific teeth of the remaining twenty-six were "restored," eight upper and five lower; the "restorations" included three specific crowns in the upper right jaw forming a fixed dental bridge, gold inlay fillings in specific teeth, a specific procelain inlay filling, and the balance of silver inlay fillings in specific teeth. The three charts therefore compared identically, with the exception of a gold inlay filling which Dr. Pallotto testified he inserted in a tooth in February 1963, which tooth the other charts showed as containing a silver inlay filling. It cannot be said that this single, minute discrepancy so affected the credibility of the chart comparison as to have rendered it wholly meaningless as a means of identification. Defendant nevertheless maintains that Dr. Zullo's comparison of the dental charts had no value for identification purposes for the reason that he failed to relate the probabilities upon which he based his opinion that the dental structure which he examined and charted could have been that of Harvey Weinstein only and of no other person. Defendant's position in this regard is based upon an article on dental identification appearing in Forensic Odontology (American Elsevier Pub. Co., 1966, at pp 29–30), which consists of a study conducted by Gosta Gustafson of the dental records of 775 Swedish school children between the ages of ten years and sixteen years; approximately nine per centum of the children surveryed were found to have had identical dental records. However, not only did that study involve persons in their tender years, whereas Harvey Weinstein was a man in early middle age who had undergone considerable dental work during his lifetime, but this was a matter of weight and credibility for the trial judge. Furthermore, on the cross examination of Dr. Zullo, defendant did not attempt to determine what probability existed that the dental structure of the burned body which Dr. Zullo examined was not that of Harvey Weinstein.[1]

The science of determining the dental facts and then basing an opinion regarding the identification of the deceased upon these facts is the work of the forensic odontologist.

Procedures for identifying an unknown body, including dental identification, are based upon a process of comparison, namely, a comparison of known facts, observations, or measurements of the putative (suspected) identity with the postmortem data in hand. The favorable comparison without incompatibility of the antemortem and postmortem data results in the achievement of positive identification. The teeth represent an excellent medium for indentification in that the teeth and dental treatment (such as fillings) are resistant to postmortem change, have been previously registered in life through dental records, and bear varying degrees of specificity as to personal identification.

The antemortem data available for the comparison procedure in dental identification consist of:

1. written dental records from the attending dentist;
2. dental or skull x-rays;
3. casts or models for the suspect dentition;
4. recollection of dentition by dentists or relatives.

Dental x-rays taken during life are especially helpful because they show specific morphologic criteria regarding filling size and shape, parameters of which are readily adaptable to objective comparison with any postmortem x-ray data. In fact, the utilization of such an x-ray comparison may enable specific identification to be based upon the x-ray findings of a single tooth only. Even nondental structures such as the adjacent jawbone pattern on an x-ray may bear enough specificity to result in positive identification.

A basic concept of dental indentification is that no two mouths are truly alike, although this theoretical approach breaks down somewhat when dealing with the extremes of age. Children, especially in areas served by a fluoridated water supply, may have no dental fillings, and, except for age differences, the mouths may be quite similar. In the elderly, where all teeth have been lost and/or dentures are present, the comparison may also be nonspecific depending upon the circumstances. The specificity of dental identification is based upon the existence of 32 adult teeth, each of which possesses five surfaces visible to the eye (as a cube on a table top), therefore providing a total of 160 surfaces per mouth for alteration by cavities (caries) and filling materials. The latter, of course, vary in substance from silver to gold to cement materials to caps of varying design. When one also introduces the loss of certain teeth from this set of 32, the various combinations and permutations of the final dental pattern represent a degree of specificity for one individual which may approach astronomical proportions. In addition, bridgework, partial dentures, and alterations in tooth position such as rotational or drifting changes also may bear certain degrees of specificity.

The greater the number of alterations or abnormalities that exist in any given mouth, the greater are the points for potential comparison in the establishment of a positive identification. The important feature of dental identification is that a positive comparison must bear no incompatibilities, and any inconsistencies must be adequately explained to effect a perfect match between antemortem and postmortem data. The final decision as to correctness or degree of credibility of the identification rests within the judgment and experience of the identification expert after consideration of all the elements and data applicable to the situation.

It is optimal to have the entire jaws available for postmortem examination. On the other hand, as is common in medicolegal cases involving bodily injury and skeletal material, certain cases may reveal a comparable set of nonspecific restoration patterns involving only one or several teeth. In such a circumstance, the expert may be left with an opinion that the postmortem findings are consistent with but not specific for the putative identity in question. The final decision involving such a case will depend upon the specificity inherent in the particular findings and upon the judgment of the investigator. X-ray comparison is most valuable in such an instance. The x-ray may serve to increase greatly the specificity value of the naked-eye findings involving tooth surface and fillings and, hence, to enable a positive identification that is specific for that one person and excludes any other possibilities.

The fact that the dental identification procedure may result in only a *consistent with* conclusion may in itself be a significant contribution. The dental comparison can be utilized in collation with other modes of identification, such as personal effects or anthropologic data, and with the circumstances of disappearance in order to elevate the credibility of the identification.

The common points of comparison utilized in dental identification include the following parameters:

1. number of teeth;
2. presence of fillings, bridgework, dentures, and so forth;
3. decay location;
4. abnormal position or rotation;
5. peculiar shapes of teeth;
6. presence of root canal therapy;
7. jaw bone x-ray patterns;
8. relationship of the bite;
9. oral diseases;
10. occupational changes and socioeconomic pattern of the dentitition;
11. sex and race determination;
12. chronologic age based upon the teeth.

Dental X-ray Comparison

To admit the confession of murder given to the police by an accused, the law first requires other objective evidence that a homicide has been committed. Once this other objective evidence, called the *corpus delicti*, has been admitted into evidence at the trial, the prosecutor can offer the confession for admission into evidence. The dental identification of the murder victim can become this crucial objective evidence. In one case, the state's dental evidence, which identified the remains of two girls, both of whom the accused confessed to having murdered, established the *corpus delicti* corroborating the defendant's confession, thus permitting his confession to be introduced into evidence. In upholding the defendant's conviction for the two murders, the court stated:

> The appellant protests that the court erred both in admitting in evidence an X-ray photograph of the teeth of Rhonda Renee Johnson and in admitting in evidence the testimony of Dr. Edith Meeks, who was Rhonda's dentist. Another skull was found in the bayou close to that of Sharon Shaw. Dr. Meeks identified X-ray photographs that she had made of the teeth of Rhonda Renee Johnson. Dr. Stimpson compared the X-ray photograph with the skull and identified the skull as that of Rhonda Renee Johnson. Both girls, who were friends, had disappeared at the same time. This evidence, of which complaint is made concerning Rhonda Renee Johnson, was blended and closely interwoven with the evidence admitted to show the death of Sharon Shaw and was therefore admissible. . . . This corroborative evidence tended to confirm as true the written and oral statements of the appellant and was also of probative value in showing that Sharon Shaw met her death by criminal means.[2]

The postmortem dental radiograph is used to enhance points of comparison and to disclose certain dental findings that are not visible upon naked-eye examination of the mouth. Such findings commonly include the performance of root canal therapy (endodontics), retained root tips resulting from previous loss of teeth, and the presence of impacted teeth (teeth submerged in the jawbone but not visible in the mouth). The use of x-ray is mandatory for the estimation of chronologic age based upon the degree of root development and/or the status of unerupted teeth. In addition, the postmortem dental x-ray of dental filling materials enables a distinct objective comparison to be made regarding the morphology of the materials compared on the ante-mortem and postmortem x-rays. A comparison of antemortem and postmortem x-rays also enables enumerable concordant points to be established regarding features of tooth morphology such as root curvature as well as the outlines of the internal portions of the tooth such as the root canal and pulp chamber. In additon, the x-ray pattern of the adjacent jawbone may bear certain specific changes. X-ray comparison also enables an analysis of intertooth relationships so as to allow a comparison of angulated teeth. In other instances, the x-ray of the healing or healed socket of a lost tooth may provide an estimate as to the time interval since tooth loss.

When concerned with the size and shape of filling materials within teeth, a comparison of antemortem and postmortem x-rays provides the dimension of depth of the filling material (an observation not visible upon mouth examination by the naked eye) as well as the possible presence of other corrective substances applied to the interior of the tooth and subsequently covered by the filling noted upon external examination. Dental x-ray comparison provides a graphic, objective method for size and shape determination inclusive of the various morphologic irregularities of the filling material.

Identification of a Living Person

The first legal problem in the identification of a suspected person through his or her bite mark is to acquire a sample of the bite mark. Can a person be compelled to provide the law with his or her bite mark? There is no constitutional protection prohibiting the police from com-pelling a person to provide an example of his or her bite mark. The legal procedure for obtaining sample bite marks from a person has been given by one court as follows:

> After the interview with the police officer, defendant was asked if he would provide samples of his fingerprints and body hair. He refused. A search warrant was obtained to secure defendant's fingerprints, body fluids, and a cast of his teeth. He refused to comply with the order. On February 12, the prosecutor told defendant that there was a court order, that he had no right to an attorney, that he had no right to refuse

to comply with the order, and that such refusal could be used against him as evidence in court. Defendant still refused to comply.

On February 12, defendant was brought before the judge who had signed the search warrant. Defendant did not request an attorney, but indicated that "he or some member of the family were in the process of arranging for him to be represented by counsel." The judge ordered defendant to comply. Defendant refused and was brought back to the court that day. He was again ordered to obey the court order and told that if he did not, he could be found in contempt of court and jailed until he did comply, and that his refusal "could be used against him in a trial." Defendant refused to comply and was jailed. On March 20, he was again brought before the court, which was advised that he was now willing to comply with the court order.

On March 20, a dentist made impressions of defendant's upper and lower teeth — later introduced into evidence. After the impressions were made, and defendant had submitted to the other tests, he was released and exonerated from contempt. The prosecutor told the detectives that the most promising area of further investigation was to exhume the victim's body and to obtain a cast of the bite mark on her nose.[3]

The next legal problem arises over whether the identification of a person through a comparison of his sample bite mark with the bite mark impression found on the victim is scientifically reliable. A valuable legal discussion was set forth by the same court:

The autopsy of the victim has been performed on February 4, and the body buried in Dallas, Texas, on February 7. On March 25, it was exhumed and impressions of the wound on the victim's nose were made.

The central issue in this case is the admissibility of expert testimony — supported by many exhibits — that the bite on the victim's nose was made by the defendant's teeth.

Three dentists testified on behalf of prosecution. One dentist testified on behalf of defendant. The three prosecution experts were: Reidar Sognnaes, a dentist and professor at UCLA medicine school; Gerald Vale, a dentist and lawyer and chief of forensic dentistry with the Los Angeles Coroner's office; and Gerald Felando, a dentist in private practice. The project of identifying the teeth which made the bite on the victim was conducted in part as a joint effort. Each of the three experts used somewhat different analytic techniques. Defendant did not testify.

Discussion

A. *The Expert Evidence*
The relevance of the expert testimony turned on two postulates: first, that, as a general rule, it is possible to identify a person from his dentition; second, that in this particular case there was enough

evidence of a "match" between defendant's dentition and the victim's wounds to enable experts to make such an identification, and, thereby, to eliminate others as suspects.

.   .   .

The real dispute on admissibility centers on the second of these premises. Defendant concedes that the science — or art — of identifying persons through their teeth is, as such, well established. Each of the three prosecution experts and even defendant's own expert had performed such identifications. While the field is relatively new and experts do not agree on the exact number of similarities necessary to made a positive identification, the prosecution experts stressed the obvious point that it is not the number of similarities, but their quality which is most helpful. Further, this being a case involving identification by bite marks, rather than by comparing a dentiton with two-dimensional X-rays and charts, the experts were able to use a virtually unprecedented three-dimensional approach.

What defendant does attack is the admissibility of the prosecution evidence insofar as it rests on the experts' asserted ability to prove identity from similarities between bite marks and the dentition of a person suspected of having made those marks.

Concededly, there is no established science of identifying persons from bite marks as distinguished from, say, dental records and X-rays. Indeed, the testimony of the three prosecution experts reflects their enthusiastic response to a rare opportunity to develop or extend forensic dentistry into the area of bite mark identification.

.   .   .

What is significantly different about the evidence in this case is this: the trier of fact, here the court, was shown models, photographs, X-rays and dozens of slides of the victim's wounds and defendant's teeth. It could see what we have seen in reviewing the exhibits to determine the admissibility of the evidence. First, for example, the extent to which the appearance of the wounds changes between the time that the autopsy was performed and the time that the body was exhumed in Dallas. Second, the extent to which the purported bite marks appear to conform generally to obvious irregularities in defendant's teeth. Thus the basic data on which the experts based their conclusions were verifiable by the court. Further, in making their painstaking comparisons and reaching their conclusions, the experts did not rely on untested methods, unproven hypotheses, intuition or revelation. Rather, they applied scientifically and professionally established techniques — X-rays, models, microscopy, photography — to the solution of a particular problem which, though novel, was well within the capability of those techniques. In short, in admitting the evidence, the court did not have to sacrifice its independence and common sense in evaluating it.

The state of the art was summed up by Dr. Sognnaes: "There have been cases where bite marks have been identified in various inure substances or, in theory, for example, a piece of chocolate found on a desk where the crime was committed or banana or marzipan or apples or even wood.

"In the case of bite marks in skin, most of the ones that have been in the literature have been on the softer portions of the body, notable in sex crimes related to the female breasts. And here, of course, there is a very soft underbase and consequently the bite marks are not very deep.

"In this particular case,...we do have a third dimension to these marks, that they are very deep indeed, which makes the comparison with the dentition that can make the bite marks much more sufficient.

"From all I have read in literature and discuss[ed] now with colleagues...this particular case will be recorded as one of the most definitive and distinct and deepest bite marks on record in human skin."

None of the prosecution experts specifically identified the other tooth bite cases. There was no evidence of systematic, orderly experimentation in the area. Moreover, in this particular case, there was the further difficulty that although the victim died on February 3, casts of her nose were not taken until March 25, after an autopsy had been performed and she had been embalmed, buried, and exhumed.

. . .

The court pointed out that if it "was making its findings based just on the bite mark as it compared to...the defendant's dentition, I am not sure that there perhaps would not be a reasonable doubt. However, taking that bit of evidence and giving it the weight to which I felt it was entitled and perhaps not in as refined a manner as the experts for the People would have liked the trier of fact to find, but in a more gross manner, I still feel that it was helpful plus all of the other evidence that was in the record here pointing to the defendant."

The trial court properly admitted the expert evidence.[4]

With such legal decision now available, it behooves lawyers and dentists to be fully aware of the scientific procedures necessary to obtain the bite mark exemplar from the suspect and to compare scientifically the two bite marks for identification of the assailant.

As a general statement, the bite mark analysis involves a comparison of a photographic reconstruction of the bitten area (subject or object) with the dental models of a suspect. Although different methods have been utilized to accomplish such a comparison, the common basic concept has been to delineate the pressure-inducing surfaces of the suspect models and to record these surfaces in such a manner that they may be superimposed or compared with the photograph of the bite mark upon the body, foodstuff, or other bitten substance at the scene of a crime.

The procedural aspects of bite mark analysis are as follows.

Examination of the Bite Mark on the Victim

Due to possible postmortem changes that may alter a bite mark injury, the registration of the bite mark (as by photograph) should begin as soon as possible following recognition of injury. Nevertheless, the passage of time in itself does not, by any means, negate the validity of any particular bite mark comparison.

A. Salivary Secretor Substance Retrieval Because approximately 80% of persons secrete protein antigenic complexes comparable to their A, B, or O blood groupings in their saliva, an attempt should be made to detect the presence of such secretor substance in the bitten area. The detection of salivary secretory antigens may further implicate or eliminate a particular suspect in any given case. The test for secretory antigens is performed by the serology section of the crime laboratory.

The bite-mark saliva sample is acquired by swabbing the involved area in concentric fashion, using a sterile cotton swab moistened with saline solution. The examiner should not handle the cotton end of the swab because he or she may contaminate it with sweat or skin secretion. The swab should then be placed in a clean, dry vial for transmission to the laboratory. The presence of dried saliva on the bitten area does not necessarily obviate the detection of secretory substance. In addition to the bite-mark area swab, a control swab, used in a similar fashion, should be applied to an unbitten skin surface of the victim. In addition, an intraoral saliva sample and blood sample of the victim should also be obtained to determine the secretor status and blood type of the decedent.

Salivary secretor substance swabs should be effected at the very outset of the bite mark examination procedure, prior to the removal of clothing and certainly before any washing or wiping of the body surfaces. Of course, any blood contamination of the saliva swab may introduce error in the results.

The analysis of salivary secretor substance from a bite-mark case usually results in an absence of any detectable secretory substance. This is a result of the current methodology available for such determinations; nevertheless, the test should be performed in every bite-mark case. If the bite mark swabs reveal an absence of detectable secretory substance, two possibilities exist — namely, the secretory substance is not detectable postmortem or the biter is a nonsecretor. If the swabs reveal a secretory type that is different from that of the decedent, the implication is that the biter was a secretor of the type identified. On the other hand, if the bite mark and control swabs disclose similar A, B, or O secretory typing for both the victim and the bite-mark area, no conclusions can be established.

B. Registration of the Bite Mark This is accomplished by one or both of the following methods: (1) the photographic method, or (2) the impression method. Both methods use models of the suspect dentition for comparison with the recorded bite mark. Registration of the bite mark is thereby accomplished by means of a photographic picture or the application of a rubber base or silicone impression material upon the bitten area. Such an impression of the bitten area is then converted to a model of the bite mark by utilizing a model substance such as plaster of paris. In this manner. the morphology and measurements of the bite mark are recorded and are suitable then for objective comparison.

The photographic registration of the bite mark should be accomplished prior to the performance of the autopsy examination and following the secretor substance swabs. The bite mark must be photographed prior to excision from the body due to dimensional changes which result from release of skin tension if the bite mark is excised. The photograph must include a rigid millimeter rule positioned next to the bite mark and upon the plane of the bite mark. The ruler is essential because the eventual comparison of the bite mark with suspect models will be made using a life-sized reproduction of the bite mark negative to enable direct comparison by measurement with the pressure-inducing areas of the suspect models. Both black and white as well as color photography should be employed in the registration of the bite mark.

If the bite mark is located upon convex surface, such as the breast or arm, it is suggested that a separate photograph of each arch pattern be taken because a single photograph may result in distortion caused by subject curvature. The film plane should be parallel to the plane of the bitten surface and, similarly, the plane of the adjacent ruler.

Photographic registration of the bite mark is a must; however, the impression of a bite mark applies only if tooth indentations are present upon the bitten skin surface. The impression method, therefore, provides a three-dimensional model with the inclusion of depth for comparison with the suspect dentition.

C. Preservation of the Bitten Tissue The anatomic area of the bite mark should be removed and preserved as evidence or for further examination. This should be done only after swab examination and registration of the bite mark. The bitten area should be excised, exercising wide latitudes of tissue resection to minimize specimen distortion caused by release of tissue tension. The bite-mark tissue should be retained in formalin solution, cognizant of the fact that a 10% to 20% shrinkage of the tissue will occur.

D. Histologic Examination Once the bite-mark tissue is fixed and suitable for histologic examination, a histologic section of a segment of the bite-mark injury should be examined microscopically by the pathologist to establish an estimate of the time of injury relative to the time of death.

E. Evaluation of Self-Biting If the bite mark upon the victim is in an anatomic location consistent with self-biting, dental impressions should be made of the decedent's dentition for evaluation of the possibility that the deceased had bitten himself (as when the arm may be forced into the mouth). In addition, if there is evidence to indicate that an assailant may have been bitten by the victim, the registration of the decedent's dentition may enable a comparison with the bite mark on the assailant.

Registration of Bite Marks from Objects Other than the Body

Bite marks inflicted upon foodstuff or other substances at the scene of the crime also provide grist for the mill of the forensic dentist. The dentist should keep in mind that the police tool-mark examination laboratory can also be of great assistance in such a case because the techniques employed are similar to those utilized in tool-mark comparison studies. A plaster of paris or rubber base impression should be made of the bitten foodstuff or object and a model of the original then constructed. A photographic comparison of the bitten object may then be made with the suspect dentition.

Registration of the Suspect's Dentition

Once registration of the bite mark has been completed, the analyst focuses his attention upon the biter. To obtain the models of a suspect's teeth for subsequent comparison with the bite-mark registration, the analyst should have a court order issued by a governing judge or a legal consent form signed by the suspect giving permission to perform the necessary medicolegal examination. Either of the above should be accomplished prior to examination because: (1) the dentist may be liable for assault upon the suspect if voluntary permission has not been granted in the absence of a court order; and (2) evidence of this nature may not be admitted at trial unless either of the above has been obtained prior to the retrieval of data.

Examination of the suspect includes a total charting of the dentition as well as photographs of the dentition. Saliva from the suspect must also be obtained for secretory antigen analysis, and a blood sample is necessary to establish the suspect blood type. The registration of the suspect's dentition utilizes a dental impression material with subsequent stone models constructed from same.

The bite characteristics of the suspected dental models are then transferred to a medium that is suitable for comparison with the photograph or model of the actual bite mark. The objective is to derive a reproduction of the biting or pressure-inducing surfaces of the suspect models and to compare the measurements and shape of the biting surfaces with the corresponding bite-mark areas of the bitten object. The writer prefers to transfer the suspect bite to a wax medium and have subsequent photographs taken of the wax medium and superimposed upon the actual bite mark. It is imperative that all photographs of the suspect bite pattern be taken or enlarged so that they are life sized and therefore suitable for direct comparison with the photographs of the actual bite mark.

Bite-Mark Comparison

In the bite-mark comparison, the analyst must always be aware that numerous variables exist in the imprint pattern of teeth biting human skin. The relative plasticity of skin, unlike a wax bite, may result in variable degrees of distortion caused by pressures of biting, sucking action, or the actual anatomic position of the bitten part of the body at the time that the bite was inflicted. The bite-mark injury observed on the human body may present as an abrasion (skin scrape), a contusion (bruise of the skin), or a laceration (tear of the skin). In addition, accessory abrasions or contusions may occur on the skin as a result of the mechanics of the bite when inflicted. Bite marks inflicted through clothing tend to reduce the degree of force exerted on the tissues and may be responsible for the absence of particular tooth injuries.

The dental expert is faced with two questions regarding the bite-mark comparison:

1. Can the suspect be excluded from consideration as having produced the bite mark?
2. If the suspect cannot be excluded, how specific are the points of comparison leading to the conclusion that the suspect alone could have produced the bite mark?

Of these two questions, the first is the easiest to answer and represents a vital contribution to the total case investigation because the comparison may confirm guilt or redirect a search for the suspect in question.

The second question raised above, namely, the specificity of the comparison, encompasses the most difficult and controversial area within the realm of forensic dentistry. In essence, the problem is whether the work is specific for the suspect alone to the exclusion of all other individuals. Classified bite-mark characteristics on large segments of the population are unavailable; therefore, the analyst must depend upon his objective and subjective interpretation of the comparison. The forensic dentist enumerates points of comparison between the bite mark and the suspect models in an effort to enhance the specificity of the comparison procedure. The number of points of comparison would depend upon the circumstances of the bite mark. Such circumstances include the quality of the mark itself, the presence or absence of possible distortion induced by postmortem or positional change, and the peculiarities of the mark as they pertain to the dentition of the suspect. The presence of multiple points of comparison in the absence of inconsistencies or incompatibilities enables a more valid conclusion to be derived regarding any given subject.

Depending upon the particular bite mark under consideration, an analysis revealing few measurable specific points of comparison may lead to a conclusion that the bite-mark injury is consistent with the particular suspect. On the other hand, a bite-mark case comparison may disclose even further degrees of specificity, so that an opinion may be expressed with reasonable certainty that the mark is extremely consistent with, if not specific solely for, the suspect in question. The writer strongly feels that the strength of the evidence in any particular bite-mark comparison must be indicated at trial. Each case, depending upon the comparison results, should be indicated as weak, strong, or extremely strong in discriminatory evidence against the suspect in question.

SUMMARY

In summary, bite-mark comparison results may represent varying degrees of incriminating evidence that must be so designated by the dental expert so the court or jury can apply the weight of the evidence in proper perspective to the total circumstances surrounding the trial. Identification of persons both living and dead is accelerating rapidly as forensic odontology matures. The administration of justice, criminal and civil, will come to rely more and more on the dental expert to resolve the vital issue of the true identification of persons.

REFERENCES

1. *People v. Mattox*, 96 Ill App 2d 148; 237 NE 2d 845 (1968).
2. *Self v. State*, 513 SW 2d 832 (1974).
3. *People v. Marx*, 54 CA 3rd 100; 126 Cal R 350 (1975).
4. Id. pp. 106–112.

14 Dispensing Drugs in Dental Practice

Oliver C. Schroeder, Jr.
Burton R. Pollack

Substances given to a patient to alter normal neurologic and physiologic functions are an integral and pervasive aspect of dental treatment. They are also emerging as a major legal concern. There are few procedures that do not require the use of a drug at some stage. The use is self-evident to the practitioner. Unfortunately, the legal aspects and ramifications arising from the purchase, storage, prescription, dispensation, and administration of drugs may not be as self-evident. The potential for the use of drugs was recognized in Roman times; since the codification of law, society has acknowledged the potential harm that could result from the intentional or negligent administration of a drug. With the industrialization and mass marketing of drugs, national and local governments have created laws designed to ensure the purity and safety of drugs while allowing for the development of new substances and techniques in treating illness. Most states and the federal government have regulatory statutes that control varying aspects of drug use.

Practitioners should determine the controls that are imposed upon them by the state in which they practice. The dental society can play an important role in this information process by acting as a legal clearinghouse for its members. It is incumbent upon the practitioner or future practitioner to be cognizant of the mandated restrictions in order to avoid both criminal and civil liability.

As seen previously, dentists may become legally liable to their patients or to the patients' families under wrongful death statutes if the dentist violates a standard of care and if death results. Liability may be established under the theory of tortious assault. If the practitioner fails to obtain an informed consert from the patient, the dentist has no right to invade the patient's body. Liability may also arise through a negligence action based upon the breach of a duty of care and competence. In many jurisdictions, a prior adjudication of criminal liability may be used as evidence of negligence in a subsequent civil suit. The dangerous nature of drugs has required the establishment of strong criminal and civil sanctions against their misuse. The practitioner must recognize the philosophical reasons behind the law and act with a standard of care and professionalism that will be above legal reproach.

CRIMINAL LIABILITY

The public has a strong interest in creating and maintaining independent controls on drugs and the processes and systems by which information reaches the ultimate consumer. Because of this strong concern, state and federal legislatures have attempted to create regulatory schemes that meet constitutional requirements and do not restrictively prevent the administration of health care. In spite of strict requirements and controls upon individuals, the courts have upheld drug statutes as valid. Because of the government's compelling interest to protect the public in an area with maximum potential for abuse, the courts are reluctant to strike down provisions of drug laws unless they are "patently offensive" to the rights of the individual.

Most jurisdictions regulate drugs according to their potential for abuse. Substances that have a great potential for abuse are not distributed freely and can be obtained only by the recommendation of and prescription from one who is trained in pharmacology. Regulation depends upon a compound's inherent strength and properties.

Uniform Controlled Substances Act States that have adopted the Uniform Controlled Substances Act (UCSA) have designated which substances are controlled and have further categorized them according to their medical utility and potential for abuse and harm. There are five schedules representing gradations in the dominant factors. Those drugs with the least utility and greatest potential for abuse and harm are placed in schedule I. The strongest controls are afforded to schedule I, and the weakest controls imposed in schedule V. The tests for the schedules are as follows:

I High potential for abuse.
— No accepted medical use in treatment in the United States, or lacks accepted safety for use in treatment under medical supervision.

II High potential for abuse.
— Currently accepted for medical use in the United States.
— Abuse of the substance may lead to severe psychic or physical dependence.

III Potential for abuse less than substances listed in schedules I and II.
— Currently accepted for medical use in United States.
— Abuse of the substance may lead to moderate or low physical or high psychologic dependence.

IV Potential for abuse low as compared to schedule III substances.
— Currently accepted for medical use in United States.
— Abuse of substance may lead to limited physical dependence relative to controlled substances in schedule III.

V Potential for abuse low as compared to schedule IV substances.
— Currently accepted for medical use in United States.
— Low abuse potential and lowest dependence potential.

Under the UCSA, schedule I drugs are prohibited, and substances falling into schedules II through V may be obtained only by prescription. To prescribe such substances, a practitioner (including a dentist) must register with the appropriate authority designated in a state's act. If the dentist fails to register, he or she will be considered an illegal dealer in controlled substances and little better in the eyes of the law than a "pusher." Distribution is legal only after the state recognizes the validity of the distribution of controlled substances under the rationale of medical treatment.

In addition to the licensing requirement, the UCSA requires the practitioner to maintain records of any controlled substance he or she purchases, receives, or dispenses. The UCSA allows the state director to promulgate regulations that goven the form, content, and preservation of the dentist's records. The UCSA also states that these records are to be available and open to inspection by enforcement officers. Naturally, under the unreasonable search limitations of the fourth amendment, the inspection is limited to items falling within the scope of the act. States attempt to control abuse by practitioners who have access to controlled substances through detailed inventory requirements. Failure to meet the requirements would serve to create a presumption of illegality; that is, that the substances have been diverted for reasons that are not genuinely medical. Rebutting the presumption is risky, costly, and may ultimately fail, resulting in criminal liability.

The UCSA also requires that before administering, dispensing, or prescribing a controlled substance in schedules II, III, or IV, the practitioner must obtain an original physical examination of the person for whom the substance is intended. To reduce potential injury to the patient, the language of the statute imposes an affirmative duty upon the practitioner to make sure the patient has had a physical examination before taking a controlled substance. A problem exists for the practitioner in interpreting "original physical examination." It is unclear whether the phrase requires an examination upon the commencement of the dentist-patient relationship, a physical before any course of treatment is commenced, or an examination within a time period reasonably calculated to expose any condition that would endanger the patient upon interaction with a controlled substance. A second ambiguity concerns the scope of the examination, that is, whether it should be limited to disclosing foreseeable conditions that particular type of drug would affect, such as an examination of the cardiovascular system in preparation for the administration of epinephrine. Despite the section's ambiguity, which could be clarified by administrative regulation, it is clear that dentists in states that have adopted the UCSA are required to have not only a medical history of the patient but also a report of a recent medical examination before administering controlled substances. Failure to comply with this requirement may result in liability extending beyond the criminal penalties.

States that have not adopted the UCSA vary widely in their approach to the control of drugs as it relates to the practitioner. Features common to most are registration and licensing requirements, inventories, storage requirements, and a good faith requirement that the substance is being administered for bona fide medical reasons.

Because the state's dominant interest is in the protection of the drug consumer, practitioners should assume strict interpretive stances when ascertaining their rights and duties in their jurisdictions. Violations of the statutes are criminal offenses that may range in severity from regulatory violations to misdemeanors or felonies. In many states, a violation threatens the licensed status of the dentist and may result in a complete destruction of the practitioner's professional future. The practitioner has an absolute duty to comply with the statutory requirements, and any diversion from that duty invites criminal sanction. It is essential that dentists take positive notice of the duties required of them by state statute.

UPDATE ON THE PRESCRIBING OF
CONTROLLED SUBSTANCES BY DENTISTS

A review by the author (BRP) of the actions taken by the Office of Professional Discipline in New York against the licensing of dentists during the past several years indicates that one of the frequent grounds for revocation or suspension is based upon violations of the controlled substances laws of the state. To comply with the law, the person for whom the drug is administered or prescribed must be a patient, and the condition for which it is administered or prescribed must relate to the dental treatment received by the patient:

> 1. No substance for which an official New York state prescription is required may be prescribed by a practitioner except on an official New York state prescription, and *in good faith and in the course of his professional practice only.*[1]

Federal Regulations The dentist should also be aware of federal regulations that overlap and supercede state statutes affecting the ordering, receipt, storage, dispensation, and administration of controlled substances. There are two acts that affect the practitioner: the Federal Drug Act and the Food, Drug, and Cosmetic Act. The first act is directed toward a comprehensive effort to regulate and prevent dangerous drugs from being diverted from legitimate pipelines into illegal markets. It is premised upon a systems analysis of the legitimate pipeline. Drugs traveling within the pipeline are easy to control through strict inventory procedures at those juctions where diversion is possible: the manufacturer, shipper, wholesaler, distributor, retailer, and health practitioner. By enforcing strict registration and accounting procedures, the enforcement agencies can better control the diversion into illegal markets. Note that the practitioner is included in this pipeline and is subject to regulation.

If the practitioner is authorized to receive and dispense controlled substances by the state in which he or she practices, then, as a matter of right, the practitioner may receive and dispense controlled substances. In *Linder v. United States*, 268 US5 (1925), the US Supreme Court held that the federal government had no valid interest in or right to regulate medical practices in a state if there was existing state regulation. Therefore, if a dentist is authorized by state law to receive and dispense substances covered in the Federal Drug Act, he or she is automatically entitled to registration under the Federal Act.

The Food, Drug, and Cosmetic Act is primarily concerned with the purity and safety of drugs. The scope of the act encompasses manufacturers and, to a limited extent, practitioners. The thrust of the regulations is to prevent impure or improperly labeled drugs from being consumed.

Drugs are one of the most heavily regulated items in our society. Federal and state regulation of drugs is a manifestation of governmental concern about the prevention of abuse and injury caused by unsafe or impure substances. The dentist's responsibility is to prevent diversion of controlled substances into markets that are not bona fide medical areas. It is essential that practitioners be aware of these regulations, because criminal liability can be imposed for noncompliance. Although cumbersome and time-consuming, the various regulations are designed to aid and to protect the public from the dangers inherent in most drugs and are vital to the safety and health of the community. Changes in these regulations can be effected through meaningful input by the professions to streamline the existing schemes.

CIVIL LIABILITY

The administration of drugs to a patient is part of the dental process. The patient relies upon the dentist's expertise to prescribe and administer drugs that will aid dental health. As in other aspects of dentistry, the dentist's duty is to use that degree of skill that is reasonable within the practicing community. Tort liability arises if the dentist is negligent or assaults or invades without consent of the patient. The practitioner faces the problems of determining the needs of the patient, the effectiveness and efficiency of particular substances, the risks of toxicity, and the ultimate benefit to the patient.

A factual hypothesis will aid in discussing legal issues. Mr T is in need of an extraction because a second mandibular molar is acutely abscessed. He is a walk-in patient who indicates in his history that he is allergic to penicillin. He has been undergoing psychotherapy and also suffers from hypertension.

In planning the treatment, there are several legal considerations. First, is Mr T of sufficient age to consent to a procedure; that is, is he 18 years or older or an emancipated person under 18 years, either by being married or living away from his family? Second, is he competent to give consent, demonstrating a rational and reasonable mind and not known to be under a court determination of being unable to care for himself? If the patient is not of legal age or mentally competent, the dentist, for legal protection, should contact the parent or guardian before proceeding, unless a severe emergency exists that demands immediate attention to safeguard the patient's life or health.

Assuming competence to consent, the next step is to determine the operative procedure, taking into account the patient's physical and psychological condition. What type of anesthetic should be administered? Naturally, the first consideration is medical. In determining this, the dentist quite logically relies on his or her training and practices accepted in the community. Failure to do so that results in an injury to the patient may result in a negligence lawsuit. The dentist is expected to know about the toxic qualities of the drug and the potential for both minor and serious side effects. If the dentist administers a drug to Mr T that is not accepted as a reasonable practice by his or her professional peers, the dentist will be liable for negligence. If the administration of the drug is proper among the existing practices, but the dentist has failed to apprise Mr T of the risks, the dentist may be guilty of tortious assault for not procuring Mr T's informed consent before administering the drug.

Informed consent is a tricky issue, and an examination of case law from jurisdiction to jurisdiction reveals no precise or absolute standard regarding the quantum of information to be supplied to the patient to assure that he or she is sufficiently aware of the risks to give an intelligent consent (see chapter 10). All drugs are toxic in some concentration. As all dentists know, the degree of toxicity that results in major or minor injurious side effects varies from person to person. Assuming that the particular dosage is reasonable, does the dentist have to warn the patient about the risks of toxicity and detail the potential side effects? The courts have generally held that foreseeable risks must be explained. The gray area is in defining what is foreseeable. Common, minor, side effects such as dizziness, nausea, and drowsiness, require warning. However, the certainty stops at that point. Does the dentist have to warn the patient of more dangerous but less frequent contraindications?

Going back to Mr T, suppose the extraction was performed and Mr T was suffering from a severe infection. The dentist reasonably believes that the administration of chloramphenicol is indicated. This dosage will be for a short duration and of low intensity. Must the dentist warn Mr T that the treatment presents a risk of aplastic anemia and subsequent leukemia? Although there is no concrete standard, the trend seems to require disclosure to the patient of possible irreversible side effects. While this may be detrimental to treatment by causing the patient to refuse treatment, it may be beneficial in the long run by forcing the dentist to look for less risky alternatives and by ensuring that the patient is given full opportunity to understand the risks and determine his or her physical destiny.

The issue of when to disclose possible allergic and idiosyncratic reactions is similar to that of when to disclose major or irreversible adverse side effects. The decision to disclose a potential allergic reaction depends on the foreseeability of the reaction. If the dentist were to propose the use of a sulfa drug for Mr T, an allergic reaction is quite foreseeable and disclosure would be required. When there are no indications that an allergic reaction might occur in this particular patient and the incidence of such a reaction is generally very low, the dentist need not disclose the negligible risk. He should disclose the statistical probability of an allergic reaction if the statistics indicate that the reaction is foreseeable. Idiosyncratic reactions are not predictable, not foreseeable, and, logically, not subject to disclosure.

There is no precise formula that may be applied to determine the threshold at which consent becomes informed. The courts have indicated that particular factors are important in determining if the consent is valid: whether the drug is experimental, whether it is widely applied in the particular treatment, the physical and psychological condition of the patients, the degree of risk, the need for treatment, the feasibility of using other drugs, and the nature of the information contained in the package inserts.

Package inserts that accompany most drugs are admissible into evidence for a variety of purposes. If, for example, an insert has a warning section advising the dentist not to utilize a particular substance for some type of treatment because of a potential for serious side effects, and, contrary to such warning, the dentist utilizes the drug, the package insert may be used as legal evidence to show that the risks were foreseeable and that administration of the medication was negligent.[2] If the practitioner can show that the practice is accepted, he may be able to avoid liability. The package insert may establish a prima facie duty of care, but if an accepted exception in the daily practice of dentistry is proven and the treatment is shown to be reasonable, liability will not arise.

Package inserts create a strong presumption of what is the proper standard of dental care. They are the result of intensive research and testing programs and are required by the federal Food and Drug Administration. It is assumed by the lay public and many members of the legal system that when a manufacturer limits the use of its product, there is validity to the claim that a use in violation of such instructions is negligent. Thus, it is important that a practitioner be aware of the limits imposed by the drug manufacturer. If its tolerances are not observed, a dentist must be prepared to justify the deviation as reasonable. Package inserts are insufficient in themselves to raise a presumption of negligence; however, they do create a strong presumption of what is reasonable and they increase the difficulty of rebutting a presumption of negligence.

Informed consent is a difficult area when dealing with drugs

160

because of the uncertainty of reaction that accompanies their use. Negligence is also a difficult issue, but it is determined by the accepted community practice standard. The doctrine of *res ipsa loquitur* is strong in the area of drug-related accidents, but the doctrine is applied primarily to grossly negligent acts, such as prescribing or administering the wrong drugs. The tough issues arise in the more exotic situations where a treatment is new or is not widely used, or where an adverse reaction causes injury and the reaction was not really expected. If dentists are properly informed about available drugs and their properties, the condition of the patient, and the potential risks, they can avoid liability.

The risk of liability in drug injuries may be greater than in nondrug procedures because of their complexity and potentially devastating capabilities. The public is wary of drug usage and is unable in many instances to comprehend the difficulty of protecting a patient from harmful adverse reactions. Dentists should inform patients of the foreseeable risks of a particular drug and take every precaution to assure that the use of a drug is accepted by their peers as a reasonable procedure

Through control programs and testing requirements, drugs are reasonably predictable in their effect. If properly used, they are not likely to cause injury. The legal system has not imposed criminal and civil standards on dentists in the administration of drugs to burden or encumber the practitioner, but rather to protect the patient.

REFERENCES

1. New York Public Health Law, Article 33, § 3332.
2. *Sanzari v. Rosenfeld*, 34 NJ 128, 167 A2d 625.

15 Contemporary Legal Issues Confronting Dentistry

Oliver C. Schroeder, Jr.
Burton R. Pollack

Editor's Note: This chapter was written by Oliver C. Schroeder, Jr, for the first edition, which was published in 1980. Because of his incisive analysis of the issues facing dentistry, and the events that took place since his writing and are currently taking place, it was decided to leave this chapter essentially intact (the previous section on Dispensing Drugs now appears as chapter 14) and to simply add updates following each section. The only substantive material added, which few people in the late 1970s anticipated would present major problems for the dental profession, concerns the great exacerbation of the dental malpractice crisis and attempts by hygienists to alter their legal relationship with dentists, thus moving in the direction of some form of independent practice.

The dynamics of modern professional practice — law, medicine, or dentistry — have generated profound problems for each practitioner as well as for each profession. A selection of several crucial issues will suffice to demonstrate the variety and the importance of the problems facing today's dentists. Five issues that will be discussed are the malpractice dilemma, professional unionization, the dentist *v* the denturist, the financing of complete dental care, and the hygienists *v* the dentist. Another issue, the dispensing of drugs, is discussed in detail in chapter 14.

THE MALPRACTICE DILEMMA

Several chapters in this volume have discussed the malpractice issue. The materials on torts, contracts, malpractice laws, and malpractice insurance have all contributed to the knowledge of how the professional malpractice issue is handled today. It is handled poorly.

Eighteenth-century common law concepts and principles are being utilized to resolve a twentieth-century health problem. Both lawyers and dentists have recognized that fact. What are we doing wrong?

We are emphasizing in the law the resolution of problems arising from bad dental care after the patient has suffered poor dental health. We should emphasize in law the prevention of poor dental care before it has been practiced.

We are emphasizing in law the payment of money to replace the dental health and well-being destroyed by poor dental care. We should emphasize in law the denial of the right of the inadequate dental practitioner to practice dentistry so that dental health well-being in the patient will not be destroyed in the first place.

We continue to emphasize in law centuries-old procedures of jury trials to resolve highly scientific and technological issues. However, the issue of whether the dentist did or did not commit an act of malpractice is generally not susceptible to a simple yes or no decision. In matters of dental health, the importance of "maybe" should not be underestimated. We should emphasize in law the harmonizing of conflicting scientific and technological issues through mediation or arbitration of the dental malpractice problem rather than through the absolute judgment rendered by a jury verdict.

The legal profession is concerned about the health malpractice dilemma confronting Americans. The American Bar Association (ABA) authorized its House of Delegates in February 1975 to establish a Commission on Medical Professional Liability. In August 1976, that Commission submitted its interim report to the House of Delegates.[1] While medical malpractice was the primary stimulus for the Commission, dental malpractice issues were a fortiori, included because, as the Commission recognized early, the whole issue is one of health.

The work of the Commission can best be understood by examining the creation of its subcommittees and the delineation of its guidelines. Subcommittees were established to deal with each of the following issues:

1. standards of care to be applied in resolving medical malpractice disputes;
2. proposed tort law changes;
3. use of arbitration or panels;
4. innovative alternatives to the resolution of malpractice problems;
5. insurance issues;
6. prevention of adverse medical incidents;
7. lawyers' professional responsibilities.

Guidelines for deliberations included:

1. that the needs of patients are of paramount inportance, and that the deliberations and recommendations of the Commission should always reflect this priority;
2. that the Commission's primary role is to search for the underlying causes of the medical malpractice crisis and to seek long-term solutions;
3. that a necessary ingredient in any solution is cooperative effort among the legal profession, the medical professions, and the insurance industry.

Immediate attention had to be given to the tort law of malpractice. Significant recommendations were:

1. Collateral payments received by or benefiting the patient (whether from government payments, individually purchased insurance, employment related insurance, or gratuitous benefits) should be deducted from the judgment amount in a malpractice action.
2. Medical societies should establish pools from which plaintiffs' and defendants' counsels can obtain expert consultants.
3. Pleadings should be eliminated on malpractice issues. Patients should not be allowed to ask for a specific total dollar amount in their lawsuit, since such figures are rarely if ever a true statement of possible damages.
4. Punitive damages should not be allowed in malpractice actions.
5. Pretrial exchange of experts' reports should be mandatory.
6. Every state should provide statutory authority to permit itemized verdicts to be used at the discretion of the trial judge, whereby the jury sets forth specific sums for each item claimed as a damage item.
7. Every state should provide statutory authority to permit the payment of damages in periodic installments at the discretion of the trial judge.
8. A decreasing maximum contingent fee schedule for the lawyer should be set by court order in each state.
9. Each state should have a two year statute of limitations with exceptions for later discovery of malpractice issues and for minors' claims (up to age 8, not age 18).
10. There should be no ceiling on recovery for economic loss,

but the Commission is still studying whether to recommend
a ceiling on recovery for pain and suffering.

The financial impact of these recommendations on the malpractice
insurance premium is tenuous, except for the recommendation which
would require that the jury verdict be reduced by the same amount as
the collateral payments received by the patient from the sources listed.
It was estimated that a 10% to 20% premium reduction could occur if
this recommendation were adopted. Others have suggested that
periodic payment of malpractice verdicts and the shorter statute of
limitations could also reduce the malpractice insurance premiums. In
actuality, tinkering with the tort law would not appear to provide an
ultimate answer.

Of greater importance is the role of the lawyer in the health
malpractice lawsuit. Frivolous lawsuits brought by attorneys who
display careless or fraudulent professional performances allegedly exist.
The Commission is wisely concentrating on this subissue. Many lawyers
are also allegedly incompetent to handle such health science and
technology cases, which could be a serious impediment to intelligent
resolution of a patient's claim. Delay and harassment techniques by
lawyers and countersuits by health practitioners based on malicious
prosecution are two other areas of great interest to the Commission.

The Commission also seeks a "cheaper, faster, less abrasive"
procedure to resolve the malpractice lawsuit. Civil procedure to resolve
the malpractice lawsuit in trial court has serious disadvantages and
appears to be wholly inadequate to provide the speedy, less expensive,
harmonizing process desired by professionals. One recommendation
approved by the ABA House of Delegates involved this aspect of the
malpractice problem. The House's official statement included the
following proposals:

1. Arbitration should be entered into, if at all, on a voluntary
   basis with full knowledge that the arbitration panel's
   decision is final and binding; once entered into, arbitration
   should be final and binding. The question of the time at
   which an arbitration agreement should be entered into is not
   concluded hereby and shall be considered at a later date.
2. All states that have not already done so should enact laws
   making arbitration agreements and awards enforceable in
   the courts under the Uniform Arbitration Act.
3. Arbitration panels in small claims cases should consist of
   only one impartial arbitrator. For claims above the small
   claims cut off, there should be three arbitrators: an attorney,
   a physician, and a layman. All three should be impartial and

acceptable to both plaintiff and defendant. (The Commission is not prepared at this time to recommend a specific monetary figure which would serve as a small claims cut off.)[2]

Fortunately, the American Arbitration Association has provided outstanding service in the United States as a private, professional group of arbitrators. It has been able to develop arbitration procedures with particular attention to a quick, inexpensive process for smaller claims that are of special importance in dental malpractice. Arbitration of dentist-patient disputes through the efficient efforts of this highly respected organization is a viable possibility.

The real thrust for resolving health malpractice claims can be identified in the Commission's concept of "continuums" at hospitals designed to deal with patients' complaints preceding patients' lawsuits. Resolving a patient's complaint in a hospital or in a dentist's office can often prevent a patient's malpractice claim in a court. The "continuum" would involve the utilization of advanced prevention techniques; an ombudsman or patient's advocate and a patient relations office; and an expert or panel of experts to advise all parties on the technical merit or lack of merit for each malpractice claim and to attempt mediation. If mediation fails, an attempt at private arbitration would follow, with costly court litigation the final procedure.

Alternative means of compensation of malpractice claims are also under study. Possible mechanisms are no-fault or elective no-fault procedures, with the patient's compensation modeled after the workmen's compensation system. Another area of study is hospital accident insurance with "designated compensable events" (DCE) reimbursable at a fixed amount:

> ... For example, if it were agreed that an injury to a patient following a given medical event would have resulted from negligence 90 percent of the time, there would be automatic compensation under the policy in all those cases, on the theory that the injury was almost always avoidable and that it is cheaper and better to pay in all cases than to incur the cost and delay of litigation in the doubtful 10 percent.
>
> This approach retains in a modified way the accountability notions of tort law because the principal criterion for determining compensability would be avoidability of the particular type of medical incident. It has the advantage of flexibility because only clearly compensable outcomes could be included at the outset, and the list could be expanded with experience. D.C.E. can be implemented experimentally in one or two hospitals on a contract basis. If the approach turns out to be sound for a hospital or a locality, it might become a county or even state-wide means for insuring and dealing with a large percentage of medical malpractice claims on a group basis.[3]

The Commission recognized the skyrocketing insurance premium for the professional practitioner as an immediately pressing problem. Statements on guiding economic and insurance principles are sought for such complex issues as:

1. Should the relative degree of risk be the sole criterion for premium classification?
2. Should legislation be enacted requiring all those who provide health care to show financial responsibility as a condition of practice? If so, how should financial responsibility be defined?
3. Are there insurable units within the present health care system other than the individual practitioner and the individual hospital that could be insured more sensibly from a rating, prevention, or cost point of view?
4. Should provider mutual insurance companies be encouraged, and if so, with what limitations as to size, capitalization, and underwriting criteria?

The proper disciplining of the health practitioner has also been recognized as a vital part of the malpractice problem. Better disciplinary procedures for physicians and dentists will prevent the unskilled practitioner from causing the malpractice incident. The ABA House of Delegates has also approved the Commission's recommendations in this area. All states are urged to enact laws granting immunity from civil liabilities for members of medical disciplinary borads, as well as for persons who complain to the broads. States are further urged to enact laws to make proceedings before disciplinary boards confidential.

That the Commission has taken a major step forward for all concerned with the health malpractice issue is evidenced by the chairman's observations on the Commission's work:

> The Commission's primary conclusion thus far is that in the long run fundamental changes in the health care delivery system and the compensation claim disposition system will be necessary to achieve a solution to the medical malpractice crisis. On the health care side, this means that the Commission will continue to look closely at hospital prevention programs, ways to improve medical disciplinary structures, and the relationship of insurance arrangements to the delivery of adequate care. On the compensation claim disposition side, the Commission will continue to explore the feasibility of basically different systems. These priorities reflect a consensus within the Commission that there are no panaceas and that our society is likely to be troubled by medical liability problems for a long time. Nonetheless, most members of the Commission would agree that the future is not entirely dark as long as talented individuals in and outside the professions are willing to work hard and cooperatively toward solutions.[4]

Update on the Malpractice Dilemma

For a thorough presentation of the current situation in the malpractice dilemma, see chapter 6. It should be noted that many of the reforms suggested in the 1970s by Schroeder and the Commission were adopted or proposed during the crisis of the mid-1980s. A review of the malpractice reform law passed by the New York State legislature in July 1985 incorporates many of the changes designed to control the runaway medical and dental malpractice situation.[5] Time will tell just how effective these changes are.

One suggestion that keeps surfacing is to establish a no-fault system of compensation for injuries that result from health care treatment. In an article published by Williams in 1985, a strong case is made for the system.[6]

While in the legislation of the mid-70s little attention was paid to the level of medical care, the legislation of the mid-80s appears to recognize that much of the cause of the problem rests with the quality of the care provided by some physicians and dentists. Dr Peter C. Williams notes the following in his article published on the subject of no-fault insurance:

> With the notable and understandable exception of health care providers, virtually everyone who has studied the malpractice crisis agrees that the single factor most highly correlated with the incidence of malpractice suits is malpractice.[7]

The malpractice reform legislation adopted in New York in 1985 and proposed in many other states recognizes the need to identify incompetent and impaired physicians and dentists and to take legal action to restrict their professional activities.

THE DENTIST v THE DENTURIST: HUMANITY OR TECHNOLOGY?

A most important contemporary professional crisis involves the conflict between humanity and technology. The cutting edges of this conflict are evident in the twentieth-century health sciences. One perceptive writer has given the analysis of the physician's subservience to technology:

> Even physicians, formerly a culture's very symbol of power, are powerless as they increasingly become mere conduits between their patients and the major drug manufacturers. Patients, in turn, are more and more merely passive objects to whom cures are wrought and to whom things are done. Their own inner healing resources, their capacities for self-reintegration, whether psychic or physical, are more

and more regarded as irrelevant in a medicine that can hardly distinguish a human patient from a manufactured object. The now ascendant biofeedback movement may be the penultimate act in the drama separating man from nature; man no longer even sees himself, his body, directly, but only through pointer readings, flashing lights and buzzing sounds produced by instruments attached to him as speedometers are attached to automobiles. The ultimate act of the drama is, of course, the final holocaust that wipes life out altogether.[8]

The same challenge faces dentists, as indicated by their growing conflict with denturists. Denturists furnish the technology of dentures for the individual, rather than therapy to meet the patient's oral hygiene needs. Until today, the preparation for and construction of dentures were services provided directly by the professional practitioner or by those under the direct supervision of the licensed dental practitioner. State licensure statutes codified this superior role of the dentist as a health practitioner serving an individual patient. The oral hygiene needs of a patient have been met by this strict control over the technological product identified as a denture.

The manufacturer of dentures, operating a laboratory to produce a product, epitomizes the complete technological control over a product which is then sold to an individual, without the involvement of the health practitioner, to meet his dental health needs. This industrialization of the denture permits lower costs per unit. Thus, the manufacturer offers a lower sales price per individual customer.

The crucial issue, however, is whether oral health for each particular person can be achieved with a product manufacturer in control rather than a health practitioner. Only a dentist serving the health needs of an individual patient can determine a patient's dental health needs. This is basically a human problem, not a technological problem. In short, the issue is whether denture wearers will be customers or patients.[9]

The conflict between humanity and technology as represented by the dentist v the denturist will not be easily resolved. If dollars are to be the paramount concern, technology through the denturist will prevail. If the dental needs are to be met with the humanity demanded of a health professional, the ultimate responsibility for the denture therapy of each patient must be concentrated in the dentist.

Update on Denturism

The movement to permit direct services by denturists to patients, and thus bypass the dentist, continues in the 1980s. As noted in chapter 11, additional states have enacted legislation to permit denturism, and more are considering the move.[10] The trend is evident. Sufficient data are not available to determine the effect of the movement on cost, quality, income of dentists, or the expansion of dental services to more people. An additional movement on the part of laboratory technicians in several states, which is somewhat less threatening to the dentists but still opposed by them, is an attempt by technicians to become licensed. They base the cause for licensure on the need to upgrade the profession, to assure the dentist of better-quality work, and, ultimately, to improve services by the dentist to the patient. Many segments of organized dentistry look on the move as the first step toward the final goal of the laboratory technician to rid the industry of control by the dominant professional master: the dentist.

FINANCING OF DENTAL CARE

Traditionally, health practitioners have been remunerated by the individual patient on a fee-for-service basis. The concept of prepaid dental care through group insurance had its beginning in the 1950s. Today, this concept is well accepted and growing rapidly. Stimulated by the marketing activities of the private insurance business, encouraged by certain federal income tax incentives, utilized by labor unions as a bargaining pawn for better fringe benefits, and accepted by many providers of dental care, group dental care plans nearly doubled in enrollment between 1970 and 1975. With 23 million persons now covered, 50 to 80 million patients are expected to be covered by 1980. One program, Delta Dental Plans, is now a sponsoring entity in 41 states.

Experts in the area have listed the following reasons for this rapid growth:

1. a recognition that group insurance offers protection against unpredictably high dental expenses;
2. the desire of many dentists to contribute to the public good;
3. the attempt to forestall federal legislation that would impose bureaucratic regulation of national health care;
4. growing public awareness of the importance of oral health to one's general well-being;
5. affluence in a society where many workers prefer untaxed fringe benefits to wage or salary increases;
6. a nearly realized ideal of painless dentistry.

The American Dental Association (ADA) has added its weight to this rapidly developing field for financing dental care. On October 5, 1975, the ADA published a 12-page supplement to *The New York Times* revealing that prepaid dental insurance had received strong impetus from the inclusion of the program in the national union labor contracts of the United Auto Workers, the United Steel Workers, and the Communication Workers of America.

Two general kinds of prepaid dental insurance plans have emerged. One is sponsored by nonprofit organizations such as Blue Cross-Blue Shield and similar service organizations. The other is sponsored by the private insurance carriers that compete for profit. The former plan services the dentists directly, while the latter indemnifies enrolled members by reimbursing the patient for dental expenses incurred.

Many varieties of prepaid insurance plans are available. The prepaid dollar amount determines the dental services to be provided. Copayment arrangements are often included, especially for extended, complicated services; under such a plan, the patient pays 10% to 50% of the dental service charge and the insurer pays the balance. Deductible provisions are frequently a part of these plans, as are maximum limits of financial obligations for the insuring organization. Generally, a minimum group, such as ten persons, is required of any given prepaid dental plan.

With the development of this form of financing, the door has been opened for the acceptance of more radical methods of financing dental health care. A federal national health insurance program has been "in the wings," ready to become a reality whenever the US Congress acts. If the federal government includes every American in its health care program, the practice of dentistry will be profoundly changed. Legal regulations and legal procedures will dominate the practice of health care. The political inevitability of a federal health care program is accepted by many. The simple truth is that if 80 million persons are financially covered for dental care in 1980, there is no reason the remaining 130 million Americans should not receive similar treatment by political legislation, if not through employment contracts.

A second development in the financing of dental care is the potential for full dental service available through medical health service organizations. One aspect of this procedure could be hospitals' providing dental care for all oral surgery. Primary control over this phase of dental care would be through the hospital facility.

What is occurring is the great impact of mass purchasing power on the practice of dentistry. The individual practitioner is now subjected to the influence of third-party payers, which is steadily becoming more intense. If full dental care is delivered by health maintenance organizations, which are now legally encouraged by congressional legislation, and/or by company or union health clinics staffed by hired dentists who are employees of a corporate entity, the profession of dentistry will be subjected to a major professional transformation. The dental student about to enter the practice, as well as the seasoned dental practitioner, faces greater legal involvements in the years ahead as the public struggles with the means of financing dental health care.[11]

Update on Financing Dental Care

See chapter 14.

PROFESSIONAL ASSOCIATIONS: TRADE ORGANIZATIONS OR LABOR UNIONS

Dentists, like physicians and attorneys, have organized professionally within the past century. The roots of such organization can be traced to Hippocrates, who in the fifth century BC prepared a code of medical ethics for his students about to enter medical practice. For attorneys, the relationship of the lawyers as officers of the English courts began in 1292 AD under Edward I. The royal decree provided for appointment of:

> ...certain attorneys and apprentices of the best and most apt for their learning skill, who might do service to the court and people; those so chosen only, and no other, should follow his court and transact the affairs thereof.

An exclusive organization for the professional duties has emerged from these ancient beginnings. The ADA and the ABA have much in common. Analysis of the current issues confronting the ABA as a professional association is fruitful. Dentists should compare the following analysis with the ADA Code of Ethics, set forth in appendix III. Issues similar to the ones confronting the bar face the professional dental association.

First, lawyers are being asked whether the ABA is a professional association or a trade organization. It has been dubbed the latter by Mark Green, coeditor with Ralph Nader of the critical volume *Verdicts on Lawyers*. Green provides ample evidence that the ABA is concerned primarily with protecting the economic rewards and gains of its law practitioners. He contends that the great issues of public justice do not receive the attention of the organized bar as represented in the ABA. According to Green, three types of major efforts articulate this trade-organization syndrome of the national lawyers' association: (1) "The ABA avoids promoting issues against its own economic self-interest." (2) "When it is progressive the ABA seems to rush in where others already have trod." (3) "There is often timidity and inconsistency."[12]

In a similar vein, Jerome A. Hockberg, formerly in the Antitrust Division, Department of Justice, and currently chairperson of the

Division of Antitrust, Trade Regulation and Consumer Affairs of the District of Columbia Bar, says:

> Just like the AMA then, the American Bar Association seeks to play a major role in the formulation of the industry's structure and regulation so as to benefit its members first and the public second. This is to be expected, for the ABA is a trade association of businessmen who sell legal services. Expected, but not endorsed. It is especially troubling that proposed programs for CLE (continuing legal education), certification, and specialization are being developed and administered by the legal profession itself. Some state programs authorize a few laymen to sit on operating committees, but the overwhelming majority of plans involve only lawyers. The self-interest of lawyers to establish rules to favor themselves can again be best appreciated by noting how doctors have kept their supply down and their incomes up.[13]

In short, the ABA has a fretful concern with its own well-being rather than a fervent desire to advance the cause of legal justice. Dentists and dental students will want to analyze the American Dental Association in a similar vein to determine whether a trade organization for dentists or a professional association for dentistry really exists.

Second, lawyers are being challenged in client relationships, which are truly the heart of professional law practice. The minimum legal fees set through bar associations have been held unconstitutional. Solicitation of clients, long a deep-seated prohibition, has been altered drastically by the efforts of labor unions to protect members in need of legal counsel; to refer union members to a special panel of lawyers recognized or retained by the union to represent individual members has been increasingly held to be a valid procedure. To make a long story short, professional legal ethics and procedures based on what is good for the profession now conflict with the constitutional and legal rights of the clients who are entitled to justice in their rights to legal representation. To serve the public rather than the profession is the high calling of a practitioner in law. Might not the same thing be true for the practitioners in dentistry and in medicine: to serve the health needs of patients and not the special needs of physicians and dentists?

The Anderson, Indiana Experience

The ultimate affiliation for action may well be the labor-union type of organization. Is there a role for unionization of dentists? A quick negative answer would appear to be in order, because labor unions have but one purpose — service to self. At least philosophically and, hopefully, practically, professional associations are to provide service to the public. But the experience of dentist unionization in Anderson,

Indiana, opens a new chapter in professional associations for dentistry. The Anderson incident demands close study for dental practitioners and students alike.

In Madison County, Indiana, 51 dentists serve more than 20,000 employees and their families in two large General Motors plants. These patients, covered by a union contract with dental care benefits, represent 80% to 95% of the dentists' clientele. The United Automobile Workers union and General Motors Corp negotiated the dental care benefit for all hourly and salaried employees effective October 1, 1974. In effect, two mammoth organizations — one management, the other labor — had a profound impact on the dentist-patient relationship. Connecticut General Insurance Co became the insurer of the dental care plan. In keeping with its interests in its business operation, the insurance company is primarily concerned with the financial impact. While the relationship between the Anderson dentists and Connecticut General has been cordial and cooperative, an insurance company has the right to determine what dental procedure can be done more cheaply. Payment based on this more economical procedure may ignore dental health concerns.

The dentists in Anderson, led by Dr David B. McClure, have become increasingly concerned over the terms of dental insurance programs, which frequently call for the "least expensive adequate" treatment. The dentist is not allowed to choose the treatment that he or she professionally believes is best for the patient. The dentists have also been concerned by the policies of some insurance companies imposing cumbersome requirements, such as basing reimbursement on submission of x-rays rather than case studies. The extensive additional paper work demanded of the dental practitioner is another growing concern.

In simple terms, Dr McClure summed up the Anderson dental community's final position:

> Since insurance contract terms affect our working conditions and our relations with our patients, we believe we should be able to negotiate with them at the bargaining table.
> They (the insurance company) have all these vague things...they try to make determinations without seeing patients.
> When the company and union make contracts without consulting us, then they're selling our labor in the marketplace without any input from us.[14]

The Indiana Dental Association, the traditional professional entity, could not provide the bargaining power for the tough negotiations envisaged as necessary in the minds of the Anderson dentists. The ADA is subject to the federal antitrust laws and would be inviting both civil and criminal actions by the US Department of Justice if it proceeded to represent all the Madison county dentists in the economic activity required to protect the dentists in their individual relationships with their patients. Labor unions are specifically exempt from antitrust actions. With this understanding, the dentists of Anderson voted overwhelmingly to organize the Indiana Federation of Dentists, Chapter 1, in August 1976. The Union adopted its charter, registered as a union with the US Department of Labor, and affiliated with the new national union, the American Federation of Physicians and Dentists, headquartered in Springfield, Missouri.

The objectives of the union as set forth in section 2 of its charter deserve thoughtful study:

Section 2. Objectives

The Indiana Federation, Chapter No. 1. shall represent, protect, maintain and advance, through activities accomplished by relevant techniques which may lawfully be engaged in by a labor organization, the interests of the dentists within its jurisdiction. The objectives of this Chapter shall include, but not be limited to the following:

(a) To represent dentists in all socio-economic matters, negotiations and grievances with employers, third and fourth parties or any group that is involved in financing or delivery of dental care. The ultimate purpose being to promote better patient care and to prevent abuses and correct inequities in the delivery of dental care to the public,

(b) To seek to insure adequate compensation and proper working conditions for dentists commensurate with their training and skill and the responsibility they bear for the life and health of their fellow human beings,

(c) The establishment of approval of appropriate utilization review or peer review procedures which do not interfere with the doctor-patient relationship and the maintenance of the highest quality of dental care,

(d) To associate together all dentists for their mutual benefit and protection,

(e) To unite the efforts of dentists in obtaining and preserving the individual freedom of action necessary for the success of their professional endeavors,

(f) To study, advise, recommend and secure the enactment of legislation in the interest of dentists,

(g) To encourage advanced education studies,

(h) To cooperate with other organizations, local, regional, statewide, national or international, which have similar objectives and aims,

(i) To hold and transfer such real and personal property as may be necessary or convenient to conduct and operate the organization,

(j) To establish, acquire and own such trademarks or copyrights as may be necessary to provide the organization with distinctive union label or insignia,

(k) To lawfully do everything necessary, suitable or proper at any time or place for the accomplishment of any of the purposes and objectives,

(l) To transact business in the State of Indiana or in any other jurisdiction in the United States of America or elsewhere, and,

(m) To have and exercise all rights and powers conferred on labor organizations under the laws of the State of Indiana and the United States of America, provided, however, that this chapter shall not, except to an insubstantial degree, engage in any activities or exercise any powers that are not in furtherance of the primary purposes of this organization.

While these objectives represent the full legal delineation of the purposes for the nation's first union of dentists, Dr McClure, the first president of the local, succinctly stated the crux of the purpose:

We want to have some influence and control over the care of our patients when other persons try to interfere with our treatment.[15]

The words of another Anderson dentist describe even more specifically the general attitude of the Madison County dental community:

I dislike someone telling me how to treat my patients. What's good for one patient is not necessarily good for another.[16]

The final agreement on which type of organization best serves the dentists of America really cannot be made at this time. The professional association, trade organization, and labor union are all viable opportunities for professional activities. The conditions of the dental community to be served, the types of dental problems to be confronted, and the legal possibilities available will all dictate which type of professional entity should be utilized. It is not a question of selecting one; it is the process of using all types to ensure better dental health care for the patient.

Update on Professional Associations

The Anderson, Indiana story continues into the 80s and finds its way into the US Supreme Court. The source of the problem is the requirement by third-party payers that dentists submit radiographs along with claims for payment to substantiate the treatment provided to beneficiaries of insurance coverage. A significant number of dentists, encouraged by the Indiana Federation of Dentists (IFD), engaged in a boycott against sending the radiographs to the insurance company. The issue is whether the actions of the IFD constitute restraint of trade. The Federal Trade Commission (FTC) issued a complaint against the IFD. The Commission determined that the IFD was engaged in restraint of trade in violation of federal antitrust statutes. The FTC based its case on "rule of reason" in the restraint of trade. The boycotting dentists claimed that dentists are permitted by Indiana law to complete a diagnosis. Their contention was that in submitting radiographs to the insurance company they were permitting nondentists to complete a diagnosis. The "rule of reason" argument was rejected in the decision of the Seventh Circuit Court of Appeals in reversing the ruling of the Commission. An appeal to the Supreme Court was taken by the FTC.

Supporting the position of the Indiana dentists through the submission of amicus briefs (not a party to the action, but a friend-of-the-court brief) were the American Medical Association, the ADA, the American College of Radiologists, and the American College of Surgeons. In opposition were the American Association for Retired Persons and the Health Insurance Association of America.

Thus, the battle lines were drawn in the highest court in our land between what the profession believes to be an exclusive health-related activity and what commercial interests believe to be an administrative function related to financial considerations.

The case was decided by the Supreme Court June 2, 1986, in favor of the FTC.[17] In a unanimous decision, the court held that a conspiracy among the Indiana dentists (IFD) to withhold patient x-rays from dental health insurers, while not illegal per se, constituted an unreasonable restraint of trade under section 1 of the Sherman Act.[18,19]

It is of interest to note that New York law prohibits the taking of posttreatment radiographs for administrative purposes. The Public Health Law, adopted in July 1979, states:

> The use of x-rays, performed in the course of dental services, shall be limited solely to diagnostic purposes and shall not be used for the purpose of verifying services performed for which requests for payment were submitted to third party payors.[20]

HYGIENISTS v THE DENTIST

Beginning in the late 1970s and extending into the 80s, hygienists began exploring their chances to change their professional and legal ties to dentists. Their efforts are directed toward the ultimate goal of establishing practice independent of the dentist. Some hygienists are working toward an independent contractor practice, while others have as their goal a completely separate practice. Either would require a change in state law that would permit hygienists to practice unsupervised by the dentist. In an independent contractor practice, the hygienists could practice without supervision, but their patients would be required to be referred by a dentist. However, they may open their own office and bill patients directly. In both situations, the hygienist would be free of direct control by the dentist — the "middle-man supervisor" would be eliminated.

Effective July 1, 1986, a bill passed by the Colorado legislature in April permitted dental hygienists to engage in unsupervised practice. It become the first state to enact such legislation. Under the sunset legislation, attention was directed on the Colorado State Board and the Dental Practice Act. Largely through the efforts of the Colorado Dental Association, the Senate passed its version that required supervision by dentists of all hygienist activities. The House, however, in its version, included provisions for unsupervised practice. The conference-committee bill permitted unsupervised practice by hygienists with limited responsibilites. The compromised version then passed both houses. Under the bill, hygienists may perform the following procedures unsupervised:

- removal of deposits, accretions, and stains by scaling with hand, ultrasonic, or other devices from all surfaces of the tooth and smoothing and polishing natural and restored tooth surfaces;
- removal of granulation and degenerated tissue from the gingival wall of the periodontal pocket through the process of gingival curettage;
- provision of preventive measure including the application of fluorides and other recognized topical agents for the prevention of oral disease;
- gathering and assembling information for use by the dentist in diagnosing and treatment planning, including fact-finding and patient history, oral inspection, and dental and periodontal charting; and
- administration of topical anesthetic to a patient in the course of providing care.

A new disciplinary clause is included in the bill that states it is unprofessional conduct for a hygienist to fail to recommend that a patient see a dentist or fail to refer a patient to a dentist when the hygienist detects a condition that requires care beyond the scope of dental hygiene.

The composition of the dental board has also been changed. The old board consisted of five dentists, two hygienists, and one consumer. The new board consists of four dentists, two hygienists, and three consumers. The dentists are outnumbered.[21] This represents a trend taking place in several states that are reconstituting their dental boards.

The Colorado law provided a list of services that may be performed by hygienists without supervision by a dentist. It also permits a hygienist to be the proprietor of a place where dental hygiene is performed and to purchase, own, or lease equipment necessary to perform dental hygiene.[21]

An action was brought by the ADA Commission on Dental Accreditation and two medically compromised dental patients in the Denver District Court to have the dental hygiene bill declared unconstitutional. On Sept 3, 1986, the judge dismissed the suit. The ADA has decided to appeal the decision to the Colorado Appellate Court.[22]

In March 1986, the *ADA News* reported that bills for unsupervised hygiene practice were pending in nine (now eight) states. Bills proposed in the states of Washington and California died in committee. At the time of the publication, bills modifying supervision of hygienists or expanding their scope of practice were under consideration in Colorado, Georgia, Florida, Massachusetts, Nebraska, Maryland, South Carolina, Utah, and Virginia.[23]

In the long run, what happens with these bills is not important. What is important is that the hygienists are making waves, and it is anticipated that eventually they will be successful in changing their relationship with dentists and their patients in many states. The changed law in Colorado will serve to encourage hygienists to extend their political activities to additional states, and to introduce legislation designed to further remove them from the control by dentists.

Some efforts are currently directed at a nonlegislative mechanism to separate hygienists from domination by dentists. Questions are being raised concerning whether the relationship of the dentist and the hygienist violates the Sherman antitrust laws. The hope is to break the existing link between the hygienist and the dentist through the courts.

Organized dentistry in the 1980s is faced with hygienists and dental laboratories seeking to break the domination of dentists in providing services and products to the public. The pressures on the profession are mounting, and how long the dentist can avoid the forces dedicated to breaking the monopoly is speculative.

Nondentist Owners of Dental Practice

In late 1985, Wisconsin passed legislation permitting nondentists to own and operate facilities that provided dental care. It was the first state to effect such legislation. Similar legislation was proposed in Hawaii and Oregon but not adopted. Virginia held hearing on the subject, but no change in legislation was proposed. According to an article that appeared in the *Journal of the American Dental Association*, March 1986, the efforts stemmed from the FTC and corporate interests. If successful, the legislation would permit large chain operations to enter the field of dentistry.

CONCLUSION

The foregoing contemporary legal issues involving dentistry are not the only ones that confront the dentist and the dental profession. They are, however, representative of the breadth and depth of current legal concerns which must be addressed with reason and dedication. As the interdependence of human beings becomes more acute in today's industrial-technological society, the professional relationship of dentist to patient must also take into account third parties: governments, unions, denturists, and insurance companies, to name a few. More importantly, modern malpractice law now demands not only higher standards for dental health care from the dentist, but also informed, voluntary consent by the patient. Today, professional dentists are contributing to these massive upgradings of health and justice in America. Tomorrow's dentistry should profit greatly from today's professional efforts.

REFERENCES

1. Tondel, L., Jr., and Crittenden, T.S. Work of the Medical Professional Liability Commission, *Am Bar Assoc J* 62:1580–1584, 1976.
2. Ibid.
3. Ibid. p. 1583.
4. Ibid. p. 1584.
5. For a detailed analysis of the new legislation in New York, see Connors, J.P., Analysis of new comprehensive medical malpractice reform law, *NY Law J*, August 13, 1985, p. 1.
6. Williams, P.C., Abandoning medical malpractice, *J Legal Med*, Vol. 5, No. 4, November 4, 1984. pp. 549–594.
7. Ibid. p. 572.
8. Weizenbaum, J. *Computer Power and Human Reason.* San Francisco: W.H. Freeman and Co., 1976.
9. Munson, J.F. Dentists and technicians battle of fitting, cost of false teeth. *Cleveland Plain Dealer*, October 21, 1976, p. 2-C.
10. Kettenbach, D. Denturists target 7 more states. *Modern Dentalab*, Vol. 4, No. 1, Dec/Jan, 1986, p. 1.
11. Johnson, R.S. Can Coloradans have complete dental care? *Empire Magazine, The Denver Post*, February 29, 1976, p. 16.
12. Nader, R. and Green, M. *Verdicts on Lawyers*, New York: Thomas Y. Cromwell Co., Inc., 1976, pp. 17–18.
13. Ibid. p. 123.
14. Showing their teeth: Community dentists form nation's first union. *The Anderson (Indiana) Herald*, Augest 26, 1976, p. 1.
15. Ibid.
16. Ibid.
17. 54 U.S.L.W. 4531 (U.S. June 2, 1986). Hereinafter cited as *FTC v. IFD*.
18. Court backs F.T.C. on dentist ruling. *New York Times*, p. D2, June 6, 1986.

180

19. Stoll, N.R., Goldfein, S. Rule of reason still has teeth. *NY Law J* p. 1, June 17, 1986.
20. *New York Public Health Law*, Article 35, §3515-a.
21. Colorado passes unsupervised practice. *ADA News*, May 19, 1986.
22. ADA to appeal dental hygiene decision. *ADA News*, Sept 15, 1986.
23. Bill for unsupervised dental hygiene practice pending in nine states. *ADA News*, March 3, 1986.

16 Legal Catechism for the Practicing Dentist

Burton R. Pollack

INTRODUCTION

In this chapter, the opinions expressed as answers to the questions presented represent majority opinions of the various state courts, and, in some cases, local state statutory law or rules and regulations of administrative boards. The opinions, therefore, are not necessarily universal throughout the 50 states. When specific questions arise that are similar to those presented in this chapter, the answers should serve as a guide. Real-life questions should be referred to an attorney or insurance company respresentatives. Slight alterations in facts might change the results.

DUTIES

1. Is the relationship between a dentist and the patient contractual in character?

Answer: Yes. Once a patient presents for care, and the dentist accepts the patient, a contractual relationship is formed, and the laws of contract apply.

2. Must the terms of the contract, because the relationship is a contractual one, be in writing to bind the patient and the dentist?

   Answer: No. If the oral agreement meets all the requirements of an enforceable contract, and there are no disputes as to the terms, an oral contract is enforceable. The written document is evidence that the parties agreed.

3. Must all of the terms of the contract be stated expressed?

   Answer: No. Simply because the parties have entered into an agreement, unless modified by express terms, there are implied duties on the part of each party — patient and dentist.

4. What are the implied duties attached to the dentist in the doctor/patient relationship?

   Answer: There is a long list of duties that are implied as a result of the contractual relationship. Among these are: to use reasonable care in the treatment of the patient, to employ competent personnel and supervise them carefully, not to abandon the patient, to maintain knowledge current with advances, to make care available during emergencies, etc.

5. What are the implied duties of the patient?

   Answer: To pay a reasonable fee in a reasonable time, to cooperate in the care, to keep appointments, to provide accurate answers to questions about their history and health, to follow instructions, and to keep the dentist informed if there is a change in their health status.

6. In the absence of an express contract, is the dentist entitled to a fee, and if so, how much?

   Answer: Yes. Even if no fee was agreed on by the dentist and the patient, the dentist is entitled to a fee for the services rendered. The amount is based on the reasonable value of the service as determined by community standards.

7. Who is responsible for services rendered to a minor child or a mental incompetent?

   Answer: The parent or legal guardian. If, however, the parent or legal guardian is unaware of the services rendered, the services must be either necessary or rendered in an emergency to hold the parent or guardian responsible.

8. If a dentist fails to perform a portion of his duties under a contract with a patient, does the patient owe a fee to the dentist for the completed services?

   Answer: Yes. The amount usually is based on a proportion of the total fee, or, when the contract is itemized, on the fee for those services completed.

9. If an individual who is not a patient of record enters a dentist's office in need of immediate care, is the dentist required by law to treat the person?

   Answer: No. A dentist is free to refuse to treat any person as long as the reason for refusal is not based on race, religion, or national origin.

10. Can claims of malpractice against a dentist legitimately be based on faulty diagnosis?

    Answer: Yes. One of the specific implied duties owed by the dentist to the patient is to complete a thorough and accurate diagnosis.

11. Is it possible for a patient to sue a dentist for breach of contract as well as malpractice (professional negligence)?

    Answer: Yes, depending upon the facts of the case. In a breach of contract suit, the patient does not have to show negligent care. In allegations of malpractice, experts are required to establish for the jury or judge the standard of care from which the defendant departed. The awards, however, for breach of contract are usually less than a plaintiff would receive if the suit were based on malpractice.

12. In actions of breach of oral contract, what is the usual Statute of Limitations (the period of time in which suit may be brought)?

    Answer: In most states, the Statute of Limitations for breach of contract is 6 years, running from the time a last payment was made or the last fee was entered, whichever is later.

13. In actions of malpractice, what is the usual Statute of Limitations?

    Answer: It varies from state to state and with wrongful death or personal actions from 6 months to 3 years.

14. When does the Statute of Limitations in actions of malpractice begin to run?

    Answer: It varies in different states, but there are generally four options: from the time the injury occurred; from the time the patient discovered or should have discovered the injury; from the time the patient-doctor relationship terminated; or from the time the specific course of treatment for which injury occurred terminated. As an example, in New York State the statute begins to run from the time of the injury and runs for 2½ years. There are two exceptions to the beginning of the running of the statute — in cases of foreign bodies and continuous treatment.

15. Have repeated and unreasonable attempts to collect fees owed by a patient resulted in counterclaims of malpractice or breach of contract by a disgruntled patient against the dentist?

Answer: Yes. On a statistical basis, it has been determined that one of the several causes of legal action against a dentist has been attempts by dentists to collect money due for treatment.

16. If a dental patient complains that the services are unsatisfactory, should the dentist refrain from presenting a bill for the services?

Answer: A dentist may bill for services completed. Not to do so might be interpreted by the courts as an admission that the services were unsatisfactory. However, the current trend is that many courts look to the return of a fee, or its abatement, as a demonstration of good faith rather than as an admission of negligence in the treatment of the patient.

17. What would be the effect on a patient's claim of malpractice if it is determined that the patient did not follow the dentist's instructions for posttreatment home care?

Answer: If an injury resulted, in part, from failure to follow reasonable posttreatment home instructions, it is probable that the dentist may be relieved of any liability. Thus, contributory negligence is often a good defense to allegations of malpractice; in many jurisdictions it is a complete defense. In others, the doctrine of comparative negligence is invoked, and the award against the dentist is apportioned based on the comparative negligence of the patient.

18. What is the legal effect of guaranteeing a result, such as stating that the patient will be "satisfied" at the conclusion of treatment?

Answer: The guarantee of a result creates a contract term that is difficult to defend in a suit brought by a patient for its breach. In some states, such as New York, guaranteeing a result is illegal. According to the Principles of Ethics of the American Dental Association, it is also unethical. Therefore, to guarantee a result in New York places the dentist in triple jeopardy: it is illegal (a crime), unethical, and might result in breach of contract in a civil suit. In some states, for a guarantee relating to health care to be enforceable it must be in writing, while in others there must be special consideration, that is, extra money paid for the guarantee.

19. What, if any, are the dentist's responsibilities for clothing left by a patient in the waiting room?

Answer: The dentist becomes the temporary custodian of articles left by patients in the waiting room. He or she has a duty to protect the articles, to seek out the owner through reasonable measures, and to return them unharmed.

20. Under what circumstances is a dentist required to treat an individual who is not already a patient?

Answer: Certain dentists practice in a contract situation, such as in the armed forces, community clinics, union clinics, hospitals, closed-panel union plans, and so forth, where the dentist must often accept patients of the institution or those referred for care. See question 9.

21. Under the following circumstances, is a dentist legally bound to perform services for:

A. A 5-year-old child, not a patient of record, who has a toothache and is accompanied by the parent?

Answer: No.

B. A 5-year-old child, not a patient of record, who has a toothache and is accompanied by a teacher?

Answer: No.

C. A 5-year-old child, a patient of record, who has a toothache?

Answer: Yes.

D. A husband with a dental emergency, not a patient of record, whose wife is a patient of record?

Answer: No.

E. A baseball player, hemorrhaging from the mouth following an injury?

Answer: No. It may be unethical and immoral to refuse such services, but by doing so the dentist will not be subject to civil or criminal sanctions.

22. Is a dentist required by law to lend assistance in an emergency situation outside the dental office?

Answer: Except in a few states, no. For example, in Vermont, the law states that anyone available must render care to a person in an accident.

23. If a dentist renders a service gratuitously, does it alter the professional responsibility of the dentist to the patient?
Answer: No. The fact that the dentist did not expect to receive some form of remuneration for services rendered or for offering casual advice does not relieve the dentist of any responsibilities.

24. Many states have enacted "Good Samaritan" laws. What are the usual four criteria for relieving a dentist of responsibility when he or she renders care at the scene of accident in these states?
Answer: That an emergency exists; that no remuneration was expected for the service rendered; that the dentist was not guilty of gross negligence (a wanton or willful disregard of the safety or health of the victim); and that the care was not provided in the office or in a health facility such as a hospital or clinic.

25. Must every dentist consider the implications very carefully before passing judgment to a patient on the treatment provided by a fellow dentist?
Answer: Yes. Dentists who express opinions about the services of another dentist without knowing all the relevant facts are placing themselves at legal risk if they are wrong. They may be subject to suit by the other dentist and even by the patient. However, if they do know all the facts and their opinion is correct, they have an ethical and legal duty to inform the patient if reasonable and prudent dental care requires such disclosure at that time.

26. During office hours, may anyone who enters the office be considered a trespasser?
Answer: Yes. Unless an individual has legitimate business to conduct in the office, he or she is trespassing. Even a landlord may be a trespasser. Patients, potential patients, those accompanying them, laboratory delivery persons, drug company representatives, the mailman, and others in the same categories are invitees, not trespassers.

CONSENT

27. What elements are essential for consent to dental care to be valid?
Answer: The patient must be an adult; he or she must be

of sound mind; the consent must be informed; and the consent must be voluntary. If obtained from someone other than the patient, he or she must be the parent, legal guardian, or one authorized by the parent.

28. May a valid consent be oral?

    Answer: Yes. As long as the consent contains the essential elements described above, an oral consent is valid. Should proof ever become necessary, a written consent may be important to the outcome of a case. In special situations, identified in many states, some consents must be in writing to be enforceable, eg, donation of human organs, acupuncture, abortion in minors, etc.

29. When a dentist renders care in an emergency to an unconscious patient, does he or she have consent?

    Answer: Yes. Consent of an unconscious patient is apparent consent, implied by law.

30. What elements are essential, in the rendering of emergency care, for apparent consent implied by law to be valid in court?

    Answer: A true emergency must exist, with care needed at once; the patient must be unconscious; consent would be given by this patient had he or she been able to consent; and a reasonable person in a similar situation would give consent.

31. A patient enters a dental office, completes a personal, medical, and dental history, sits in the dental chair, and says nothing about the care he or she is to receive. Has this patient given consent to an examination of the oral cavity?

    Answer: Yes. In the situation described, the consent is termed apparent consent, implied by the actions of the party.

32. In summary, how is consent classified?

    Answer: Actual — written or oral; or apparent — implied by law or implied by the actions of the party.

33. A child of 13 years enters the dental office with mild pain that has been present for several days. The child consents to care and neither parent is available. Is the consent valid?

    Answer: No. In the case described, consent must be obtained from the parent or guardian.

34. If the child in the situation described in question 33 was 19 years of age, is the consent valid?

    Answer: Yes. By statute, all states have lowered the age of majority to 18 years of age.

35. A pregnant, unmarried female, 17 years of age, is pre-

sented with a dental treatment plan. The patient agrees, but the parent does not. The dentist completes the care. The parent claims the consent of the child is not valid. Is the parent correct?

Answer: No. The minor child has been emancipated by pregnancy and is able to give a valid consent. However, the parents are not responsible for payment.

36. If the patient is a 17-year-old male and either married or living alone and working, is his consent valid if the parent objects to the care?

    Answer: Yes. The minor child is emancipated. An emancipated minor is one who is not dependent on the parent for support, is married or pregnant, and can therefore consent to dental treatment independent of the parent or guardian.

37. In the absence of an emergency, under what circumstances can a 16-year-old, who is neither married nor pregnant and not independent of the parent, consent to dental care without the consent of the parent or guardian?

    Answer: There is a trend in many jurisdictions to consider the consent given by a mature minor as valid. The lowest age limit to which this recent trend has been extended is 14 years. The test is whether the patient understands the nature of the treatment and the risks involved. It has been called the "Mature Minor" rule.

38. Should a dentist, when treating a 16-year-old who fits the category of a mature minor, have the consent only of the child, only of the parent, or both?

    Answer: In all cases of consent obtained when treating anyone under 18 years of age, it is best to have both the child and the parent or guardian give consent. When a minor is involved, it is important to get the consent in writing.

39. Is the minimum age of consent the same in all states?

    Answer: No. Although in most states the age at which a child may grant a valid consent is 18 years, it is not so in all states. For example, in Alabama, the minimum age of consent to health care, independent of parental consent, is 14 years of age.

40. What legal action is available to a dental patient when a valid consent has not been obtained? Is it possible to take criminal action against the dentist in cases of lack of consent?

    Answer: The civil actions that may be available for

treatment of a patient when a valid consent has not been obtained are actions in battery, breach of contract, and malpractice. In some jurisdictions (eg, New York) actions in battery arising from lack of consent are treated as malpractice. It is difficult to sustain a criminal action in battery because of lack of consent due to the fact that it is almost impossible to show an intent to harm, and proving the intent to harm is essential in a criminal allegation of battery.

41. What is the general rule regarding information that must be given to a patient in order to obtain consent that is informed and meets the test of self-determination?

Answer: The patient must be given enough information about the procedure and its benefits and risks to make an intelligent decision.

42. Are there any specific requirements set out in judicial decisions or statutes as to the extent of information that must be given to a dental patient in order for the patient to make an intelligent decision in giving consent?

Answer: Yes. In judicial decisions, there have been many cases setting out the requirements. These requirements are: the treatment to be completed must be described to the patient, the benefits must be presented; the material risks must be stated; alternatives must be described; the prognosis if no care is provided must be presented; and the information must be presented in a manner that the patient can understand. Many states have enacted statutes setting out requirements similar to case law. In situations in which federal money is used to support the care, there are additional federal regulations concerning consent.

43. If a dentist learns some facts about a patient as he or she performs dental service, may the dentist disclose this information to anyone without the patient's consent?

Answer: No. By disclosing such information, the dentist would commit a breach confidentiality and an invasion of the patient's right to privacy — a right carefully protected by law in contemporary society. In order to release confidential information, including records, the dentist should obtain a written waiver from the patient. In some states, the unauthorized release of information obtained from the patient in the course of treatment is a crime.

44. In a trial of a patient, must a dentist reveal information

obtained in the course of treatment of the patient?

Answer: At common law (legal precedent), a dentist was required at a trial to release information obtained from a patient during treatment. Thus, the information was not privileged. By state law, in some jurisdictions, information obtained by a dentist in the course of treatment is privileged and, unless the patient waives the privilege, the dentist is not permitted to release the information.

45. Is there any information obtained by the dentist in the course of treatment that the dentist is required to disclose?

Answer: Yes. By law, in most jurisdictions a dentist is required to report patients with communicable diseases and cases of suspected child abuse to the appropriate state agency.

STANDARD OF CARE

46. When treating a patient, must the dentist use ordinary care, or is he or she held to the level of care of the best dentist?

Answer: The standard of care to which a dentist is held is that of a reasonable dentist. Therefore, the dentist is expected to use ordinary care.

47. How have the courts described the standard of care expected of the dentist?

Answer: A dentist is held to the standard of a reasonable and prudent dentist from the same school of practice in a community similar to the one in which the care was rendered.

48. Are dentists who are specialists held to the standards of other specialists or to the standards of general practitioners who perform the same services?

Answer: A specialist is held to the standards of other specialists in the same field.

49. Are local standards or national standards applied to general dentists and specialists?

Answer: At the present time, both general dentists and specialists are held to local standards; however, in some jurisdictions the trend is to hold specialists to a national standard.

50. Is a customary local standard automatically acceptable in court?

Answer: Recently, some courts have rejected the customary standard in favor of an acceptable standard. This novel way of looking at standard of care resulted from situations where the local or customary standard was thought by the court to be negligent and therefore unacceptable.

51. Are standards of care established by professional societies recognized by the courts as acceptable standards?

Answer: No. The level at which professionals are expected to provide care is established by the courts. It is what dentists do that establishes standards, not what their organizations say they should do.

52. If a general dentist undertakes orthodontic treatment, is he or she held to the standard of care of an orthodontist or to that of a general dentist?

Answer: To the standard of a general dentist. However, there seems to be a legal trend toward holding the generalist to the standard of a specialist when he or she is treating a patient who should have been referred to a specialist, or if the generalist suggested that the patient seek the services of a specialist.

53. If a dentist fails to refer a patient to a specialist when he or she should, will the dentist be liable to the patient for negligence?

Answer: Yes. Such liability is becoming more frequent. It is known as failure to make a timely referral.

54. What risk does a dentist run when failing to inform a patient in his or her care of an incident that might be injurious, such as a fractured root tip, a broken file left in a canal, and so forth?

Answer: This type of fraudulent behavior could extend the Statute of Limitations and/or be actionable at law by itself for malpractice. There is also a danger of punitive damages being awarded by the court for the fraudulent concealment, and punitive damages are not covered by professional liability insurance.

55. In rendering care, what types of civil suits might be brought by a patient against a dentist?

Answer: Professional negligence (malpractice), battery (trespass to the person), fraudulent misrepresentation, false imprisonment, invasion of privacy, defamation, breach of confidentiality, abandonment. These are all torts, although only negligence is classified as an unintentional tort. The others are intentional torts. There is also the possibility of a breach of contract lawsuit under contract law.

56. In order to win a suit in malpractice against a dentist, what must the patient prove?

    Answer: That a duty was owed by the dentist to the patient (ie, a dentist-patient relationship existed); that the duty was breached; that an injury resulted; that the breach of duty was the direct cause of the injury; that the injury resulted in damages; and, in some jurisdictions, that the patient did not contribute to the injury.

57. If a dentist loses a malpractice case, does the court ever require the dentist to redo the service?

    Answer: No. Only money damages are awarded.

58. What must a defendant-dentist show to avoid losing a case of malpractice brought by a patient?

    Answer: To win the case, the dentist must show either: (1) there was no duty owed (no doctor/patient relationship; (2) there was no departure from the standard of care; (3) there was no injury; or, (4) if there was an injury, the departure from the standard of care was not the direct cause of the injury; and (5) in some jurisdictions, that the patient contributed to the injury.

59. If a general dentist refers a patient to a specialist who has a good reputation, and the specialist commits a negligent act, can the referring dentist be held liable?

    Answer: No. Only when the specialist has a reputation for incompetence or if the referring dentist benefited in some material way from the referral can the referring dentist be held liable.

60. If a dentist causes an accidental injury to a patient, such as cutting the patient's tongue, does this injury constitute negligence?

    Answer: The word "accident" defeats a claim of negligence. Accidents that can be avoided are not accidents but are acts of negligence. In the stated case, because the injury is described as accidental, there is no negligence.

61. When a dentist administers the wrong drug to a dental patient, causing injury, does he or she commit a tort?

    Answer: Yes. Drug administration should be most carefully monitored. Even if the drug container was mislabeled by the manufacturer, the dentist is liable to the patient for such an action. Of course, the dentist could then sue the drug manufacturer to recover for the losses paid to the patient.

62. Following the injection of a local anesthetic agent, a

dental patient falls out of the dental chair onto the floor and suffers a concussion of the skull. Would this patient be the subject of a tort committed by the dentist?

Answer: If it can be shown that the fall resulted directly from the injection of the local anesthetic (allergic reaction or hyperadrenergic state), and the dentist should have known that this might occur and did not take the necessary precautions to prevent the fall, a tort was committed. If, however, the history and experience were negative and the result was completely unexpected, no tort was committed, no matter how serious the injury.

63. Would a dentist who fractures a patient's jaw in the course of dental surgery have committed a tort?

Answer: If the fracture was caused by the negligence of the dentist, a tort was committed. If, however, the fracture was unavoidable (unforeseeable or hardly likely to occur), no tort was committed. Not all injuries to patients are torts — only those acts where negligence or willfulness can be shown. Unavoidable accidents and/or unavoidable injuries are not torts.

64. If a bad result occurs from treatment, does this imply or prove negligence?

Answer: No. The bad result must be shown to be caused by a negligent act.

65. Are there rules of law in some states that may relieve the dentist of liability for malpractice in specific cases?

Answer: Yes, where the "Good Samaritan" acts apply; where there is contributory negligence on the part of the patient (in some states); or where there is a prior settlement of the patient's claim with another party who has assumed liability.

66. Are errors in judgment grounds for malpractice?

Answer: No, provided the error was honestly and reasonably made.

EMPLOYEES

67. If a dental assistant commits an act of negligence without the knowledge of the dentist, and the patient elects to sue the dentist, can the patient collect from the dentist?

Answer: Yes. The dentist is held liable under the theory of *respondeat superior* (vicarious liability) for the negligent acts of employees when the acts are performed within the general scope of employment.

68. How does the legal doctrine of *respondeat superior* apply to individuals in the dental office?

    Answer: Under the doctrine of respondeat superior, the individual in a superior position must pay for the negligent acts of persons in an inferior position. Thus, a dentist must pay for the negligent acts of employees under the legal principle of vicarious liability.

69. If a dental assistant commits an act of negligence for which the dentist must by court order pay money damages to an injured patient, can the dentist sue the assistant for indemnification?

    Answer: Yes. The dentist will probably win the suit, although this is rarely done.

70. A dentist tells the employee hygienist never to use instruments unless they are sterilized. The hygienist does not follow the orders of the dentist and as a result a patient suffers an infection. In a suit by the patient against the dentist, will the dentist be required to pay money damages for the negligence of the hygienist?

    Answer: Yes. The legal theory is that the dentist placed the hygienist in a position to commit the act. The dentist benefits from the care provided by the hygienist and should therefore bear the burden of risk. Both legal theories are compatible with the doctrines of vicarious liability and *respondeat superior*.

71. Suppose the act performed by the hygienist in the above situation is illegal, and the hygienist is aware of it, while the dentist is unaware that the hygienist committed the act. Will the result be the same?

    Answer: Yes, for the same reasons given above.

72. Knowing that the dentist is responsible for the acts of employees, why would an attorney for the patient sue the negligent employee as well as the dentist?

    Answer: When the employee is considered a defendant, the plaintiff's attorney gains considerably more procedural benefits than if the employee only appears as a witness. The attorney can ask a defendant leading questions and can be certain that the employee will appear in court.

73. If an employee (hygienist or assistant) of a dentist performs a dental service for a patient that is illegal, can the patient win a malpractice suit against the employee or against the dentist?

    Answer: If the procedure is done properly, the patient cannot win a suit in malpractice against either the dentist or his or her employee.

74. In the case described in question 73, is there any civil cause of action?

    Answer: Yes, possibly in breach of contract, fraudulent misrepresentation, or battery.

TERMINATION OF SERVICES

75. What procedure should a dentist follow to avoid legal risk when prematurely terminating treatment of a patient?

    Answer: The dentist should notify the patient in writing by certified mail of the intention to terminate treatment; provide the patient with sufficient time to secure comparable substitute services; make the records and radiographs available to the substitute dentist; and inform the patient of the consequences of delay beyond a reasonable period of time in securing substitute services.

76. If a dentist terminates care without proper notice, what is the legal liability?

    Answer: A dentist who terminates care without proper notice is guilty of abandonment and may be required to pay damages to the patient. The dentist may also be open to suit in breach of contract or malpractice. In some jurisdictions, to abandon a patient is a criminal act.

77. If the dentist when terminating care without good cause completes the requirement for proper and timely notification, he or she is not at legal risk for a claim of abandonment. However, may the dentist be open to some other legal risk?

    Answer: Yes, breach of contract. To avoid this secondary risk, the cause for termination must have some good basis in fact. Usually, failure on the part of the patient to complete his or her duties, such as failure to keep appointments, to follow directions, to pay bills on time, and so forth, will suffice.

RECORDS

78. Is a dentist required by law to maintain patient records?

    Answer: Yes. Case law establishes that adequate and accurate records are required. In many jurisdictions they are also required by state regulation.

79. What advantages does a dentist derive from keeping good records, other than compliance with the law?

Answer: Patients' records may serve as evidence in legal disputes.

80. How long should records, including radiographs, be kept by the dentist?

Answer: Ideally forever, practically for 10 years. In the case of minors, records should be kept for at least 10 years after the minor reaches the age of majority. In many states, there are regulations as to how long records should be kept, but it should serve as the minimum time for retention of patient records.

81. Who owns the records, including the radiographs, of a patient?

Answer: The ownership of patient records varies from state to state. The trend is that the patient is entitled to the information on the record, while the doctor has custodial rights to the record. In some jurisdictions, New York for example, on the patient's written request the dentist must provide the patient with a copy of the records and radiographs. The dentist may charge a reasonable fee to duplicate the record and radiographs, but may not withhold them for payment of a prior bill. The request to furnish records to someone other than the patient should be in writing; if not, the dentist may be guilty of invasion of privacy for releasing the records. Under no circumstances, except by court order, should the dentist surrender the original records or radiographs.

82. What risk does a dentist invite by altering a record after there is an indication that a suit may be entered against him or her?

Answer: Considerable. Altering charts in preparation of a suit can be a serious transgression in the civil suit and may result in a criminal charge against the dentist. It may constitute criminal fraud, and the insurance company may withdraw from the defense of the claim.

83. What should a good dental record contain?

Answer: A complete personal, medical, and dental history; the results of any tests performed, including an interpretation of radiographs; a thorough diagnosis; a thorough treatment plan; accurate and complete treatment notes; and any consents to care. The record also should include any special instructions to the patient, drugs prescribed and administered, laboratory work authorizations, and the outcome of care. Where consultations are requested, the reports of such consultations should be included in the record.

84. What is the best way for a dentist to manage a situation in which a patient refused to submit to recommended radiographs and the dentist wishes to treat the patient?

Answer: The dentist should have the patient sign a statement indicating refusal to submit to radiographs against the advice of the dentist. The risks of not obtaining radiographs also should be set out in the statement. However, it is best for a dentist to refuse to treat a patient who refuses to submit to diagnostic procedures that the dentist believes are essential to the proper care of the patient.

85. What procedure should a dentist follow if he or she wishes to use photographs, records, and/or radiographs of a patient in case reports, texts, or scientific presentations?

Answer: A written release should be obtained from the patient; and the identity of the patient should be concealed in the photographs and records.

86. Who has title (ownership) of a denture during its fabrication?

Answer: The dentist.

87. Does title to a denture pass from the dentist to the patient when it is completely paid for, or when it is inserted as completed?

Answer: When it is completed. Even if money is still owed by the patient, the title to the denture passes when final insertion is made (after the final adjustment).

88. Must dentists accept the return of a denture in lieu of payment when the patient claims the denture is unsatisfactory?

Answer: No. Although dentists may accept the denture in lieu of payment, they are not obliged to do so.

89. If a patient surrenders a denture to a dentist 6 months after completion for adjustment and money is still due for the fabrication of the denture, may a dentist retain the denture until the original fee is paid?

Answer: No. Title has passed and the denture is owned by the patient. A dentist who keeps the denture is guilty of conversion. He may, however, retain the denture until the fee for the adjustment is paid.

90. When a dentist places a denture in a patient's mouth and dismisses the patient, stating that no more appointments will be necessary, does the denture belong to the patient?

Answer: Yes. The title has passed because the dentist delivered the goods and indicated by the statement that the denture has been completed.

INSURANCE

91. Does malpractice insurance ordinarily cover dentists when they are sued for battery due to lack of informed consent?
    Answer: Professional liability (malpractice) insurance ordinarily does not cover a dentist for any torts other than professional negligence. Thus, intentional torts, such as breach of contract, defamation, invasion of privacy, or battery are usually not covered by malpractice insurance. In some states (eg, New York) lack of informed consent is considered malpractice and therefore covered by malpractice insurance. In many jurisdictions, actions against health providers based on lack of informed consent is considered negligence. Some courts treat complete lack of consent as a battery. However, if the consent obtained is not informed, it is usually considered as negligence, in which case the typical professional liability insurance will provide coverage.

92. Should liability policies for dentists have a consent to settlement clause which stipulates that the insurance company will not settle or compromise any claims or lawsuits without the written consent of the dentist?
    Answer: Absolutely. It is the dentist's reputation that is at stake. The dentist is the client of the insurance company and should insist on agreeing to settlement negotiations with the plaintiff. Unfortunately, the trend in newer policies is to deprive the dentist of this right, reserving it for themselves.

93. May a liability policy taken out by an individual dentist agree to pay damages caused by the dentist, dental assistant, partner, anesthetist, nurse, or any other person in the dental office?
    Answer: Yes. The terms of the liability policy are set by the contracting parties. Thus, if the dentist wants this type of coverage and the company agrees, then those are the terms. However, companies usually have standard terms and to arrange others can be difficult and costly. Most policies cover employees who are not licensed without having to name them.

94. A dentist requests that an employee (hygienist or assis-

tant) provide an illegal service for a patient. The service is provided negligently, and the dentist is sued by the patient. Will the dentist be protected under malpractice insurance?

Answer: No. Insurance companies will not protect a dentist in a suit for a tort where the tortfeasor (wrong-doer) is engaged in illegal activities.

95. In a state in which it is against the law for a dentist to supervise illegal treatment, and the dentist does in fact supervise an employee (hygienist or assistant) in performing illegal acts, will the dentist's malpractice insurance cover him or her in a criminal case?

Answer: No malpractice insurance or any other insurance will cover a dentist or anyone else against a criminal charge. It is against strong public policy, and is illegal to do so.

96. A dentist, while at a social gathering, is called to the dental office to treat an emergency patient. The dentist had several alcoholic drinks at the party. While treating the patient, the dentist commits an act of negligence and is sued by the patient. Will the malpractice insurance policy provide coverage?

Answer: No. Performing services while intoxicated or under the influence of drugs is a standard exclusion in malpractice policies.

97. A dentist states that his service is "guaranteed to satisfy." The patient believes the result promised is not achieved and enters suit against the dentist. Will this suit be covered by malpractice insurance?

Answer: Probably not. Most policies exclude coverage where results are guaranteed. In some jurisdictions, guaranteeing results in health care is a violation of the law. It is also in violation of the Principles of Ethics and Code of Professional Conduct of the American Dental Association.

PARTNERSHIP

98. Two dentists are in a partnership. One dentist commits an act of negligence. If the patient should elect to sue the other dentist, will this other dentist be liable?

Answer: Yes. Regarding third parties (in this case, the injured patient), each partner is liable for the negligent acts of the other. Between the partners, however, they can agree privately and by contract to indemnify each other for losses suffered innocently. Based on this concept, all partners should be insured by the same company.

99. A patient wins a lawsuit in negligence against one dentist in a partnership, and the dentist cannot satisfy the judgment. The patient then attempts to seize the personal property of the partner. Can the patient succeed?

Answer: Yes. Under partnership law, all assets of each partner are subject to legal seizure for acts committed by any partner on behalf of the partnership.

100. A partner treats a patient for an emergency after office hours. The other partner is unaware of the treatment and is never told about it. The patient sues and wins a case in malpractice against the treating dentist. Can the other partner also be held liable?

Answer: Yes. Lack of knowledge of the acts of one partner is not a bar to recovery if the patient wins the suit against the other partner. In partnership practice, each partner is held vicariously liable for the negligent acts of all other partners.

101. If two or more dentists form a professional corporation, does it alter the liability of the "innocent" dentist?

Answer: Yes. In most jurisdictions, if a negligent act is committed by one member of a professional corporation, other members of the corporation are not held liable. However, the corporation, as a legal entity, also may be liable.

102. What are the advantages of a written dental partnership agreement?

Answer: The individual duties, liabilities, and rights can be spelled out for each dentist before entering into the relationship; and certain valuable rights can be spelled out in the contract to survive after the death of a partner to benefit both the surviving partners and the deceased partner's heirs.

SETTLEMENTS AND LITIGATION

103. How should dentists respond to offers of settlement of a claim by a patient?

Answer: Offers of settlement may frequently result in avoidance of legal actions. However, any offers of settlement of a claim should be referred to the insurance company. Some policies specifically prohibit the dentist from entering into settlement negotiations without the knowledge and consent of the company.

104. Are offers to settle a dental lawsuit out of court considered by the court as an admission of guilt?

Answer: No. Courts always encourage litigants to settle differences prior to making appearances. To support this attitude, offers to settle are not admitted into evidence at trial and are not considered as admissions of guilt or liability. In some jurisdictions, settlements in malpractice suits are reported to the state licensing agency and may affect licensure.

105. Is a release for settling a dental claim a legally binding resolution of the claim?

Answer: Yes. Unless there is fraud, once a patient signs a release for the settlement of a dental claim, the cause of action is legally terminated and cannot be revived. Additional terms may be added to the settlement agreement, such as to keep the settlement and the amount confidental.

106. May any dentist be summoned to appear in court as a principal, expert witness and/or general witness?

Answer: Rules of procedure provide for the request (demand) for the appearance of any legitimate party to a suit. This would include the dentist as a principal (plaintiff or defendant), as an expert witness, or as a general witness. Failure to appear can result in contempt of court proceedings against the dentist, which have serious consequences. The courts, however, are cooperative, and if proper notice of difficulty in scheduling the appearance is given, the courts will generally adjust their schedule to meet the dentist's needs.

108. Can dentists be excused from jury duty?

Answer: Yes. Although dentists may be called to serve, they may be excused. As health providers, their community would be better served in the uninterrupted care of their patients. Most states recognize that the need of the community for dental care and the availability of others to serve outweighs the need for dentists to serve as jurors.

109. Can a dentist serve on the jury of a dental or medical malpractice suit if he or she elects to do so?

Answer: No. Physicians and dentists would not be permitted to serve on a jury in any suit involving a health practitioner. However, when called upon to do so, they may appear as expert witnesses.

110. A dentist, without thinking, says to a patient that an instrument slipped and damage was done, for which the dentist is sorry. The statement is made immediately after the injury. The dentist is sued and the patient wants to enter the statement into evidence during the trial. Considering that the statement is hearsay, can it be entered into evidence?

    Answer: Yes. The statement would be admissible under an exception to the hearsay evidence rule. Statements made immediately after an incident and against the interest of the party (*res gestae* exception and a declaration against interest exception) are admissible into evidence.

111. Once a suit against a dentist is either threatened or begun, and the attorney for the patient wishes to speak to the dentist to ask seemingly innocent questions, how should the dentist respond?

    Answer: By referring the attorney either to the dentist's own lawyer or to the insurance company. The dentist should not respond directly to any request for information or for records. Nor should any of his or her employees, partners, or associates respond to questions put to them by the attorney of the plaintiff/patient.

112. How soon after a lawsuit is threatened or started should the dentist notify his insurance company?

    Answer: Immediately! Some policies impose a time requirement during which notice must be given. Where there is none stated, notice should be given within a reasonable amount of time. Notifying the insurance company immediately is always the best course of action. Notice should be given by phone followed by a letter giving the details of the manner of notice of suit or threatened suit. A signed receipt of the letter should be requested.

113. Most professional liability policies require that "unusual occurrences" be reported to the company at the earliest possible time. What constitutes an "unusual occurrence?"

    Answer: Polarized situations, such as the need to report a crown that has been aspirated or a lip that has been lacerated and requires a dozen stitches, are easy to define. There are many situations that may or may not be considered "unusual occurrences," and the dentist should use his or her professional judgment as to what incidents should be reported.

114. A dental assistant states to a patient that the dentist is

excellent and will complete the treatment on a given date and to the satisfaction of the patient. Is the dentist held to these conditions?

Answer: Yes. Statements made by the employee of a dentist are treated the same as statements made by the dentist. This also applies to statements of the employee to the effect that a "mistake" was made by the dentist.

115. What is the "conspiracy of silence" that is often referred to by lawyers and courts, and how does it affect the trial of malpractice suits?

Answer: It is an unspoken agreement between health practitioners not to testify against one another or to assist in any way with a suit against a fellow professional. In almost all suits in malpractice, an expert witness is needed by the complaining patient. If the attorney cannot obtain the services of an expert witness to appear for his or her client, the suit is lost. To engage in a "conspiracy of silence" is unethical and illegal, but most difficult to prove.

116. Is a dentist under any obligation to testify on behalf of a patient when requested to do so?

Answer: Yes. The Principles of Ethics and Code of Professional Conduct of the American Dental Association sets out this obligation. When the court makes this request, the dentist is under a legal duty to testify.

117. How does the doctrine of *res ipsa loquitor* apply to the trial of malpractice cases?

Answer: If a patient is injured and has no way of determining the event which led to the injury (for example, the patient was unconscious at the time, due to general anesthesia), the patient can request the court to invoke the doctrine of *res ipsa loquitor*. In effect, this means the patient is relieved of the initial burden of proving negligence; negligence is presumed because without negligence there would have been no injury. The dentist now has the burden of presenting evidence to show that he or she was not negligent. In some states, courts are reluctant to permit the use of *res ipsa loquitor* in malpractice litigation.

EPILOGUE

Any book on jurisprudence is primarily concerned with relationships between and among people. These relationships are directly affected by laws and the legal processes. For dentistry, jurisprudence today means significant changes, dynamic expansions, and conflicting demands.

The dental patient has become a health consumer, demanding better dental practices and, at the same time, lower dental health costs. The government, which previously functioned as merely a public licensure agency, now profoundly affects the dental practitioner by financing dental education and research and by debating national health insurance. The individual dentist is probing the desirability of new legal associations for the practice of dentistry.

During the past 6 years, since the first edition of this text was published, dentists have been exposed, as never before, to the judicial system and the work of attorneys. Most of the experiences have been threatening. A lack of understanding by dentists of the operation of the legal system and how lawyers conduct their business in representing clients has led to a breakdown in communication between these two noble professions. The dental malpractice crisis that surfaced in the early 1980s brought the effects of lack of understanding to the surface. Most dentists blame the legal profession for the escalation in dental malpractice litigation. Reliable studies on the subject demonstrate that the lawyers are not at fault. Education of both professions about their respective roles is the most effective way to heal the wounds created by the adversarial system of malpractice litigation. This book is designed for the dental profession with that goal in mind.

The crisis also brought to the surface the need for dentists to know what is expected of them by society, as reflected in court decisions and legislation, to minimize the risk of allegations of malpractice and illegal practice. Much of the text of this book is devoted to educating dentists and dental students about these subjects.

In short, the dental professional is moving into a new relationship with human society, one that must be concerned with the social well-being of a patient and not merely with his or her physical and mental well-being. Furthermore, the dentist has become enmeshed in the political processes of government that seek to provide the economic well-being for better dental health in America. Finally, the dentist seeks to adjust basic relationships with patients to meet the new demands and accelerating changes. This relationship is the keystone in the practice of a health profession.

Law, a vital tool to achieve just, fair, and equitable relationships between dentists and patients, now demands that each and every dentist and dental student understand legal concepts, principles, rules, and procedures. This text attempts to contribute to such understanding. Law must not be feared by dentists as an enemy. Law should be used as a tool to harmonize the relationships among dentists, patients, governments, and third-party interests. It establishes, for the practitioner, the parameters in which the practice of dentistry may be conducted to conform to reasonable standards for the dentist and the patient. Only in this utilization of law by the dental profession can an environment of better justice be achieved in a nation that strives constantly to provide better dental health.

Oliver C. Schroeder, Jr.
Burton R. Pollack

RISK MANAGEMENT IN DENTAL PRACTICE*

Burton R. Pollack

The purpose of this appendix is to "bring it all together" in one place. Although much of the material is contained in other sections of the book, its repetition links the information directly to risk management activities and thus increases the effectiveness of the recommendations. It also eliminates the need for the reader to check back in the book to find the legal principles that support the risk management advice.

BACKGROUND

Following the crisis in medical and hospital malpractice in the early 1970s, risk management concepts borrowed from industry were adapted to the health field — particularly to hospitals. Lately, risk management principles have been applied to individual practice settings. They are designed primarily to protect the financial resources of an industry (hospital, private practitioner, etc) from losses resulting from legal action. An effective risk management program includes:

1. loss identification (exposure to legal claims);
2. loss analysis (evaluation of loss experience);
3. loss avoidance or reduction;
4. loss financing (financing claims exposure).

Three activities are associated with risk management:

1. identifying areas of legal vulnerability;
2. instituting corrective or preventive measures;
3. purchasing liability insurance.

This appendix is designed to supply information related to the first two listed activities. It is based on a thorough review of cases brought against dentists, and opinions of the courts in deciding medical and

---

* Reprinted in part by permission of the National Society of Dental Practitioners, Suite 900, 1275 K Street NW, Washington, DC 20005.

dental malpractice suits. The text summarizes the areas of legal vulnerability associated with the practice of dentistry. The highlighted risk management rules (recommendations, suggestions, etc) represent corrective or preventive measures associated with the subject matter of the text. The third activity, purchasing liability insurance, is a personal matter that includes cost, scope of coverage, and amount of indemnification of losses, and is covered in chapter 6.

Risk management principles are applied to professional and general liability. However, this appendix will focus on professional liability.

INTRODUCTION

An effective risk management program will do much to control the cost of malpractice insurance and protect the reputation and resources of the practitioner.

This appendix will provide dentists with information about the legal risks of practice and methods designed to eliminate or reduce them. The goal is to enable dentists to practice in a worry- and claims-free environment.

To maintain an effective dental risk management program, it is not essential that the practitioner know how the courts are organized, the history of the development of consent laws, procedural laws of evidence, or the many other legal principles that contribute to the operation of law and the legal system. For that information, the reader may refer to the many available texts listed in the bibliography. Instead, the sole purpose of this appendix is to guide dentists in what to do and what not to do in the area of risk management, without the burden of explaining why, except when necessary.

CAVEATS IN RISK MANAGEMENT AND THE LAW

There are 51 jurisdictions in the United States; 50 states and the federal government. Each of the 50 states has exercised its right to regulate the health professions including dentistry. In addition, Puerto Rico, the Virgin Islands, and the District of Columbia regulate health practices. The federal government also regulates some elements of health practice. Therefore, there are 54 separate jurisdictions that regulate the practice of dentistry. Except for federal regulations that apply to practitioners in all states, each jurisdiction has independent regulations. Except for some federal laws, there is no generic law in the United States. There are, however, legal principles that apply nationwide. The legal principle of the statute of limitations is the same in all jurisdictions but the statute may begin to run at different times and for different lengths of time in each individual jurisdiction.

The caveat is that for a practitioner to know the specifics of the regulation of dental practice, he or she must know local law. The same act may be legal in one state and illegal in another: In New York it is legal for a dental laboratory to select a shade for a crown. In Massachusetts it is illegal for a dentist to refer a patient to a laboratory for the purpose of selecting a shade. Therefore, a dentist in New York who sends a patient to a dental laboratory for the selection of a shade is not in violation of the law. The same act performed by a dentist in Massachusetts would be in violation of the law. Except for the purpose of presenting examples, this appendix will describe generic legal principles. Local attorneys, government agencies, or a local dental society should be of assistance in determining the law of the jurisdiction in which you conduct your practice.

THE REGULATION OF DENTAL PRACTICE

As stated above, each of the 54 jurisdictions has exercised its right to regulate dental practice. Except for federal regulation, the mechanism for regulation is similar. The elected body, the legislature, enacts legislation designed to regulate dental practice. Because the members of the electorate have neither the time nor the expertise to exercise control over the daily activities of the profession and the details of practice, they enact additional legislation (enabling legislation or statutory authority) establishing an administrative agency to further regulate the profession and grant to that agency the power to adopt rules and regulations to carry out its mission.

Each state may vary the name of the administrative body and adopt any organizational structure to accomplish the goal of regulating the health profession, but the general regulatory structure is the same. In New York, for example, there are two administrative agencies regulating dentists and other health professionals: the State Education Department and the Board of Regents. The Commissioner of Education is empowered by legislative act to adopt regulations; the Board of Regents, to adopt rules. In New York, the State Board for Dentistry is not authorized to adopt rules or regulations for the purpose of regulating dental practice. It serves as an examining body, recommends licensure, advises the Commissioner and the Board of Regents on dental matters, and serves as an administrative body to hear violations of the rules and regulations. In New Jersey, one administrative agency regulates the practice of dentistry — the Board of Dentistry. It combines all the functions assigned to the three agencies in New York.

A combination of the statutes and the rules and regulations make up the body of black letter law referred to as the Dental Practice Act. However, in all jurisdictions there are many other laws that affect the practice of dentistry. These may be found in the public health law, the sanitary code, the education law, and others. The practitioner should be aware that the laws regulating dental practice are spread throughout the statutes and administrative laws of the state. In addition, there are a multitude of federal laws that exercise control over dental practice. The old adage that ignorance of the law is no excuse should not be ignored.

The risk management principles are: Know the laws of the jurisdiction in which you practice and federal laws that apply to the practice of dentistry, and do not break them!

AREAS OF LEGAL VULNERABILITY IN DENTAL PRACTICE

Legal vulnerability in dental practice may be divided into two broad categories: criminal and civil. Each category has subcategories as shown on the next page.

CRIMINAL AND QUASI-CRIMINAL VULNERABILITY

Violations of statutory law are termed crimes. They constitute acts that are deemed by the government to be against the public interest. They may be defined as misdemeanors or felonies. Violations of that part of the Dental Practice Act that is statutory are classified as crimes, and may include penalties such as loss or suspension of license, mandatory psychiatric counseling, drug rehabilitation, mandatory continuing education, fines, or even jail. If the legislature declares the violation a misdemeanor, the jail sentence may be less than if it classifies the violation a felony. In New York, for instance, aiding or abetting an unlicensed person to perform a service that requires a license is classified a class E felony, punishable by up to 3 years in jail. In other jurisdictions, it is classified as a misdemeanor.

Violations of administrative laws (rules or regulations of administrative agencies, eg, the state board, the state education department, the board of regents), are termed quasi-crimes. Penalties may include all actions that are possible under crimes, except loss of personal freedom (jail).

One of the major differences between a violation of a statute and that of an administrative law is the degree of evidence necessary to convict. In allegations of criminal behavior, the state must prove "beyond a reasonable doubt" that the law was violated. For violations of administrative law, the proof necessary may only be "substantial

LEGAL VULNERABILITY IN DENTAL PRACTICE

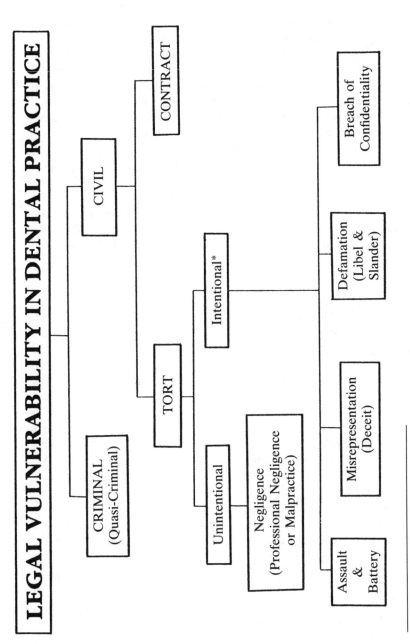

* The intentional torts listed on the chart are those most frequently associated with dental practice. There are others, eg, false imprisonment, abuse of process, trespass to real property, conversion, interference with performance of a contract, and others that are recognized in law but have little relevance in dental practice.

evidence," which may be less than 50%. (In civil actions, the burden on the plaintiff is to prove by a "fair preponderance of the evidence" [more than 50%], that the defendant is guilty.)

In all dental practice acts, there is authority granted to an administrative agency to impose punitive sanctions against a dentist who is found guilty of a violation. Therefore, a dentist who is found guilty of violating the law regulating the prescription or the administration of controlled substances may have an additional action taken by the dental board, or if the violation occurs in New York, by the Board of Regents, against the license of the offender.

At the present time, professional liability insurance does not provide protection against either criminal or quasi-criminal allegations. However, if there is an allegation of negligence attached to a violation of the law, either criminal or quasi-criminal, the defense of a civil suit based on an injury resulting from the alleged illegal act becomes more difficult because of trial practice procedures.

The risk management admonition again is: Don't break the law!

THE DOCTOR-PATIENT CONTRACT

When the Doctor-Patient Relationship Begins

The legal foundation of the doctor-patient relationship is contract law. At the moment a dentist expresses a professional opinion, the doctor-patient relationship begins, and the doctor is burdened with implied warranties (duties). The fact that no fee is involved does not affect the relationship that attaches to the contract or the duties.

The example best demonstrating the moment the relationship begins, and the duties that attach, is a situation where a dentist gives a fellow party-goer dental advice at a social gathering. If the advice results in an injury, the dentist may be held liable for negligence. It is not a defense that no fee was charged or expected. The dentist would be held to the standard that patients should not be given dental advice unless an examination and a history are completed.

The risk management principle is: In social settings, never provide anyone, unless he or she is a bona fide patient, with advice regarding dental problems.

Must you accept anyone who presents to you for care? The answer is a qualified no. You may refuse to treat a patient for any reason except race, creed, color, or national origin. As long as the person is not a patient of record, you may refuse to provide emergency care. It may be unethical, but it is not illegal, nor can it form the basis of a civil suit. However, remember, as stated above, that just as soon as you express a professional judgment, or perform a professional act, the doctor-patient relationship begins, and duties begin to attach.

When the Doctor-Patient Relationship Ends

The relationship ends when:

1. both parties agree to end it;
2. either the patient or the dentist dies;
3. the patient ends it by act or statement;
4. the patient is cured; or
5. the dentist unilaterally decides to terminate the care.

The dentist unilaterally terminating the relationship may support an abandonment claim by the patient unless the dentist follows a procedure acceptable to the courts. In some jurisdictions, abandoning a patient is a violation of the law. In all jurisdictions, abandonment may lead to a civil suit.

The risk management rule to avoid findings of abandonment when you wish to discontinue treatment of a patient is to: Give the patient sufficient time to find alternate care, and assure the patient that you will cooperate by making the patient's records, radiographs, and other diagnostic aids and reports available to the succeeding dentist.

It is best to have the patient select the substitute dentist.

The major causes that contribute to a decision to terminate treatment before it is complete are: the patient has not fulfilled the payment agreement; the patient has not cooperated in keeping appointments; the patient has not complied with home care instructions; or there has been a breakdown in interpersonal relationships. Any of these is ample justification for the dentist to terminate treatment.

A risk management rule is: Discontinue treatment of patients who do not cooperate in their care, become antagonistic, or exhibit a litigious attitude.

The procedure recommended to discontinue care begins with a discussion of the problem with the patient. Advise the patient that it is in their best interest to seek care elsewhere. Assure the patient that you will cooperate by making the records available. Note the conversation on the patient's record. Follow up the conversation with a certified letter stating the above, signed receipt requested.

A risk management caveat is: Do not discontinue treatment at a time when the patient's health may be compromised. The decision is professional rather than legal.

Express Terms

An express term is one in which both parties are in agreement. Putting the term in writing is not required to make it enforceable, although to avoid misunderstandings a written agreement is always preferred. Usually, the express terms define items such as the fee, the treatment, and the manner in which payments are to be made.

The risk management principle is: When in doubt, write it out! It may be done on separate forms or entered into the record of the patient. It is best done on a separate form because the treatment record should contain only treatment notes and patient reactions to treatment.

Guarantees

Guarantees made by the dentist or an employee constitute an express term in the contract. In some jurisdictions, guarantees attached to health care are illegal. They are also in violation of the Principle of Ethics and Code of Professional Conduct of the American Dental Association. You will be held to a guarantee even if the treatment meets acceptable standards of care. A statement made by a dentist to the patient that he or she will be satisfied with the treatment is a guarantee. If the patient is not satisfied, the dentist has breached the contract in spite of the excellent quality of the service. Therapeutic reassurances are rare in dentistry, except in unusual situations and usually when related to oral surgery.

Risk management rule: Never guarantee a result!

Implied Warranties (Duties) Owed by the Doctor

Attached to the doctor-patient relationship are additional duties that are implied, unless the express terms serve to void them. They are enforceable although not written or stated. Over the years the courts have identified many of these implied duties. In accepting a patient for care, the dentist warrants that he or she will:

1. be properly licensed and registered;
2. employ competent personnel and supervise them carefully;
3. provide care that will meet acceptable standards;
4. keep patients informed of their treatment status;
5. remain current with recent advances in the profession;
6. provide emergency care for patients of record.

A complete list of implied duties owed by the dentist is contained at the end of this appendix.

The list generates a host of risk management rules. They are all important, but one appears to be of considerable influence in deciding malpractice cases and is neglected by many practitioners: *Actively participate in continuing education.*

Implied Duties Owed by the Patient

In accepting care the patient warrants that:

1. home care instructions will be followed;
2. appointments will be kept;
3. bills for services will be paid in a reasonable time;
4. the patient will cooperate in the care;
5. the patient will notify the dentist of a change in health status.

It is best to make the last listed duty part of the express terms of the agreement. This can be done by placing the statement at the end of the history form and reminding the patient of the need to notify the office of a change in health status.

If the patient breaches any of these duties, notes to that effect should be made in the patient's record.

TORTS

Introduction

A tort is a civil wrong or injury, independent of a contract, that results from a breach of duty. The tort may be unintentional or intentional. An unintentional tort is one in which harm was not intended, as is the case in the tort of negligence. As the name implies, the intentional torts contain the element of intended harm.

Negligence is an unintentional tort. If the negligence involves an act that is performed in a professional capacity, it is termed professional negligence, or malpractice. Thus, if a dentist is accused of negligence in the performance of dental treatment, the allegation is one of malpractice.

The intentional torts of major concern to the dentist include trespass to the person (assault and battery), defamation, breach of confidentiality, and misrepresentation (deceit).

Malpractice (Professional Negligence) and Standard of Care

Only malpractice related to dentistry will be presented. The New York courts have provided the most comprehensive definition of malpractice as it relates to physicians and dentists. Although it is lengthy, the definition is reprinted because it is required reading for those interested in risk management. Included are some editorial changes and updating; important risk management concerns are highlighted.

A doctor's responsibilities are the same whether or not he is paid for the services. By undertaking to perform a medical (dental) service, he does not — nor does the law require him to — guarantee a good result. He is liable only for negligence.

A doctor who renders a medical (dental) service is obligated to have that reasonable degree of knowledge and ability expected of doctors (or specialists) who do that particular (operation, examination) treatment in the community where he practices, or a similar community (the trend in some jurisdictions is to apply a national standard).

The law recognizes that there are differences in the abilities of doctors, just as there are differences in the abilities of people engaged in other activities. To practice his profession, a doctor is not required to be possessed of the extraordinary knowledge and ability that belongs to a few men of rare endowments, but *he is required to keep abreast of the times and to practice in accordance with the approved methods and means of treatment in general use.* The standard to which he is held is measured by the degree of knowledge and ability of the average doctor (or specialist) in good standing in the community where he practices (or in a similar community).

In the performance of medical (dental) services the doctor is obligated to use his best judgment and to use reasonable care in the exercise of his knowledge and ability. The rule requiring him to use his best judgment does not make him liable for a mere error in judgment, provided he does what he thinks is best after careful examination. The rule of reasonable care does not require the exercise of the highest possible degree of care; it requires only that he exercise that degree of care that a reasonably prudent doctor (or specialist) would exercise under the same circumstances.

If a patient should sustain an injury while undergoing medical (dental) care and that injury results from the doctor's lack of knowledge or ability, or from his failure to exercise reasonable care or to use his best judgment, then he is responsible for the injuries that are the result of his acts.[1]

Courts do not require that all dentists use the same modality of treatment. The standard can be met if a "respectable minority" of practitioners use the same treatment method. Therefore, the Sargenti method in endodontic treatment and the Keyes technique in periodontal therapy would probably be acceptable to the courts as meeting the standard of reasonable care. It should be noted that the standard to which a dentist is held is the standard set by other dentists, not what a text, article, or a guideline from a professional organization recommends.

Additional risk management principles applied to malpractice prevention are:

1. *Do not undertake treatment beyond your ability and training even if the patient insists that you provide the care.*

2. *If, in your professional judgment, you believe that specialty care is required prior to the care you intend, do not undertake your treatment unless the patient follows your recommendation to obtain specialty care.* This is of importance when the patient needs to receive periodontal therapy prior to the fabrication of crowns or fixed bridges.

3. *If you recommend to the patient that specialty care is required, and the patient refuses to follow your recommendation, the legal risk is increased if you undertake the care that, by your own admission, should have been provided by a specialist.*

4. *If you believe that certain tests or diagnostic procedures should be completed before you undertake treatment and the patient refuses, as in the case of the need for radiographs, the legal risk is markedly increased if you treat the patient without the diagnostic aid you recommend.*

In 2, 3, and 4 above, you have established for yourself a standard of acceptable care. If you accede to the patient's refusal to follow your recommendations, and treat the patient, even at the patient's request, you have departed from your own standard. This action presents a situation that is difficult to defend. Having the patient sign a statement to the effect that he or she is aware of the risk of noncompliance somewhat reduces the risk but does not eliminate it. A court might declare the statement exculpatory, and void as against public policy. An exculpatory statement excuses an individual from liability for negligence. Agreements entered into by patients that relieve health practitioners from responsibility for negligent acts have not been enforced by the courts.

Trespass to the Person (Assault and Battery)

The civil counterpart of the criminal act of assault and battery is trespass to the person. It constitutes a threat to harm (assault) and unauthorized touching (battery). Traditionally, lack of informed consent to care was treated as assault and battery. Recent decisions classify lack of informed consent as negligence. The change resulted in part from the recognition by the courts that, except in the most unusual cases, doctors do not intend to harm their patients, even though the touching was not authorized by the patients. In some jurisdictions if the consent is present, but faulty, the rules of malpractice will apply. If there is a total absence of consent the case will be treated as assault and battery.

Assault and battery cases not associated with lack of consent have occurred in dentistry. The use of force or unnecessary physical restraints in the treatment of uncooperative children has led to allegations of criminal assault and battery and civil trespass to the person. Dentists should be aware that if the allegation is criminal, professional liability insurance will not provide coverage. In some older professional liability policies, civil actions of assault and battery are covered. The newer policies limit coverage to professional negligence.

The risk management principle applied to trespass to the person is: Avoid the use of physical force or unnecessary restraints in the treatment of children. If you feel that such measures are necessary, discuss the matter with the parents, and have them present in the operatory.

Misrepresentation (Deceit)

Patients must be kept informed of their treatment status. This is one of the implied duties that the courts have attached to the doctor-patient relationship. However, when information is withheld that places a patient's health in jeopardy, or deprives the patient of the legal right to bring suit against the practitioner, a legal action in deceit (fraudulent concealment) may result. In the civil action of deceit, the statute of limitations may be extended, and professional liability insurance may not provide coverage. In addition, a criminal action of fraud may also be alleged. The problems in dentistry most frequently associated with deceit include the failure to inform the patient when an instrument breaks off in a root canal, when a root is fractured and the tip remains in the jaw, and when the dentist is aware that the success of the treatment will be compromised because of lack of cooperation by the patient.

The risk management rule is: Never lie to patients about their treatment, and keep patients informed about their health status while in your care.

Third party payment coverage has led to many allegations of deceit. It is usually associated with passing off one metal for another in the fabrication of prosthetic appliances by substituting nonprecious for precious metals. Actions in criminal fraud also may result. Insurance companies are alert to such activities and are relentless in their pursuit of suspected dentists. The patient may also institute an action for the same act against the errant practitioner. Actions in fraudulent misrepresentation overlap actions in breach of contract. The choice is left to the plaintiff's attorney, and the one most damaging to the dentist's interests will be selected.

The risk management rule is worth repeating: Never lie to or deceive a patient or an insurance company!

Defamation

The intentional tort of defamation is not of major concern in dentistry because most dentists are aware of the problem and its consequences.

The risk management admonition is: Keep your opinions about your patients to yourself unless they are essential to the successful treatment of the patient. Expressions about the mental health of a patient are particularly risky.

Keep in mind that intentional torts are usually not covered by professional liability insurance.

Breach of Confidentiality

Breach of confidentiality was not known as a tort under English common law. It is a product of recent case law and black letter law.

Information obtained from the patient in the course of diagnosis or treatment must remain confidential. Unless the patient waives confidentiality, a breach may lead to a suit. Patients may waive confidentiality by their actions or words. It may also be waived by action of law, as in the case of the requirement to report certain communicable diseases to government agencies. When a patient visits a specialist or another health practitioner at your request, you are expected to inform that practitioner of the health status of the patient. In going to the specialist, the patient, by his or her action, has waived confidentiality. A patient who seeks care from a group practice and is aware that the practitioners practice as associates has waived confidentiality. There are many other situations in which confidentiality is waived, but there are many situations that a practitioner should be aware of when a specific waiver is required.

The risk management rule is: Never reveal any information about a patient to anyone without first obtaining permission from the patient — preferably in writing.

In some jurisdictions, information related to sexual activity obtained from a minor must not be revealed to the parent without the minor's consent. Both criminal and civil actions may result from the breach of confidentiality.

PATIENT RECORDS

Introduction

The patient's medical (dental) record is a legal document. It serves many purposes in the judicial process. It contains information about the patient's complaint, health history, and basis for the diagnosis, and it reports all treatment rendered, the patient's reaction to treatment, and the results of the treatment. Case law (law as stated by courts in deciding cases — also called common law), requires that these records be kept. They constitute an essential part of patient care. Treating a patient without maintaining accurate records represents a serious departure from acceptable care. Some jurisdictions require that accurate records be kept as part of black letter law.

The outcome of many suits against dentists are decided on the content and quality of patients' records. For the treating doctor, the record is the only documentation of the course of treatment of the patient, and the patient's reactions to the treatment. Memory alone is often viewed as self-serving, and the shortest written word lasts longer than the longest memory. In cases where the doctor and patient disagree on what took place and there is no written documentation of the event, the question may be settled in court by who makes the most credible witness. It becomes a risky affair for the doctor.

In summary, failure to keep accurate records may constitute negligence, and in some jurisdictions, a violation of law. In addition, failure to keep accurate records markedly increases the risk of losing a malpractice suit.

The risk management rule is: Accurate and complete records must be maintained for each patient you treat.

Ownership

The right to ownership of the patient's treatment record has undergone considerable change in the past decade. Courts have separated the physical record from the right of the patient to its contents. At one time, doctors had the exclusive right to the possession of the record and its contents. Today, after many suits, the law has evolved so that the doctor is considered the custodian of the record while the patient has a property right in it contents. Some jurisdictions have codified court decisions.

If the patient demands in writing the treatment record, or demands that the record be sent to another practitioner, comply with the request — but only supply copies. The term "record" includes the treatment record, radiographs, casts, results of tests, consultation reports, etc.

If you believe that the patient has litigation against you in mind, report the request to your insurance carrier. If there is no local black letter law in your jurisdiction, do not comply with the request unless the carrier approves.

The risk management rules that are generated by the new view of the courts about the patients' rights of ownership are: On the patients' written request for their records, comply, but only supply copies; and *if you believe a patient intends to sue, before you comply, contact your insurance carrier for advice.*

Form and Content

The changing law on ownership of patient records has had a profound effect on the form and content of the record. If you keep in mind the fact that what you write on the record can be seen by the patient, it will serve as a guide to what should be entered on the record. Other facts will assist you in maintaining good patient records. Records are your documentation of the care the patient has received. They are essential to your defense if you are accused of negligence. Currently, patient records are treated as legal documents and must be regarded as such.

Financial information has no place on the treatment record. Separate records should be kept to record charges and payments.

The treatment record should be written in black ink, or ball-point pen. It should be neat, well organized, and easily read. A sloppy record implies a sloppy dentist.

You are referred to a list at the end of the appendix for suggestions on form and content of record-keeping.

How Long Should You Retain Your Patient Records?

In many jurisdictions, there are laws specifying the minimum time period for retention of patient treatment records. Failure to comply brings with it risk of allegations by the state agency of criminal or quasi-criminal violations.

On the civil side, practitioners are advised to keep the original treatment records for as long as possible. Although the statute of limitations runs for a specific period, the exceptions dictate that the records be kept for a period considerably longer than the statute. For example, if you are accused of lying to a patient about a mishap in treatment, the courts may extend the statute based on fraudulent concealment. In addition, in many jurisdictions the statute does not begin to run until the patient discovered, or should have discovered, the act that produced the injury. Two thirds of the states have the discovery rule. The rest have the time-of-injury rule. But even in those, there are exceptions, as noted above. Without records, it is virtually impossible to defend a suit.

In the case of minors, the statute, in many jurisdictions, does not begin to run until the minor reaches majority.

The risk management rule is: You should retain your original patient treatment records, including radiographs and all other documents related to the diagnosis and treatment of the patient, for as long as possible.

Histories

The Medical History An area of growing concern for dentists in malpractice liability relates to the health history. There have been major financial losses due to the failure by the dentist to discover information about the patient's past medical history. The primary cause of the omission is the design of the self-administered health history form. The typical form, and that suggested for use by the American Dental Association, has led to considerable difficulties. There are two columns in which patients may indicate whether they present a particular problem in their treatment. They are asked to place a check mark in a Yes or No box. In many cases, there have been disputes about who placed the check mark in the box, notwithstanding the fact that the patient signed the form. Facts in dispute lead to problems for the defense attorney in the trial of a case.

The risk management rule is: If you use a self-administered health history form in which the patient is to respond by marking a box, have them initial the appropriate box, rather than using a check mark.

Other problems have arisen with the self-administered health history form. Did the patient understand the questions? Did the patient know the answer at the time the form was completed? Was the patient aware of the importance of the question to his or her care? If the answer to any of these questions is no, the patient may leave a blank in place of an answer. Blanks are dangerous. If a self-administered health form is used, there should be four columns instead of two, to avoid a possibility of a blank space. The column headings should be Yes, No, Don't Know, and Don't Understand The Question.

Another problem concerns the manner in which the dentist follows up the self-administered health history. It is normal for the dentist to question the patient further about positive answers to the questions and to ignore negative responses. This process may lead to major errors. The patient may have misinterpreted or not understood the question, and incorrectly answered in the negative. This is the cause of major malpractice losses, eg, particularly to the general practitioner who failed to discover that his or her patient had a history of rheumatic fever, and thus took no precautions in treatment.

Risk management rule: If you use a self-administered health history form and the choices to the patient are two — Yes or No — follow up on the No answers as well as the Yes answers to make certain the patient understood the questions and the reason the questions were being asked. Don't leave it to patients to decide if the answers to the questions on the health history are important to the success and safety of their care.

The best policy for the use of a self-administered health history form is not to use it. It leaves too much to chance in discovering medical problems that may compromise the successful and safe treatment of the patient. There is much more at stake than legal liability. When a history of rheumatic fever is not discovered, no matter who is at fault, the consequences to the patient and the dentist may be disastrous.

A much more effective way to determine past medical history is to have someone take the history who has been trained in the procedure and who has the background to interpret the responses — preferably, the treating dentist. If the history is elicited by someone other than the treating dentist, the dentist should review the history with the patient.

Another type of history-taking form is simple to design. Use a blank sheet of paper with a reminder list of the questions to be asked in the left margin. It is better to spend the extra time this takes than to have a patient suffer permanent injury because of your negligence as a result of the use of an inadequately designed form.

Updating the Medical History Good dental practice requires that the patient's health history be updated at regular intervals. The frequency at which it should be done is a professional decision. The process is simple and effective: allow the patient to review the history that was obtained at the last history-taking visit and ask if there are any changes. Make notes of the procedure and the patient's responses in the patient's record.

The risk management rule is: Update the health history at appropriate intervals and document the process and responses.

If you continue to use a self-administered health history form, place the following statement before the signature: "I understand that in the event there is any change in my health status, I should notify your office at the earliest possible time." It places some of the burden on the patient as an express term in the doctor-patient contract, but will not completely relieve the doctor of responsibility for updating the history.

Follow-Up on Positive Findings It is essential to good patient care, and to risk management concerns, that positive findings in the medical history be followed up by consulting the patient's physician. It is best to have consulting reports in writing. If this is inconvenient, findings should be noted on the patient's record.

The risk management rule is: Document all conversations with other health practitioners that are, or were, involved in the treatment of your patient.

The Dental History The dental history presents few problems to the dentist. However, one issue not as yet addressed by the courts deserves attention. Dental disease is chronic and almost everyone suffers from it. It does not begin when the patient presents to the dentist. Most patients change dentists several times throughout their life. To have a complete picture of the cause of the patient's disease and the history of their treatment, it is essential that, in addition to the history obtained from the patient, the treating dentist should make every effort to obtain the records of the previous dentists. It is possible that the previous dentists' notes may reveal a health risk to the patient, an abnormal reaction to the administration of a drug, the level of cooperation in care by the patient, breaking of appointments, delinquencies in the payment of fees, etc. Not obtaining information that is available and may be essential in the treatment of the patient may constitute malpractice.

A good risk management practice is: Obtain the records and radiographs of prior dentists and other health care providers who have treated your patient. Determine if there is some law in the state that enables patients to secure copies of their records and radiographs.

EXAMINING THE PATIENT AND COMPLETING A TREATMENT PLAN

"Failure to diagnose" represents a growing area of legal vulnerability. A thorough clinical examination and radiographic review should be completed on each patient. The results should be recorded on the patient's record.

It is difficult to successfully defend a case when many of the questions on the form used to record the dental examination have been left blank. It is impossible to determine if the blank indicates that the question was mistakenly omitted in the examination or if the result was within normal limits. If the form you use has questions that are not germane to your practice habits, or seldom answered, design your own form or purchase one that is more suitable.

Many recent cases involve failure to diagnose periodontal disease. Periodontal issues present a major problem if there is no evidence that the patient was examined to determine periodontal needs, eg, pocket depth, plaque scores, OHI. If periodontal disease was diagnosed, was the patient told of periodontal needs? Was the need for periodontal care neglected? Was a recommendation made for the patient to seek the services of a periodontist? The latter represents another growing risk: failure to make a timely referral.

Acceptable dental practice includes completing a treatment plan, both the recommended one and a reasonable alternative. Either have the patient initial the accepted plan or make a note of the acceptance in the record.

Good risk management practice includes completing a thorough dental examination and treatment plan before treatment is begun. The results should be accurately recorded, and all questions on the dental examination form should be answered. There should be documentation that the treatment plan was accepted by the patient.

CONSENT

Issues of consent have played an increasingly important role in malpractice litigation. Because of its complexity, consent appears to be little understood by many dentists. Much of the problem is caused by its convoluted legal evolution (see chapter 10). For our purposes here, it is simpler to list the current thinking of the courts and legislatures.

For consent to be valid it must meet the following tests:

1. It must be freely given.
2. All descriptions must be in language the patient understands.
3. It must be informed.

To be informed, the following elements are required to be included in the presentation to the patient:

1. The procedure must be described along with the prognosis.
2. Alternatives to the recommended treatment must be presented along with their prognoses.
3. Foreseeable and material risks must be described.
4. Patients must be given an opportunity to have their questions answered.

Capacity to consent is essential for informed consent to be valid. In the absence of an emergency, the only person with capacity to consent for a mentally competent adult patient, is the patient. The spouse does not have the capacity to consent, nor does the adult child of an aged parent.

If the patient is a minor, only the parent has the capacity to consent — not the grandparents, nor the teacher in the school where the child patient is a student, nor a sibling of the patient. However, parents may grant the right to consent to the health care of their children to others.

The age at which a minor is granted the capacity to consent to health care may vary in each jurisdiction. Generally it is 18 years of age. Consent to care in emergency situations and telephone consent are discussed below in Emergencies and the Good Samaritan Law.

If informed consent becomes an issue in the trial of a malpractice case, documentation that consent was obtained may decide the outcome. As a general rule, the more invasive the procedure or the greater the risk, the more attention must be paid to the elements of an informed consent and the need for documentation. In situations where there is little or no risk and the procedure is noninvasive, implied consent may be sufficient.

Documentation of informed consent may take many forms, from a note on the record with or without the patient's signature or initials, to a signed form having witnesses to the signature of the patient. The nature of the treatment and the disposition of the patient should dictate the degree of documentation necessary.

In some jurisdictions, the matter of informed consent to health care has been codified. However, the rules cited above should satisfy all case, statutory, and administrative law.

The risk management rule attached to the issue of consent is: Obtain the informed consent for the examination and treatment of the patient, and document that consent was obtained.

EMERGENCIES AND THE GOOD SAMARITAN LAW

The Good Samaritan law, enacted in all states, provides immunity from suit for specified health practitioners who render emergency aid to victims of accidents. Generally, the statutes require that the aid is provided with no expectation of financial remuneration. Should an injury result from negligence, the victim is precluded by law from instituting a suit, provided there was no evidence of gross negligence. Gross negligence is defined as the failure to exercise slight care.

Immunity does not extend to acts performed in the office or in any health facility.

The standard to which the good samaritan is held is based upon his or her education and experience. Therefore an act performed by an oral and maxillofacial surgeon may constitute gross negligence, while the same act performed by a general practitioner may not be considered negligence at all.

Not all states include dentists in the Good Samaritan law.

The risk management rule is: Determine if the jurisdiction in which you practice includes dentists in the Good Samaritan law. Be guided by the answer in rendering emergency aid at the scene of an accident.

An emergency is defined as any situation when care must be provided at once to preserve the life or health of the patient. Because the interpretation is broad in most states, dental care may fall within the definition. In cases where a dental emergency exists, and consent cannot be obtained because of a time constraint, consent to care is implied by operation of law.

The risk management rule in dealing with emergencies in which a minor is involved and brought to the office by someone other than a parent is: Efforts should be made to obtain the consent of the parent before treatment is begun.

Telephone consent will be valid provided the following rules are observed:

1. The situation must fall within the definition of emergency.
2. The dentist or one of the auxiliaries in the office should make a conscientious effort to contact one of the parents (either parent may grant consent for a minor child).
3. If a parent is contacted, he or she should be told that a third party is listening to the conversation on the phone.
4. The dentist or the auxiliary should explain the situation to the parent and include all the elements required for the consent to be valid.
5. Notes should be made in the child's record of all that took place, and should be signed by all parties to the telephone event.
6. A follow-up written consent form should be sent to the parent for signature and when returned, placed in the minor's record.

If neither parent can be located, notes should be placed in the minor's record about the nature of the emergency, why immediate care was necessary, the care provided, and that all attempts to reach the parents failed.

Recall that a dentist is free to reject an individual who is not a patient of record, even in an emergency situation. One of the duties owed by the dentist to patients of record, by case law and in some jurisdictions by black letter law, is to make care available to patients in emergency situations. Generally, the patient determines what constitutes an emergency.

The risk management rule in emergency situations for patients of record is: The availability of care is a 24-hours-a-day, 7-days-a-week, responsibility. If on vacation, someone must cover for you.

MISCELLANEOUS ISSUES

Package Inserts

Inserts in drug packaging have been accepted into evidence in malpractice cases. Dentists and physicians have been found guilty of negligence for not following the warnings contained on the package inserts. Statements contained in the *Physicians' Desk Reference (PDR)* have also been admitted into evidence.

The risk management rule is: Read all drug package inserts and the PDR *before administering or prescribing a drug. Because inserts and the* PDR *are updated frequently they should be consulted regularly.*

What to Do When Doctors Disagree

Situations may arise when the treating dentist and the patient's physician disagree on what prophylactic measures should be taken with a cardiac-compromised patient. The physician may recommend that no preventive measures be taken, or that measures be taken that are not consistent with those the dentist feels are appropriate. If the physician's advice is followed and an injury results, it is difficult for the dentist to claim immunity based on the physician's recommendation. The patient is a patient of the dentist, and the dentist operates on his or her own license. Dentists are not employees of physicians, nor are they required to carry out a physican's orders if they believe the orders are not consistent with the patient's needs. Whatever care is rendered by a dentist to the patient is interpreted as what the dentist, in his or her best judgment, thinks should be done.

If the dentist does not follow the advice of the physician and an injury occurs, the dentist will be judged on what other dentists in the community would do under similar circumstances, and not what the physician recommended. If the dentist's care meets acceptable community standards, there may be no liability.

The risk management rule is: Exercise your own judgment when deciding on the dental care of the patient. Use advice by others, including physicians, as recommendations that you may either accept or reject. The final decision as to what is done is yours and the patient's.

Associates and Employees

There are several important legal issues involved with associates and employees of the dentist. Some have an impact on legal vulnerability and will be discussed in this section. It is important for dentists to be aware that the more complex the arrangements of practice, the more exposure there is to legal entanglements.

Associations in practice may take many forms, some of which increase legal risk. The employer-employee relationship between dentists make the employer-dentist individually or jointly liable for the negligent acts of the employee dentist. The legal doctrine for this transfer of liability to the employer, an innocent party, is known as *respondeat superior* (the person in the superior position, the employer, must answer for the acts of the one in an inferior position, the employee, to injured third parties). It is a form of *vicarious liability* (the substitution of an innocent party for a guilty one in the matter of liability to third parties). However, the employer may sue the employee for indemnification of his or her losses. If both are insured by the same professional liability insurance company, complications may be avoided.

The same principle of *respondeat superior* applies to all employees of the dentist, including hygienists, dental assistants, receptionists, and others. The employer-dentist is held liable for all acts performed by an employee in the course of conducting the business of the employer-dentist, even if the acts are specifically prohibited or illegal.

Another form of associateship between dentists is the partnership. All partners are individually liable for the negligent acts of one partner. The choice of who to sue is exercised by the plaintiff or the plaintiff's attorney. If a generalist, who is low risk, has a partner who practices oral and maxillofacial surgery, which is high risk, the generalist may be held liable for the negligent acts of the surgeon. It is not unusual for all partners to be joined in the suit. Vicarious liability is supported by the legal theory that all partners are united in interest (each benefits from the acts of others). To avoid serious complications, all should be covered by the same professional liability insurance company. From the standpoint of legal liability for negligent acts, practicing in a partnership agreement brings with it serious risks. In several cases, courts have stated that if the patient considers the practice to be a partnership, the courts will treat it as such. Even if the agreement among a group of dentists is to practice as solo and independent practitioners, if they engage in sharing to the extent that the arrangement appears to be a partnership, they may take on the risks of a partnership.

The third form of associateship is the professional corporation. This relationship represents the lowest level of legal risk. Innocent shareholders are not liable for the negligent acts of other shareholders. Only the guilty practitioner and the corporation are liable. However, all shareholders and the corporation should be insured by the same professional liability insurance company.

The independent contractor is the final form of associateship to be considered. With this arrangement, the principal hopes to avoid liability for the negligent acts of the independent contractor. The courts examine the arrangement between the parties before determining the liability of the principal — just how independent is the independent contractor from control by the principal, and whose patients are they? Having the same professional liability insurance company avoids many complications.

In summary, the lowest level of legal risk in associateship practice is to practice as a professional corporation and, in any form of joint practice, for all parties to be insured by the same professional liability insurance carrier.

The acts or statements made by nondentist employees present other forms of legal risks to the employer-dentist than those described above. An employee of a dentist is treated by the courts as an agent of the dentist when the employee is serving in the capacity for which he or she was employed. Thus, if a receptionist, hygienist, or assistant assures a patient that following treatment the patient will be satisfied with the result, an express guarantee has been made to which the dentist may be held.

The risk management advice is: Educate your employees to the precise role they are to play in communicating and dealing with patients. Supervise them carefully and monitor their activities at regular intervals. Remain current on changes in the law that affect dental auxiliaries.

Interpersonal Relationships

A deterioration in good interpersonal relations between patient and dentist, or patient and staff, still ranks as one of the leading causes of malpractice allegations despite the emphasis placed on behavioral science in the dental literature, continuing education programs, and dental education.

When a patient becomes angry, upset, or frustrated, instituting a lawsuit is one of the methods available for retaliation. The resulting annoyance to the dentist may be reason enough to sue, regardless of the merits of the claim. For the patient, it works. For the dentist, it becomes a real problem involving time, effort, and emotional distress. Too often, efforts of the auxiliary staff made in the interest of shielding the dentist from complaints of difficult patients or patients with annoying problems, result in a patient seeking redress through the courts. Most of these situations can be defused by an understanding and compassionate staff. The dentist must be accessible to patients, particularly to those with perceived problems. The judgment of the staff as to what is important to the patient should not be substituted for the patient's judgment of what is important.

The risk management advice is: Monitor the staff in their inter- personal relationships with patients. Listen to your patients! Make certain that patients with problems have access to you. Don't hide from your patients — arrange for substitute care when absent for extended periods. If all efforts fail to restore a cordial relationship with a difficult patient, the safest course to follow is to discontinue treatment.

Return of a Fee and Suing to Collect One

At one time, courts viewed the return of a fee by a doctor as an admission of wrongdoing. Today, it is viewed as an expression of good faith. If you feel that the return of a fee, or part of it, will appease a hostile patient and defuse a difficult situation, it is best to do so. With a patient who threatens to sue unless the fee is returned, and you decide to return the fee, it is best to have the patient execute a release from further claim with the acceptance of the returned fee. You should weigh the refusal to return the fee with the trauma and loss of time in defending a claim of malpractice — you might even lose the case.

One of the major causes of malpractice allegations is response to an attempt by a doctor to collect a fee. Patients who are delinquent or refuse to pay are inclined to claim poor quality of care as the reason. Should the doctor press to collect, especially through the courts, the patient is likely to countersue for malpractice. Weighing the risk of a countersuit in malpractice should guide the dentist before suing to collect the fee.

If you use a collection agency to act on your behalf for fee collection, review all correspondence sent to a patient. Usually there is more at stake for the practitioner than the fee.

The risk management advice is: Think of what might be avoided if a fee is returned and of the possible consequences if a suit is instituted to collect a fee. Don't let pride and principle interfere with making a practical decision.

Selling and Buying a Practice

It is customary in the sale of a dental practice to deliver the patients' records to the purchaser. This act may invite many legal difficulties. Without each patient's consent, confidentiality may be breached and a civil suit may follow. In those states where a health practitioner may be required by law to retain patients' records for a specified time, the transfer may invite an action by the state for violation of the law. Perhaps the most important consequence may arise if a lawsuit is instituted against the seller-dentist by a former patient. The records may be difficult to obtain from the buyer-dentist. Without the records the suit will undoubtedly be lost. The solution to the problem is not simple. It might be of some use to include in the contract of sale that the records shall be made available to the seller in the event they are needed to defend a lawsuit. However, this strategy will not recover records that are lost or destroyed.

The safest mechanism, although complex and difficult, is to transfer to the buyer only the original records of patients who have not been treated for a period of time exceeding the statute of limitations for malpractice or contact actions, whichever is longer. For those patients treated within the statute, transfer only copies of records.

A fool-proof risk management rule to protect the seller-dentist in the sale of a practice that requires the transfer of records is difficult to design. A clause in the contract of sale requiring the purchaser to make patient records available to the seller may reduce the risk, but will not eliminate it. The sole method to further reduce the risk is to transfer only copies of the records to the purchaser.

There is good reason to demand the originals rather than copies. Courts insist on originals of all records that are to be entered into evidence. Altered entries on original records are more easily discovered than on copies.

CURRENT TARGETS IN MALPRACTICE LITIGATION

The traditional problems leading to allegations of malpractice are still with us: ill-fitting dentures and the extraction of wrong teeth. The ill-fitting denture problem is often linked with statements made by the dentist that constitute guarantees of satisfaction or serviceability (see previous section on Guarantees). In wrong-tooth extraction cases, most are the result of poor office management and, in situations that involve oral and maxillofacial surgeons, inadequate communication with the referring dentist.

Over the past several years, new grounds of vulnerability have been discovered by patients and their attorneys. In addition, risks have increased because of the introduction of new and more sophisticated techniques into dental practice. New fertile grounds of litigation include:

1. failures in treating problems related to the temporo-mandibular joint;
2. failures associated with blade implants;
3. failure to diagnose — especially periodontal disease;
4. failure to treat periodontal disease;
5. failure to obtain the informed consent of the patient by not informing him or her of the risk of failure and its consequences, eg, in endodontics;
6. failure to take necessary precautions (rubber dam, use of assistants, etc) to prevent mechanical injury to the patient, eg, aspiration of foreign bodies (crowns and instruments) and lacerated soft tissues;

7. continuing to treat when the dentist is aware that the result will not be satisfactory, eg, in orthodontics when the patient is not cooperating in home care;
8. failure to identify a patient with a compromised medical history, eg, rheumatic fever, heart murmur, allergies;
9. failure to take precautions to protect a patient having a compromised medical condition, eg, to prevent subacute bacterial endocarditis;
10. performing a service at the insistence of the patient that is not in the best interest of the patient and will not produce acceptable results, eg, treating periodontal disease that should be treated by a specialist — the same holds true in oral surgical cases.
11. not performing a service, at the insistence of the patient, that should be performed before certain treatment is undertaken, eg, radiographs prior to any treatment, periodontal care by a specialist prior to fabrication of fixed prostheses;
12. failure to inform the patient about the risk of paresthesia following surgical procedures;
13. failure to provide follow-up care after surgery, eg, abandonment;
14. failure to consult the patient's physician when the patient's health is compromised.

The risks are significantly increased for failure to maintain adequate records or remain current with new advances in the profession. A deteriorating interpersonal relationship between patient and doctor or patient and office staff, or attempts by the dentist to collect the fee, may be causes of the patient seeking redress in the courts.

REPORTING INCIDENTS AND CLAIMS TO THE INSURANCE CARRIER

Problems for the dentist have arisen from failure to report incidents to the insurance carrier that may generate claims of malpractice. One of the terms of the professional liability insurance policy is the burden placed on the policy holder to report unusual incidents to the insurance carrier at the earliest possible time (the exact wording varies in each policy, but the intent to have timely reporting of occurrences that may lead to suits is the same). This requirement presents a dilemma for the dentist. If every incident, no matter how minor, that might result in an allegation of malpractice were reported to the insurance carrier, then most of the working hours of the dentist would be spent in writing reports. In addition, if all incidents are reported, the dentist's risk profile may cause the insurance company to have second thoughts at renewal time. Alternately, the dentist is faced with the fact that if timely reports are not made, the provision to report may be breached and coverage may not be provided. For the insurance company and the dentist, early reporting and timely action by the insurance company may head off claims.

There are a host of unusual occurrences that must be reported. If a patient aspirates a bur, or a lip is lacerated and requires sutures, it should be reported at once. It is not necessary to report each time a patient feels faint following the administration of a local anesthetic. However, there are many gray-area unusual occurrences. The practitioner should exercise reasonable judgment about the likelihood of a suit following a gray-area occurrence. It is better to overreport than underreport.

How the report is made to the insurance company, what is written in the patient's treatment record, and what is told to the patient are very important.

To the insurance company: First read the provision in the policy and follow the instructions. Report by telephone and follow with a registered letter, signed receipt requested. Report all you know about the incident. Make a note for the file that you reported the incident. Do not make any entry on the patient's record that a report to the insurance company has been made.

To the patient: It is important that the patient be told of the occurrence. However, tell it in an impersonal manner, and accept no blame. Be extremely careful in what you say. Full disclosure is necessary. Provide follow-up care and do what is needed to reduce the injury and calm the patient. If specialty services are required, make the referral at the earliest possible time. Follow the advice of the insurance company as to what course of action you should take in paying for any care the patient requires as a result of the incident. Keep in touch with the patient and exhibit concern for his or her health.

In the treatment record: Record in objective terms what occurred, the patient's reaction, and what immediate care was rendered as a result of the incident. It is important to include any instructions given to the patient designed to reduce the effects of the injury. If there was a witness to the occurrence, have the witness sign the entry on the record. If you make follow-up calls to determine the condition of the patient, make entries of the calls and the patient's responses on the treatment record.

If a patient threatens suit, it should be reported to the insurance carrier in the same manner as described above. The same is true if you receive a letter from an attorney threatening suit. Make a copy of the letter, and send the copy to the insurance company.

If you receive a summons and complaint, follow the same reporting procedure described above. Include a copy of the summons and complaint.

The risk management rules are:

1. *As soon as possible, report to your insurance carrier all incidents related to the care of your patients that may result in allegations of negligence.*
2. *If an accident occurs during treatment, don't panic and don't make an admission of fault against your interest. Do everything you can to care for the patient. Record what occurred objectively in the patient's record.*
3. *Follow the advice of the insurance company and its attorney in dealing with the situation and with any events that follow.*
4. *If the patient or an attorney threatens suit, notify the insurance company at once.*
5. *Always use certified mail, with signed receipt requested, in correspondence related to legal matters.*

IF YOU ARE SUED

Do...

- At the earliest time after receiving the summons and complaint, report it to your insurance carrier by phone.
- Make a copy of the papers and send the originals to your carrier.
- Write a summary of the treatment of the patient using the treatment record to refresh your memory. Include all you recall, even if it is not on the record.
- Make a copy of the records, including radiographs, reports, and the summary — lock the originals in a safe place.
- Tell your staff about the suit and instruct them not to talk to anyone asking questions about the case without obtaining your permission.

Don't...

- Tell the patient or his or her representative that you are insured.
- Agree to or offer a settlement.
- Agree to or offer to pay for specialist's services.
- Alter your records in any way.
- Lose any of your records.

- Discuss the case, or the treatment of the patient, with anyone except representatives of your insurance company or their attorney.
- Admit fault or guilt to anyone.
- Contact any other practitioner about the case even if the practitioner has written a report.
- Agree to or treat the patient-plaintiff during the course of the action.

IMPLIED DUTIES (WARRANTIES) OWED
BY THE DENTIST TO THE PATIENT

In the absence of express conditions stated in a contract, the courts, in a series of cases, have identified duties owed by dentists to their patients that are based on the doctor-patient relationship.

In accepting the patient for care, the dentist warrants that he or she will:

1. use reasonable care in the provision of services as measured against acceptable standards set by other practitioners with similar training in a similar community;
2. be properly licensed, registered, and meet all other legal requirements to engage in the practice of dentistry;
3. employ competent personnel and provide for their proper supervision;
4. maintain a level of knowledge in keeping with current advances in the profession;
5. use methods that are acceptable to at least a respectable minority of similar practitioners in the community;
6. not use experimental procedures;
7. obtain informed consent from the patient before instituting an examination or treatment;
8. not abandon the patient;
9. ensure that care is available in emergency situations;
10. charge a reasonable fee for services based upon community standards;
11. not exceed the scope of practice authorized by the license, nor permit any person acting under his/her direction to engage in unlawful acts;
12. keep the patient informed of his/her progress;
13. not undertake any procedure for which the practitioner is not qualified;
14. complete the care in a timely manner;

15. keep accurate records of the treatment rendered to the patient;
16. maintain confidentiality of information;
17. inform the patient of any untoward occurrences in the course of treatment;
18. make appropriate referrals and request necessary consultations;
19. comply with all laws regulating the practice of dentistry;
20. practice in a manner consistent with the code of ethics of the profession.

RISK MANAGEMENT RULES
FOR PATIENT RECORD-KEEPING

Note: No amount of documentation is too much and no detail is too small.

1. Entries should be legible, written in black ink or ball-point pen.
2. In offices where there is more than one person making entries, they should be signed or initialed.
3. Entries that are in error should not be blocked out so that they cannot be read. Instead, a single line should be drawn through the entry, and a note made above it stating "error in entry, see correction below." The correction should be dated at the time it is made.
4. Financial information should not be kept on the treatment record.
5. Entries should be uniformly spaced on the form. There should be no unusual or irregular blank spaces.
6. On health information forms, there should be no blank spaces in the answers to health questions. If the question is inappropriate, draw a single line through the question, or record "not applicable" (NA) in the box. If the response is normal, write "within normal limits" (WNL).
7. Record all cancellations, late arrivals, and change of appointments.
8. Document consents, including all risks and alternative treatments presented to the patient. Include any remarks made by the patient.
9. It is important to inform the patient of any adverse occurrences or untoward events that take place during the course of treatment, and to note on the record that the

patient was informed.

10. Record all requests for consultations and responses.
11. Document all conversations held with other health practitioners relating to the care of the patient.
12. All patient records should be retained for at least the period of the statute of limitations equal to that of contract actions. In most jurisdictions it is 6 years. In the case of minors, it would be until the person reaches the age of 24. Check for special laws in your local jurisdiction. If at all possible, keep records forever.
13. Records should not be transferred to the purchaser of a practice without the consent of each patient.
14. Do not include subjective evaluations, such as your opinion about the patient's mental health, on the treatment record unless you are qualified and licensed to make such evaluations.
15. Guard confidentiality of information contained on the record.
16. *Never* surrender the original record to *anyone*, except by order of a court.
17. *Never* tamper with a record once there is some indication that legal action is contemplated by the patient.
18. Instruct your heirs that they must retain the records of your patients and offer to comply with any written request for a copy.

REFERENCE

1. *New York Pattern Jury Instructions — Civil*, ed 2. Rochester, NY, The Lawyers Co-operative Publishing Co, 1974, vol 1, updated by pocket part, February 1986.

SPECIFIC LEGAL CONCERNS OF DENTISTS
AS ELICITED BY QUESTIONNAIRE

We are surveying nationwide a select group of dentists to determine their concerns in matters involving law and dentistry. May we request that you, as a dental practitioner, indicate by a check mark (√) which matters concern you listed below. NO NAMES OR ADDRESSES NEEDED unless you desire a compilation of the responses. Insert this questionnaire in the enclosed envelope and mail at your earliest convenience. Thank you.

Oliver Schroeder, Director

MALPRACTICE MATTERS

148 Negligent care of patients
130 Informed consent by patient
 51 Negligent act of nurse
 84 Negligent act of dental assistant
 17 Negligent maintenance of dental office
 76 Negligent care in team dentistry

 68 Negligent care of minors
 71 Negligent act of dental hygienists
 54 Negligent act of receptionist
 77 Negligent act of other employee
 59 Negligent maintenance of dental equipment

Others (please indicate) _____

_____

_____

CONTRACT MATTERS

Dentist-Patient Contracts

108 Fees
 88 Work to be done
 49 Truth-in-Lending

 48 Dentist-employees' contracts
 29 Dentist-suppliers' contracts
 54 Dentist-landlords' contracts

Dentist-Third Party Payor

 63 Medicare
 51 Workmen's compensation
 79 Labor unions

 74 Medicaid
126 Insurance companies
 59 Employer contracts for
    employees

Miscellaneous Contract Matters

 57 Contracts limiting
    geographic areas of practice
 46 Contracts limiting time
    period of practice
 43 Contracts for assuming
    dental practice of another

 61 Contracts creating
    partnerships
 78 Contracts creating
    professional practice
    corporations

Other (please indicate) _____

_____

_____

GOVERNMENTAL REGULATION MATTERS

131 Licensure of dentist
 60 Licensure of dental
    hygienists
 76 Definition of dental practice
 68 Regulations for dispensing
    or use of drugs
 67 Regulations for nitrous
    oxide

 71 Licensure of dental
    assistants
 33 Licensure for nurses
 55 Regulations for dental
    research
 27 Regulations for use of gold
 45 Regulations for zoning of
    dental practice

Other (please indicate) _____

_____

_____

PROFESSIONAL DISCIPLINE MATTERS

 97 License revocation or
    suspension
 91 Professional dental society
    for unethical practices
 70 Advertising

 87 Use of auxiliary personnel
 50 Commissions/rebates/split
    fees

Other (please indicate) ————————————————————————

——

——

**Dentist Participation as Expert Scientific
Witness in the Administration of Justice, Both
Civil and Criminal**

<u>100</u> Prepare and submit dental records and report to an attorney of a
  patient
<u>96</u> Testify in civil litigation   <u>65</u> Testify in criminal
<u>76</u> For plaintiff   prosecution
<u>68</u> For defendant   <u>51</u> For prosecution
                                        <u>65</u> For accused

Other (please indicate) ————————————————————————

——

——

AMERICAN DENTAL ASSOCIATION
PRINCIPLES OF ETHICS AND CODE OF
PROFESSIONAL CONDUCT*

The maintenance and enrichment of professional status place on everyone who practices dentistry an obligation which should be willingly accepted and willingly fulfilled. While the basic obligation is constant, its fulfillment may vary with the changing needs of a society composed of the human beings that a profession is dedicated to serve. The spirit of the obligation, therefore, must be the guide of conduct for professionals. This obligation has been summarized for all times in the golden rule which asks only that "whatsoever ye would that men should do to you, do ye even so to them."

The practice of dentistry first achieved the status of a profession in the United States when, through the heritage bestowed by the efforts of many generations of dentists, it acquired the three unfailing characteristics of a profession: the primary duty of service to the public, education beyond the usual level, and the responsibility for self-government.

Principle — Section 1

SERVICE TO THE PUBLIC AND QUALITY OF CARE.

The dentist's primary obligation of service to the public shall include the delivery of quality care, competently and timely, within the bounds of the clinical circumstances presented by the patient. Quality of care shall be a primary consideration of the dental practitioner.

Code of Professional Conduct

1-A. PATIENT SELECTION.

While dentists, in serving the public, may exercise reasonable discretion in selecting patients for their practices, dentists shall not refuse to accept patients into their practice or deny dental service to

---

* By permission of the American Dental Association.

patients because of the patient's race, creed, color, sex, or national origin.

1-B. PATIENT RECORDS.

Dentists are obliged to safeguard the confidentiality of patient records. Dentists shall maintain patient records in a manner consistent with the protection of the welfare of the patient. Upon request of a patient or another dental practitioner, dentists shall provide any information that will be beneficial for the future treatment of that patient.

Advisory Opinion

1. A dentist has the ethical obligation on request of either the patient or the patient's new dentist to furnish, either gratuitously or for nominal cost, such dental records or copies or summaries of them, including dental X-rays or copies of them, as will be beneficial for the future treatment of that patient.

1-C. COMMUNITY SERVICE.

Since dentists have an obligation to use their skills, knowledge, and experience for the improvement of the dental health of the public and are encouraged to be leaders in their community, dentists in such service shall conduct themselves in such a manner as to maintain or elevate the esteem of the profession.

1-D. EMERGENCY SERVICE.

Dentists shall be obliged to make reasonable arrangements for the emergency care of their patients of record.

Dentists shall be obliged when consulted in an emergency by patients not of record to make reasonable arrangements for emergency care. If treatment is provided, the dentist, upon completion of such treatment, is obliged to return the patient to his or her regular dentist unless the patient expressly reveals a different preference.

1-E. CONSULTATION AND REFERRAL

Dentists shall be obliged to seek consultation, if possible, whenever the welfare of patients will be safeguarded or advanced by utilizing those who have special skills, knowledge, and experience. When patients visit or are referred to specialists or consulting dentists for consultation:

1. The specialists or consulting dentists upon completion of their care

shall return the patient, unless the patient expressly reveals a different preference, to the referring dentist, or if none, to the dentist of record for future care.

2. The specialists shall be obliged when there is no referring dentist and upon a completion of their treatment to inform patients when there is a need for further dental care.

1-F. USE OF AUXILIARY PERSONNEL.

Dentists shall be obliged to protect the health of their patient by only assigning to qualified auxiliaries those duties which can be legally delegated. Dentists shall be further obliged to prescribe and supervise the work of all auxiliary personnel working under their direction and control.

1-G. JUSTIFIABLE CRITICISM.

Dentists shall be obliged to report to the appropriate reviewing agency as determined by the local component or constituent society instances of gross and continual faulty treatment by other dentists. Patients should be informed of their present oral health status without disparaging comment about prior services.

Advisory Opinion

1. A dentist's duty to the public imposes a responsibility to report instances of gross and continual faulty treatment. However, the heading of this section is "Justifiable Criticism." Therefore, when informing a patient of the status of his or her oral health, the dentist should exercise care that the comments made are justifiable. For example, a difference of opinion as to preferred treatment should not be communicated to the patient in a manner which would imply mistreatment. There will necessarily be cases where it will be difficult to determine whether the comments made are justifiable. Therefore, this section is phrased to address the discretion of dentists and advises against disparaging statements against another dentist. However, it should be noted that where comments are made which are obviously not supportable and therefore unjustified, such comments can be the basis for the institution of a disciplinary proceeding against the dentist making such statements.

1-H. EXPERT TESTIMONY.

Dentists may provide expert testimony when that testimony is essential to a just and fair disposition of a judicial or administrative action.

1-I. REBATE AND SPLIT FEES.
Dentists shall not accept or tender "rebates" or "split fees."

1-J. REPRESENTATION OF CARE AND FEES.
Dentists shall not represent the care being rendered to their patients or the fees being charged for providing such care in a false or misleading manner.

Advisory Opinions

1. A dentist who accepts a third party* payment under a copayment plan as payment in full without disclosing to the third party* payer that the patient's payment portion will not be collected, is engaged in overbilling. The essence of this ethical impropriety is deception and misrepresentation; an overbilling dentist makes it appear to the third party* payer that the charge to the patient for services rendered is higher than it actually is.

2. It is unethical for a dentist to increase a fee to a patient solely because the patient has insurance.

3. Payments accepted by a dentist under a governmentally funded program, a component or constituent dental society sponsored access program, or a participating agreement entered into under a program of a third party* shall not be considered as evidence of overbilling in determining whether a charge to a patient, or to another third party* in behalf of a patient not covered under any of the aforecited programs constitutes overbilling under this section of the Code.

4. A dentist who submits a claim form to a third party* reporting incorrect treatment dates for the purpose of assisting a patient in obtaining benefits under a dental plan, which benefits would otherwise be disallowed, is engaged in making an unethical, false, or misleading representation to such third party*.

5. A dentist who incorrectly describes on a third party* claim form a dental procedure in order to receive a greater payment or reimbursement or incorrectly makes a noncovered procedure appear to be a covered procedure on such a claim form is engaged in making an unethical, false, or misleading representation to such third party*.

6. A dentist who recommends and performs unnecessary dental services or procedures is engaged in unethical conduct.

---

* A third party is any party to a dental prepayment contract that may collect premiums, assume financial risks, pay claims, and/or provide administrative services.

Principle — Section 2

EDUCATION.
The privilege of dentists to be accorded professional status rests primarily in the knowledge, skill, and experience with which they serve their patients and society. All dentists, therefore, have the obligation of keeping their knowlege and skill current.

Principle — Section 3

GOVERNMENT OF A PROFESSION.
Every profession owes society the responsibility to regulate itself. Such regulation is achieved largely through the influence of the professional societies. All dentists, therefore, have the dual obligation of making themselves a part of a professional society and of observing its rules of ethics.

Principle — Section 4

RESEARCH AND DEVELOPMENT.
Dentists have the obligation of making the results and benefits of their investigative efforts available to all when they are useful in safeguarding or promoting the health of the public.

Code of Professional Conduct

4-A. DEVICES AND THERAPEUTIC METHODS.
Except for formal investigative studies, dentists shall be obliged to prescribe, dispense, or promote only those devices, drugs, and other agents whose complete formulae are available to the dental profession. Dentists shall have the further obligation of not holding out as exclusive any device, agent, method, or technique.

4-B. PATENTS AND COPYRIGHTS.
Patents and copyrights may be secured by dentists provided that such patents and copyrights shall not be used to restrict research or practice.

Principle — Section 5

PROFESSIONAL ANNOUNCEMENT.
In order to properly serve the public, dentists should represent themselves in a manner that contributes to the esteem of the profession.

Dentists should not misrepresent their training and competence in any way that would be false or misleading in any material respect.*

Code of Professional Conduct

5-A. ADVERTISING.

Although any dentist may advertise, no dentist shall advertise or solicit patients in any form of communication in a manner that is false or misleading in any material respect.*

Advisory Opinions

1. If a dental health article, message, or newsletter is published under a dentist's byline to the public without making truthful disclosure of the source and authorship or is designed to give rise to questionable expectations for the purpose of inducing the public to utilize the services of the sponsoring dentist, the dentist is engaged in making a false or misleading representation to the public in a material respect.
2. The Council on Bylaws and Judicial Affairs believes it would be of service to the members to provide some insight into the meaning of the term "false or misleading in a material respect." Therefore, the following examples are set forth. These examples are not meant to be all-inclusive. Rather by restating the concept in alternative language and giving general examples, it is hoped that the membership will gain a better understanding of the term. With this in mind, statements shall be avoided which would: a) contain a material misrepresentation of fact, b) omit a fact necessary to make the statement considered as a whole not materially misleading, c) contain a representation or implication regarding the quality of dental services which would suggest unique or general superiority to other practitioners which are not susceptible to

---

* Advertising, solicitation of patients or business, or other promotional activities by dentists or dental care delivery organizations shall not be considered unethical or improper, except for those promotional activities which are false or misleading in any material respect. Notwithstanding any ADA PRINCIPLES OF ETHICS AND CODE OF PROFESSIONAL CONDUCT or other standards of dentist conduct which may be differently worded, this shall be the sole standard for determining the ethical propriety of such promotional activities. Any provision of an ADA constituent or component society's code of ethics or other standard of dentist conduct relating to dentists' or dental care delivery organizations' advertising, solicitation, or other promotional activities which is worded differently from the above standard shall be deemed to be in conflict with the ADA PRINCIPLES OF ETHICS AND CODE OF PROFESSIONAL CONDUCT.

reasonable verification by the public, and d) be intended or be likely to create an unjustified expectation about results the dentist can achieve. 3. The use of an unearned or nonhealth degree in any general announcements to the public by a dentist may be a representation to the public which is false or misleading in a material respect. A dentist may use the title Doctor, Dentist, DDS, or DMD, or any additional earned advanced degrees in health service areas. The use of unearned or nonhealth degrees could be misleading because of the likelihood that it will indicate to the public the attainment of a speciality or diplomate status. It may also suggest that the dentist using such is claiming superior dental skills.

For purposes of this advisory opinion, an unearned academic degree is one which is awarded by an educational institution not accredited by a generally recognized accrediting body or is an honorary degree. Generally, the use of honorary degrees or nonhealth degrees should be limited to scientific papers and curriculum vitae. In all instances state law should be consulted. In any review by the council of the use of nonhealth degrees or honorary degrees, the council will apply the standard of whether the use of such is false or misleading in a material respect.

4. A dentist using the attainment of a fellowship in a direct advertisement to the general public may be making a representation to the public which is false or misleading in a material respect. Such use of a fellowship status may be misleading because of the likelihood that it will indicate to the dental consumer the attainment of a specialty status. It may also suggest that the dentist using such is claiming superior dental skills. However, when such use does not conflict with state law, the attainment of fellowship status may be indicated in scientific papers, curriculum vitae, third party payment forms, and letterhead and stationery which is not used for the direct solicitation of patients. In any review by the council of the use of the attainment of fellowship status, the council will apply the standard of whether the use of such is false or misleading in a material respect.

5. There are two basic types of referral services for dental care: not-for-profit and the commercial.

The not-for-profit is commonly organized by dental societies or community services. It is open to all qualified practitioners in the area served. A fee is sometimes charged the practitioner to be listed with the service. A fee for such referral services is for the purpose of covering the expenses of the service and has no relation to the number of patients referred.

In contrast, experience has shown that commercial referral services generally limit access to the referral service to one dentist in a particular geographic area. Prospective patients calling the service are referred to the single subscribing dentist in the geographic area and the respective dentist is commonly billed for each patient referred. Commercial referral services often advertise to the public stressing that there is no charge for use of the service and the patient is not informed of the referral fee paid by the dentist. There is a connotation to such advertisements that the referral that is being made is in the nature of a public service.

A dentist is allowed to pay for any advertising permitted by the Code, but is generally not permitted to make payments to another person or entity for the referral of a patient for professional services. While the particular facts and circumstances relating to an individual commercial referral service will vary, the council believes that the aspects outlined above for commercial referral services violate the Code in that it constitutes advertising which is false or misleading in a material respect and violates the prohibitions in the Code against fee splitting.

5-B. NAME OF PRACTICE.

Since the name under which a dentist conducts his practice may be a factor in the selection process of the patient, the use of a trade name or an assumed name that is false or misleading in any material respect is unethical.

Use of the name of a dentist no longer actively associated with the practice may be continued for a period not to exceed one year.*

5-C. ANNOUNCEMENT OF SPECIALIZATION AND LIMITATION OF PRACTICE.

This section and Section 5-D are designed to help the public make an informed selection between the practitioner who has completed an accredited program beyond the dental degree and a practitioner who has not completed such a program.

The special areas of dental practice approved by the American Dental Association and the designation for ethical specialty announcement and limitation of practice are: dental public health, endodontics, oral pathology, oral and maxillofacial surgery, orthodontics, pediatric dentistry, periodontics, and prosthodontics.

Dentists who choose to announce specialization should use "specialist in" or "practice limited to" and shall limit their practice exclusively to the announced special area(s) of dental practice, provided at the time of the announcement such dentists have met in each approved specialty for which they announce the existing educational requirements and standards set forth by the American Dental Association.

Dentists who use their eligibility to announce as specialists to make the public believe that specialty services rendered in the dental office are being rendered by qualified specialists when such is not the case are engaged in unethical conduct. The burden of responsibility is on specialists to avoid any inference that general practitioners who are associated with specialists are qualified to announce themselves as specialists.

GENERAL STANDARDS.

The following are included within the standards of the American Dental Association for determining the education, experience, and other appropriate requirements for announcing specialization and limitation of practice:

1. The special area(s) of dental practice and an appropriate certifying board must be approved by the American Dental Association.

2. Dentists who announce as specialists must have successfully completed an educational program accredited by the Commission on Dental Accreditation, two or more years in length, as specified by the Council on Dental Education, or be diplomates of an American Dental Association recognized certifying board. The scope of the individual specialist's practice shall be governed by the educational standards for the speciality in which the specialist is announcing.

3. The practice carried on by dentists who announce as specialists shall be limited exclusively to the special area(s) of dental practices announced by the dentist.

STANDARDS FOR MULTIPLE-SPECIALTY
ANNOUNCEMENTS.

Educational criteria for announcement by dentists in additional recognized specialty areas are the successful completion of an educational program accredited by the Commission on Dental Accreditation in each area for which the dentist wishes to announce.

Dentists who completed their advanced education in programs listed by the Council on Dental Education prior to the initiation of the accreditation process in 1967 and who are currently ethically announcing as specialists in a recognized area may announce in additional areas provided they are educationally qualified or are certified diplomates in each area for which they wish to announce. Documentation of successful completion of the educational program(s) must be submitted to the appropriate constituent society. The documentation must assure that the duration of the program(s) is a minimum of two years except for oral and maxillofacial surgery which must have been a minimum of three years in duration.*

Advisory Opinion

1. A dentist who announces in any means of communication with patients or the general public that he or she is certified or a diplomate in an area of dentistry not recognized by the American Dental Association or the law of the jurisdiction where the dentist practices as a specialty area of dentistry is engaged in making a false or misleading representation to the public in a material respect.

5-D. GENERAL PRACTITIONER ANNOUNCEMENT OF SERVICES.

General dentists who wish to announce the services available in their practices are permitted to announce the availability of those services so long as they avoid any communications that express or imply specialization. General dentists shall also state that the services are being provided by general dentists. No dentist shall announce available services in any way that would be false or misleading in any material respect.*

Interpretation and Application of 'PRINCIPLES OF ETHICS AND CODE OF PROFESSIONAL CONDUCT'

The preceding statements constitute the PRINCIPLES OF ETHICS AND CODE OF PROFESSIONAL CONDUCT of the American Dental Association. The purpose of the PRINCIPLES AND CODE is to uphold and strengthen dentistry as a member of the learned professions. The constituent and component societies may adopt additional provisions or interpretations not in conflict with these PRINCIPLES OF ETHICS AND CODE OF PROFESSIONAL CONDUCT which would enable them to serve more faithfully the traditions, customs, and desires of the members of these societies.

Problems involving questions of ethics should be solved at the local level within the broad boundaries established in these PRINCIPLES OF ETHICS AND CODE OF PROFESSIONAL CONDUCT and within the interpretation by the component and/or constituent society of their respective codes of ethics. If a satisfactory decision cannot be reached, the question should be referred on appeal to the constituent society and the Council on Bylaws and Judicial Affairs of the American Dental Association, as provided in Chapter XI of the ByLaws of the American Dental Association. Members found guilty of unethical conduct as

prescribed in the American Dental Association CODE OF PROFES-
SIONAL CONDUCT or codes of ethics of the constituent and
component societies are subject to the penalties set forth in Chapter XI
of the American Dental Association ByLaws.

BIBLIOGRAPHY

1. American Dental Association. *International Conference on Forensic Dentistry*, New York. Chicago: ADA, 1970.
2. Cameron, J.M., and Sims, B.G. *Forensic Dentistry*. Edinburgh: N. Livingstone Church, 1973.
3. Carnahan, C.W., Howard, W.W., and Parks, A.L. *The Dentist and the Law*. 3rd Ed. St. Louis: C.V. Mosby Company, 1973.
4. Childs, L. *Law for the Dentist*. 2nd Ed. Philadelphia: Dental Cosmos, 1934.
5. Cohen, I. (Ed.). *Medical and Dental Malpractice: Techniques of Gathering Proof; Informed Consent; Plaintiff's Viewpoint; Dental Malpractice*. New York: Practicing Law Institute, 1970.
6. Curry, A.S. (Ed.). *Methods of Forensic Science*. New York: Interscience Publishers, 1965.
7. Durard, R.W. *The Law and Ethics of Dental Practice*. London: Modder and Stoughton, 1950.
8. Furuhata, T., and Yamamoto, K. *Forensic Odontology*. Springfield, Ill.: Charles C. Thomas, 1967.
9. Gladfelter, I.A. *Dental Evidence; A Handbook*. Springfield, Ill.: Charles C. Thomas, 1975.
10. Grustafson, G. *Forensic Odontology*. New York: Elsevier North-Holland, Inc., 1966.
11. Harvey, W. *Dental Identification and Forensic Odontology*. London: Kimpton and Sons, 1976.
12. Holz, F.M., and Johnson, D.W. *Legal Provisions on Expanded Functions for Dental Hygienists and Assistants Summarized by State*. Rockville, Md.: National Institutes of Health, 1974.
13. Loeb, B.F. *Legal Aspects of Dental Practice*. Chapel Hill, N.C.: North Carolina Institute of Government, 1972.
14. Lott, J.N., and Gray, R.H. *Law in Medical and Dental Practice*. Chicago: Foundation Press, 1942.
15. Louisell and Williams. *Medical Malpractice*. Albany, NY: Matthew Bender, 1986.
16. Rosoff, A.J. *Informed Consent*. Rockville, Md.: Aspen System Corporation, 1981.
17. Luntz, L.L., and Luntz, P. *Handbook for Dental Identification Techniques in Forensic Dentistry*. Philadelphia: J.B. Lippincott Company, 1973.
18. Miller, S.L. *Legal Aspects of Dentistry: A Programmed Course in Dental Jurisprudence*. New York: G.P. Putnam's Sons, 1970.
19. Moenssens, A.A. (Ed.). *What's New in Forensic Sciences?* Rockville, Md.: American Academy of Forensic Sciences, 1965–1973.
20. Morris, W.O. *Dental Litigation*. Charlottesville, Va.: Michie, 1972.
21. Motley, W.E. *Ethics, Jurisprudence, and History for the Dental Hygienist*. 3rd Ed. Philadelphia: Lea and Febiger, 1983.
22. Nordstrom, N. *The Rights and Rewards of the Medical Witness and Medical and Dental Appraiser*. Springfield, Ill.: Charles C. Thomas, 1962.
23. Sarner, H. *Dental Jurisprudence*. Philadelphia: W.B. Saunders Company, 1963.
24. Schroeder, O., Jr. *The Forensic Sciences in American Criminal Justice: A Legal Study Concerning the Forensic Sciences Personnel*. Rockville, Md.: The Forensic Sciences Foundation, 1974.

256

25. Seear, J.E. *Law and Ethics in Dentistry*. Bristol, England: John Wright and Sons, 1975.
26. Sopher, I.M. *Forensic Dentistry*. Springfield, Ill.: Charles C. Thomas, 1975.
27. Willig, S.H. *Legal Considerations in Dentistry*. Baltimore: The Williams and Wilkins Company, 1971.
28. Wood, L.B. *Handbook of Dental Malpractice*. Springfield, Ill.: Charles C. Thomas, 1967.